CAN
ORGANIZATIONS
CHANGE?

DANIEL A. MAZMANIAN
JEANNE NIENABER

CAN
ORGANIZATIONS
CHANGE?

Environmental Protection, Citizen Participation,
and the Corps of Engineers

THE BROOKINGS INSTITUTION
Washington, D.C.

Copyright © 1979 by
THE BROOKINGS INSTITUTION
1775 Massachusetts Avenue, N.W., Washington, D.C. 20036

Library of Congress Cataloging in Publication Data:

Mazmanian, Daniel A   1945–
    Can organizations change?
    Includes bibliographical references and index.
    1. Environmental policy—United States—Citizen
participation.   2. United States. Army. Corps
of Engineers—Civil functions.   3. Organizational
change—United States—Case studies.   I. Nienaber,
Jeanne, joint author.   II. Title.
HC110.E5M39   301.18′32   78-27767
ISBN 0-8157-5524-4
ISBN 0-8157-5523-6 pbk.

9 8 7 6 5 4 3 2 1

THE BROOKINGS INSTITUTION is an independent organization devoted to nonpartisan research, education, and publication in economics, government, foreign policy, and the social sciences generally. Its principal purposes are to aid in the development of sound public policies and to promote public understanding of issues of national importance.

The Institution was founded on December 8, 1927, to merge the activities of the Institute for Government Research, founded in 1916, the Institute of Economics, founded in 1922, and the Robert Brookings Graduate School of Economics and Government, founded in 1924.

The Board of Trustees is responsible for the general administration of the Institution, while the immediate direction of the policies, program, and staff is vested in the President, assisted by an advisory committee of the officers and staff. The by-laws of the Institution state: "It is the function of the Trustees to make possible the conduct of scientific research, and publication, under the most favorable conditions, and to safeguard the independence of the research staff in the pursuit of their studies and in the publication of the results of such studies. It is not a part of their function to determine, control, or influence the conduct of particular investigations or the conclusions reached."

The President bears final responsibility for the decision to publish a manuscript as a Brookings book. In reaching his judgment on the competence, accuracy, and objectivity of each study, the President is advised by the director of the appropriate research program and weighs the views of a panel of expert outside readers who report to him in confidence on the quality of the work. Publication of a work signifies that it is deemed a competent treatment worthy of public consideration but does not imply endorsement of conclusions or recommendations.

The Institution maintains its position of neutrality on issues of public policy in order to safeguard the intellectual freedom of the staff. Hence interpretations or conclusions in Brookings publications should be understood to be solely those of the authors and should not be attributed to the Institution, to its trustees, officers, or other staff members, or to the organizations that support its research.

Foreword

DURING the late 1960s and early 1970s many American citizens became unwilling to accept without question important policy decisions made by "bureaucrats" in "far-off" Washington. Numerous minority and special-interest groups began to demand greater participation in making public policy and carrying out public programs. At the same time, the environmental movement was alerting the nation to the dangers of air and water pollution. As it happened, some of the worst offenders against the environment were government agencies such as the Atomic Energy Commission (now the Nuclear Regulatory Commission and the Energy Research and Development Administration), the Forest Service, the Department of Transportation, the Department of the Interior, and the Army Corps of Engineers.

As one response, Congress in 1969 passed the far-reaching National Environmental Policy Act that required all federal agencies to consider the environmental effects of their activities. The guidelines that implemented the act further required the agencies to provide greater citizen involvement in decisions affecting the environment. Even so, major organizational and programmatic changes did not occur. Daniel A. Mazmanian and Jeanne Nienaber discovered when they began this study in the early 1970s that despite legislation, administrative rules, and public pressure, little had changed in the decisionmaking and environmental practices of most federal agencies.

There was, however, at least one apparent exception. The Army Corps of Engineers seemed to be making a concerted effort to comply with both the spirit and the letter of the law, calling for greater public involvement and environmental awareness in the decisionmaking process. The authors therefore focused their study on the Corps, using five case studies to show how the agency's apparently atypical response to demands for change affected its missions, organizational structure, planning, and field activities. Their purpose was to test the validity of the widely held belief that the prospects for great change in large organizations are dim at best. While the experience of one agency is not enough to refute that generalization, the detailed analysis in this book does illustrate how a large, well-established agency can change at least in some measure if it makes a serious attempt.

Mazmanian, a research associate in the Brookings Governmental Studies program when the study was carried out, is an associate professor of government at Pomona College; Nienaber is an assistant professor of political science at the University of Arizona and a former member of the Brookings associated staff. They are grateful to the many staff members of the Corps of Engineers and to citizen participants in Corps projects whose assistance made this study possible. Special thanks go to James R. Hanchey of the Corps' Institute for Water Resources and to Richard Waugh of its Board of Engineers for Rivers and Harbors, who unselfishly gave innumerable hours of their time to the research effort. Gilbert Y. Steiner, director of the Brookings Governmental Studies program during the early stages of the study, and James L. Sundquist, director during its completion, provided the encouragement, support, and patience needed to bring the study to fruition. The manuscript benefited from the careful reading and comments of Herbert Kaufman, Paul A. Sabatier, and several anonymous readers. Tadd Fisher edited the manuscript, which was checked for accuracy by Ellen W. Smith. Judy L. Cameron assisted in preparing the maps, and Diana Regenthal prepared the index. The maps and figures were drawn by Clare and Frank Ford.

The views expressed in this study are those of the authors and should not be ascribed to the trustees, officers, or other staff members of the Brookings Institution.

BRUCE K. MAC LAURY
President

February 1979
Washington, D.C.

Contents

CAN
ORGANIZATIONS
CHANGE?

CHAPTER ONE

Introduction

THE ARMY CORPS OF ENGINEERS is a rich, powerful, and influential federal agency. It is frequently praised for having contributed to the economic productivity of the nation. The Corps stands for progress. So do the vast majority of Americans. But during the late 1960s and early 1970s the Corps found itself on the defensive when, along with numerous other federal agencies, it came under sharp and sustained attack. New concerns were being aired and new demands were being made on the bureaucracy.

First came the demand for a more open decisionmaking process. Citizens evidently were no longer content with being the passive recipients of important policy decisions made in Washington. Groups that felt they had previously been excluded from participating in important decisions— the poor, ethnic minorities, women, environmentalists—demanded access to participation. Citizen involvement, ranging from sit-ins at the Bureau of Indian Affairs to sophisticated academic critiques of the lack of participatory democracy within the bureaucracy, became the focus of much attention.

Second, a major new public policy concern came to the fore during this period. It had to do with what many perceived to be the deteriorating quality of the environment. Though vague as an issue and encompassing a number of specific concerns, the environmental movement, as it came to be called, developed rapidly throughout the nation. In 1969 Congress passed broad, far-reaching legislation, the National Environmental Policy Act (NEPA), which among other things required all federal agencies to consider the environmental effects of their activities. Thus Congress was asking the government to put its own house in order, since the federal bureaucracy itself was guilty of some of the most offensive abuses to the environment. The most frequently cited offenders included the Atomic Energy Commission (now reorganized into the Nuclear Regulatory Com-

1

mission and elements of the Department of Energy), the Forest Service, the Department of Transportation, the Department of the Interior, and the Army Corps of Engineers. Nuclear power plants, flood control dams, superhighways, and careless regulation of the government's enormous landholdings all had profound effects on the environment. Moreover, many of the government's activities that were deemed offensive were ostensibly being carried out for the benefit of the general public. A vocal segment of the public, however, seriously questioned this. Throughout the 1970s, court battles based on the NEPA requirements became commonplace, with environmental groups attempting to halt what they considered to be the most flagrant abuses of the environment.

But legislation and implementing presidential directives unfortunately are insufficient in themselves to effect major programmatic changes. Policy changes must filter down to the operating levels of government, the departments and agencies, which not only administer programs but apply and interpret and hence in effect make policy. It is at this level of the executive branch that changes in policy either succeed or fail. But it is a difficult task to reform any large, well-established bureau. The literature on organizational change reflects a profound pessimism about the likelihood of directing bureaucracies, let alone redirecting them. Bureaucracy takes on a life of its own, largely unaffected by the world outside.[1]

As observers of the policy process, we thus discerned a potentially interesting situation. On the one hand, substantive and procedural changes in bureaucratic behavior were being demanded. On the other hand, the bureaucratic laws of behavior that act to hinder or nullify change were presumably still in operation. How would bureaus respond to these new pressures for change, pressures that certain agencies regarded as threats to their basic missions?

An initial examination of several federal agencies corroborated the conventional wisdom: in many instances, nothing much had changed. En-

---

1. For a more detailed discussion of the problems of introducing even slight changes into organizations, let alone dramatic ones, see James G. March and Herbert A. Simon, *Organizations* (John Wiley, 1958); Anthony Downs, *Inside Bureaucracy* (Little, Brown, 1967); Herbert Kaufman, *The Limits of Organizational Change* (University of Alabama Press, 1971); Neal Gross, Joseph B. Giacquinta and Marilyn Bernstein, *Implementing Organizational Innovations: A Sociological Analysis of Planned Educational Change* (Basic Books, 1971); and Gene W. Dalton, Paul R. Lawrence, and Larry E. Greiner, eds., *Organizational Change and Development* (Richard D. Irwin, 1970).

vironmental impact statements required by NEPA were indeed being written, and the language of project proposals had changed somewhat. Most agencies, however, were still bent on accomplishing their missions as prescribed decades ago. They paid lip service to environmentalism and citizen involvement but nonetheless regarded environmentalists and other citizens' groups as adversaries out to destroy the agencies. Many therefore resisted these new demands for change.

We discovered at least one exception: the Army Corps of Engineers. Since the Corps spends over a billion dollars annually in a massive construction effort and is viewed by many as the epitome of a well-entrenched bureaucracy, it certainly had felt the brunt of the citizens' movements. Yet contrary to what its critics expected, the agency seemed to be making a conscious and serious effort to accommodate itself to the spirit of the environmental movement as well as to the letter of the law. Thus it appeared that much could be learned from examining this possible exception to the rule of bureaucratic behavior that change takes place at a glacier-like pace.[2] Understanding the dynamics of change in the Corps might also shed light on how change in agencies with similar missions could be accomplished. At least a case study of the Corps would suggest the key issues that must be addressed if major changes are attempted.

Measuring Organizational Change

In reality few organizations are either stagnant or in a perpetual state of change. While the modal position is undoubtedly closer to the static end of the spectrum, organizational change does take place. But how, exactly, does one rank organizations along a spectrum, especially public agencies such as the Corps of Engineers? What degree of change is to be considered incremental as opposed to radical? What measures can be used? The task of evaluating change in large, complex organizations is difficult because it requires, first, a decision on the proper criteria to be

2. As it happened, we were in a unique position to study the Corps. We not only had excellent access to the agency but were encouraged by it to study and critique its response to the environmental and citizens' involvement issues. During fiscal year 1973–74 Nienaber served as a resident scholar in the Corps, which is divided into civil and military components. We examined only the civil works branch, since its activities were the ones under attack. Our field work was completed during the critical period of change in the agency in 1973 and 1974, but our material has been updated wherever possible.

used, and second, a systematic measurement of the extent to which these criteria are met. A number of scholars have addressed these issues from time to time,[3] but despite much recent interest in the topic of organizational change, as yet there is no general set of indices by which to measure change.

In the absence of any widely accepted set of criteria we suggest four factors that appear to be reasonably reliable indicators of change. While the first three are applicable for measuring change in virtually any organization, the fourth is primarily of relevance in measuring change in public agencies.

Setting New Goals. Setting new goals and promising new programs and services constitute a necessary first step, yet this step is such a minimal or subjective kind of change that it has not attracted much serious attention by students of organization. To our knowledge, no effort has been made to systematically measure changes in pronouncements of new agency goals. Only when such claims are coupled with structural, procedural, and output changes can they be reliably evaluated. New goals then serve as a criterion by which to judge the extent of change that occurs. The more interesting cases are perhaps those that hold promise of a dramatic or radical change and thus serve as a test of the ultimate capacity of organizations to change.

Reorganization. The second criterion, reorganization, has received extensive attention. Gawthrop, a prominent scholar of bureaucracy and the administrative process, sees reorganization as an inevitable part of the change process.[4] The nature of the reorganization varies widely, however. In some instances emphasis is placed on shifting authority to small work groups as functioning units. In other cases new administrative layers are added to provide a clearer chain of command. Often people and units are transferred up or down, in or out, in order to disrupt established modes of behavior and patterned routines and thus to shake up the informal authority structure.

The infusion of new personnel who have different values and training is a part of the reorganization process. Through them, ideas once regarded as unorthodox may legitimately be voiced from within. Moreover,

---

3. See, for example, David Braybrooke and Charles E. Lindblom, A *Strategy of Decision: Policy Evaluation as a Social Process* (Free Press, 1963).

4. Louis C. Gawthrop, *Administrative Politics and Social Change* (St. Martin's Press, 1971), p. 91.

new personnel have less vested interest in traditional practices and procedures. Indeed, their future is often tied to the success of the change effort.

Changes in Output. Universal measures of whether a public agency has actually improved its delivery of a product or service are difficult to agree upon. In the private sector improvements in a product or service are often measured in one or both of two ways: higher productivity or higher profit. The success of structural or procedural changes in an industrial organization are thus typically measured by a more efficient use of men and machinery, an improved internal flow of goods and communications, and better means of assembling products. These in turn are linked to an improved return on investment.[5] For public agencies (or voluntary organizations), however, measuring changes in output by profit or productivity is usually not feasible. At best it is only a partial answer. While making money is the primary goal of a private firm, government and voluntary agencies provide services to the consumer either at no cost or at below market value. Changes in output—the provision of goods and services—must therefore be measured not only by a monetary criterion but by other means as well. Sometimes change can be measured by the provision of better services or of new services. But what precisely does "better" mean? The problem is easier regarding new services; they either are or are not provided. Even so, appraisals are apt to be more subjective than is the case when one can rely on a quantifiable criterion such as profits.

A fundamental difficulty is that the desired optimum level for the production of goods and services for a public agency is ultimately a political decision. Economic criteria can provide only part of the solution. For instance, the Corps of Engineers builds dams that provide flood protecttion, water supply, recreational, and hydroelectric benefits. Some people think that the unrestricted building of dams would make the Corps a better and therefore more successful public servant. Others strongly disagree. The question, then, is what level of dam production is socially desirable? Only when this question is resolved can changes in output be measured against it; and since the levels of demand and supply for most

5. See Stanley E. Seashore and David G. Bowers, *Changing the Structure and Functioning of an Organization: Report of a Field Experiment,* Monograph 33 (Survey Research Center, Institute of Social Research, University of Michigan, 1963); Robert R. Blake and others, "Breakthrough in Organization Development," *Harvard Business Review,* vol. 42 (November-December 1964), pp. 133–55; and Robert H. Guest, *Organizational Change: The Effect of Successful Leadership* (Richard D. Irwin, 1962).

public goods are constantly shifting and open to question, one is led back
to a procedural criterion to evaluate organizational changes.

Open Decisionmaking. In the private sector, consumer demand, as
measured by sales and profits, is obviously crucial to the operation of an
enterprise. If a firm's profits are low and the public is not buying a particular product or service, something must be changed to prevent the firm from
being driven out of business. Likewise, when a public agency receives increasing criticism and opposition, public satisfaction with a given policy,
project, or service is obviously lacking, and a substantive or procedural
change is in order. For obvious reasons, government agencies must be
sensitive to criticism, but they generally attempt to neutralize opposition.
Recently, one way of doing so has been through a greatly expanded public
participation program.

We therefore posit a link between an open decisionmaking process and
an agency's commitment to change. A fairly reliable indicator that an
organization is serious about adopting new missions and also, perhaps,
about changing its customary patterns of behavior is when it opens its
doors to those previously ignored or excluded. Otherwise its traditional
constituencies, which were instrumental in determining its current level
and nature of activities, will inevitably prevail. Irrespective of the exact
procedures used, if significant changes are going to occur, the views of new
and often hostile constituencies must be incorporated into the agency.
The extent to which these views are incorporated, both procedurally and
substantively, can be gauged and serves as an important factor in assessing
the degree of organizational change.

These new constituencies in turn help redirect traditional missions, set
new goals, and ultimately define a new, socially acceptable level of service. Thus the extent to which the agency's actions satisfy previously ignored or excluded constituencies is probably one of the best measures
currently available in determining whether it has successfully changed to
meet new demands emanating from its environment.

The Study Plan

Our task therefore has been not only to gauge the extent of change in
objectives, internal structure, programs, and decisionmaking, but also to
decide whether a different level of service, or a new service altogether, is in

accord with the needs and preferences of the agency's political environment.

In chapter 2, the change in the Corps' stated objectives and promised services are gauged in light of the agency's traditional missions and activities. Structural changes are assessed in chapter 3 by the extent of reorganization, new recruitment patterns, and changed attitudes that took place within the Corps in approximately a three-year time span. Chapters 4 through 6 contain five case studies and focus on (1) changes in decision-making at the operating, or field, level, measured largely by the extent and effect of public participation efforts; and (2) output changes, in this instance the kind of projects the Corps now undertakes. More specifically, the case studies involve a detailed examination of several of the Corps' new and expanded public participation programs and of how they in turn relate to changes in agency output and to public satisfaction. Chapter 7 provides a summary view of the Corps' efforts at new participatory planning and an explanation of its results. Our conclusions and reflections are contained in chapter 8.

CHAPTER TWO

Prospects for Change in the Corps of Engineers

MEASURING THE DEGREE of change in the Corps of Engineers requires a baseline. What, traditionally, has been the Corps' role in water resources? And what have been its decisionmaking policies with respect to clientele groups and interested citizens? This chapter begins with an overview of the Corps' traditional activities, operations, and decisionmaking process. It then addresses how these were challenged during the 1960s. The final section is a discussion of the agency's pledge in the early 1970s to reorganize its structure, open its decisionmaking, and change its substantive activities in a way that it hoped would satisfy mounting criticism.

A Historical Baseline

Few federal agencies can trace their lineage to the founding of the Union. An exception is the Army Corps of Engineers, which had its origins in the Continental Army. The unit was given formal status in 1802, when President Thomas Jefferson established the Corps of Engineers and the United States Military Academy at West Point. In 1824 Congress created a Board of Internal Improvements for the purpose of planning a national land and water transportation system, and President James Monroe assigned two army engineers to the three-member board, marking the beginning of the Corps' expansion into civil works activities. This was the inception of the Directorate of Civil Works of the Corps of Engineers. From this modest beginning the Corps has grown into an enormous public bureaucracy, with over 35,000 employees involved in the civil works program.

The civil works program is directed by a staff of some 300 military officers drawn from the top 8 percent of the Army's West Point graduates. The agency's headquarters is the Office of the Chief of Engineers (OCE), located in Washington, D.C. Like other resource-managing agencies, however, the Corps is a substantially decentralized organization. The management of its civil works program therefore is distributed among 11 division offices (regional headquarters), and 36 district, or local, offices.[1]

As a branch of the U.S. Army, the Corps is directly under the secretary of the Army and is therefore a part of the executive branch. But in practice the civil works branch of the Corps has functioned with an unusual degree of autonomy from the executive-military community, largely because of the Corps' unusually close relationship with Congress.[2]

By 1974, which marked the first 150 years of the civil works program, nearly 3,400 projects and project modifications had been completed. Some 280 projects remained under construction, with completion costs estimated at $22 billion (in 1974 dollars). Meanwhile more than 330 projects remained in active backlog status and would cost an estimated $12 billion (1974 dollars) to complete. Finally, there were 600 projects either deferred for further study or classified by the agency as inactive.[3] In fiscal year 1979 appropriations for ongoing work of the Corps totaled almost $2.5 billion.[4] By any objective standard—budget, number of projects under way or under study, number of people employed—this agency is clearly the model of a powerful bureaucracy.[5]

Traditional Missions

Initially the Corps was assigned responsibility for improving navigational facilities on the nation's waterways. In the first half of the nineteenth century it made surveys for work on a number of canals and rail-

1. Data from Lt. General W. C. Gribble, Jr., "Perspectives on the Army Engineers Water Management Mission," *Water Spectrum*, vol. 6, no. 3 (1974), p. 2; and Don Moser, "Dig They Must: The Army Engineers—Securing Allies and Acquiring Enemies," *Smithsonian*, December 1976, pp. 40–51.

2. In his celebrated book, *Muddy Waters: The Army Engineers and the Nation's Rivers* (Harvard University Press, 1951), Arthur Maass amply documents the Corps' independence from the executive branch and its close alliance with Congress.

3. For project and budget data, see Gribble, "Perspectives on the Army Engineers," p. 2.

4. *The Budget of the United States Government, Fiscal Year 1979*, p. 332.

5. For a comparison of the Corps with other resource agencies, see Jeanne Nienaber, Helen Ingram, and Daniel McCool, " 'The Rich Get Richer' Phenomenon: Compar-

roads; helped to make the Ohio, Missouri, and Mississippi rivers navigable; and opened harbors for steamships on the Great Lakes. Following the Civil War these operations spread west and south, providing benefits to all sections of the reunited nation. Then in 1879, with the creation of the Mississippi River Commission, the Corps was assigned the added function of supervising local efforts for flood control; in 1917 it was authorized to undertake flood control work on the Mississippi and on the Sacramento River in California. In 1936 Congress made the Corps responsible for flood protection along all the nation's rivers. This proved to be the agency's greatest single impetus to grow and explains the impressive budget authority associated with the Corps today.

Having the federal government build dams and reservoirs in the 1930s was, of course, part of President Franklin D. Roosevelt's plan for economic recovery from the depression. In the Flood Control Act of 1936 (49 Stat. 1570), Congress declared that this was a proper and essential federal activity and that structural improvements to prevent flooding were in the public interest. Hence the cost of such improvements would be borne by the federal government. The Corps was assigned primary responsibility for implementing the act.

The Flood Control Act of 1938 expanded this authority so that the Corps' flood control structures might include the installation of facilities for power use—penstocks and turbines—when agreed upon by the Federal Power Commission. Thus by the mid-1940s the Corps had acquired statutory authority to produce and market surplus hydroelectric power from its projects, to dispose of its surplus water for domestic and industrial use, and to allow its reservoirs to be used for irrigation purposes in the 17 western, water-poor states.[6] Despite a number of ancillary functions that have been delegated by Congress to the Corps, planning and constructing navigation and flood control projects have proved to be the Corps' most important mandated and internally promoted activities. It is these activities that have won the Army engineers recognition and reward and that have brought them a secure niche in the federal establishment.[7]

---

ing Innovation in Six Federal Agencies" (paper presented at the Annual Meeting of the Midwest Political Science Association, Chicago, April 29–May 1, 1976).

6. The Flood Control Act of 1944 provides for these activities.

7. The Corps did not rise to preeminence in the field of flood control unchallenged, however. Intensive struggles over the agency's prerogatives and autonomy from executive branch control often occurred between the Corps and the Department

In essence, then, by the late 1940s and early 1950s the Corps had effectively meshed its new mission of flood control with its traditional one of maintaining the navigable inland waterways. The agency thus emerged as the undisputed guardian of the public welfare in both of these important resource development areas.

The Corps and Congress: Cementing Implementation Techniques

Much of the controversy surrounding the Corps of Engineers is concerned as much with the agency's methods or techniques as with its basic missions. For example, environmental groups may not always criticize the agency's attempt to control flooding but will attack the Corps' method of providing that protection: constructing dams rather than zoning for floodplain management.

Historically, however, the methods selected to implement the agency's basic missions were dictated by both engineering and political considerations. Channelization and dredging were selected as the best methods for the maintenance and development of the nation's rivers and harbors. Similarly, the construction of dams was perceived to be the most suitable solution to the problem of flood control. These techniques were chosen to the almost total exclusion of other alternatives because at the time of their selection they made both good engineering and good political sense, however outmoded they may appear today.

Building dams, channelizing rivers, and dredging harbors have been the kinds of methods Congress explicitly directed the Corps to use. As one observer of the agency noted:

A grant of planning responsibility to an agency authorized to implement only a limited range of solutions suffers an inherent institutional limitation. *Congress requires the Corps to examine such needs as water supply, water quality, and outdoor recreation facilities, but rarely authorizes the Corps to alleviate these needs except by means of multiple-purpose reservoirs whose purposes include flood control.* Even with respect to its supposedly primary

---

of the Interior, especially when the latter was under the leadership of Secretary Harold L. Ickes. The Corps and the Bureau of Reclamation, and the Corps and a series of presidents, including Franklin Roosevelt and Harry Truman, engaged in frequent skirmishes. See Maass, *Muddy Waters*; and Henry C. Hart, *The Dark Missouri* (University of Wisconsin Press, 1957). Even on technical points of engineering the Corps has known virile criticism, especially about its hesitance to incorporate hydroelectric power facilities into its dams. See Arthur E. Morgan, *Dams and Other Disasters: A Century of the Army Corps of Engineers in Civil Works* (Porter Sargent, 1971).

role of reducing flood losses, the Corps has been restricted largely to building structures for flood water retention. . . . The self-interest inherent in a continuation of its construction program causes difficulty for the agency in weighing objectively other means of achieving desired ends [emphasis added].[8]

One can easily appreciate the reasons behind the selection of alternatives. For example, dams and reservoirs that control flooding, that turn the downstream floodplain into productive and valuable land, and that were thought to give a general economic boost to the affected region are obviously considered advantageous by both the Corps and Congress. Over the years a symbiotic relationship evolved; the Corps needed and received congressional support in its struggle with other federal agencies for a large share of the public works budget. In turn, congressmen seeking public works projects for their districts needed and received sympathetic consideration from the Corps. The more powerful and prestigious the congressmen, especially those on the House Public Works and Appropriations committees, the greater the sympathy received.[9] The relationship is perpetuated through the classic practice of logrolling whereby a congressman will not speak out against a project proposed for a colleague's district, regardless of the project's merits, in order to be rewarded in kind in the future. As a means of ensuring this "sharing of the pork," both Congress and the Corps adamantly hold on to a "regional development" criterion as a basis of judging proposed projects. For Congress this means that projects will be spread around geographically, and for the Corps it provides a rationale for spreading them around.

If this were not sufficient to lock the Corps into perceiving only dam-building solutions to problems of flooding, the economic incentives are such that the local citizenry also usually see the wisdom of the structural solution and then request it of the Corps. This resulted from the cost-sharing formulas for public works projects that Congress has written into law over the years. These formulas provide that the federal government will pay (1) up to 100 percent of the costs of construction, land rights, relocation and alteration of utilities, as well as operating and maintenance costs for reservoirs and water quality projects; (2) up to 100 percent of the costs of the construction, maintenance, operation, and replacement of

8. Roger W. Findley, "The Planning of a Corps of Engineers Reservoir Project: Law, Economics, and Politics," *Ecology Law Quarterly*, vol. 3 (Winter 1973), p. 42.

9. See John A. Ferejohn, *Pork Barrel Politics: Rivers and Harbors Legislation, 1947–1968* (Stanford University Press, 1974), chaps. 8, 9.

navigation projects; (3) up to 100 percent of the construction costs of local flood protection projects; and (4) from 50 to 100 percent of the costs for recreation and fish and wildlife enhancement.[10]

With a few exceptions, until 1974 these generous cost-sharing schemes did not apply to nonstructural flood control alternatives such as flood-proofing buildings, floodplain zoning, public acquisition of the floodplain, and the federal flood insurance program.[11] The government does not provide federal dollars for the hydroelectric power or municipal and industrial water supply components of a project. Only partial funding is provided for irrigation and recreational benefits.

Confronted with these different cost-sharing rules, local citizens concerned with alleviating problems of flooding have had to choose between a federally funded Corps dam and reservoir or an alternative for which the state or local community must pick up most of the tab. That is, they can accept the federal government's "free" solution or finance some other alternative, which on merit alone they might have preferred. Thus, while dams and reservoirs may not have been the most economical or desirable solution to flooding from a national policy perspective, as some have argued, or even the solution with the broadest support from a local community, they have undoubtedly been the cheapest solution to the local community because of the built-in biases in cost-sharing.

Economic Justification for Public Works Projects

The political accommodation among the Corps, Congress, and local proponents is rarely the public justification given for the construction of a Corps project. Rather, all project proposals must pass through a series of stages, beginning with an initial feasibility study at the district level and ending with in-house engineering and cost reviews at the division and Washington levels. These studies and reviews stress the importance of economic justifications for construction; all projects must have a benefit-cost ratio of one or better. This means, theoretically, that for every dollar expended by the federal government more than a dollar of benefits

10. See Harold E. Marshall and V. L. Broussalian, *Federal Cost-Sharing Policies for Water Resources*, National Bureau of Standards Report 10-666, prepared for the National Water Commission (U.S. Department of Commerce, NBS, December 1972), table 4.1, pp. 100–101.

11. Section 73 of the Water Resources Development Act of 1974 (88 Stat. 32) makes cost-sharing for nonstructural flood control alternatives comparable to that for structural ones.

will be generated.[12] It turns out that most project proposals requested for study by the Corps are rejected because they fail to meet the benefit-cost criterion.

Even so, upon close examination the benefit-cost ratio is not invulnerable to outside criticism or to differing calculations. Many projects that have survived agency and congressional scrutiny can be shown to have a ratio of less than one. Here is another instance, as in the nuclear safety argument, of disagreement among the experts. Much depends on who does the calculation and which factors are considered as benefits and which as costs. The realization that benefit-cost analysis is not as objective as it once appeared has convinced the recent generation of Corps opponents that it is nothing more than the Corps' way of translating its politically based priorities into a bureaucratic rationale clothed in the garb of economic rationality.

For its part the Corps has not taken the challenge to its benefit-cost calculations lightly, though it is quick to recognize and admit that political as well as economic reasons for its projects indeed exist. While the agency does not have to justify its projects in an open market, it nevertheless is required to prove, in what it claims is a rigorous and unbiased manner, that a recommended project has a net dollar surplus.

In the world of textbook economics the concept of benefit-cost is clear: "A given project will result in net benefits for an economic system to the extent that it moves the system closer to what the professionals call 'pareto-optimality' which we can translate into 'maximally efficient utilization of available resources.'"[13] If this formula is used to evaluate a Corps flood control project, to the extent that the project "prevents pre-

12. The Corps' method of judging the benefits and costs of water projects was set forth in *Policies, Standards, and Procedures in the Formulation, Evaluation, and Review of Plans for Use and Development of Water and Related Land Resources*, S. Doc. 97, 87 Cong. 2 sess. (Government Printing Office, 1962), pp. 5–12. In 1973 President Richard Nixon approved a new set of guidelines prepared by the Water Resources Council over a five-year period of review during which it held ten public hearings. The new guidelines, "Principles and Standards for Planning Water and Related Land Resources," appeared in the *Federal Register*, vol. 38 (September 10, 1973), pp. 24778–869, and were modified by Congress in 1974 in section 80 of the Water Resources Development Act of 1974 (88 Stat. 34).

13. Allan S. Krass, "Flood Control and the Tocks Island Dam," Report 2 (Center for Environmental Studies, Princeton University, August 1973), p. 43. See also Robert H. Haveman, *Water Resource Investment and the Public Interest* (Vanderbilt University Press, 1965).

mature destruction of capital and the attendant non-utilization of labor, and to the extent that it enhances the productive capacity of previously under-productive land it would seem to provide obvious economic benefits to society."[14]

In practice, however, the accurate estimate of benefits and costs is extremely hard to determine even when the basic concept is not challenged, as recently it has been. For example, neither the benefits nor the costs of a flood control project accrue at a single point in time but rather over the life of the project. Benefits and costs must then be apportioned accordingly. But since the actual life of a project is uncertain, how are benefits and costs to be apportioned? The Corps' solution has been to choose either 50 or 100 years as the life of its projects. This serves as a useful basis for computation, but nevertheless it is an arbitrary one. The problem of calculation is compounded when one considers the probable growth rate of the proposed project location or its potential for economic development. It is hard enough to forecast these factors 5 years hence, let alone 50 or 100 years. Yet calculating benefits and costs over this long time span is required. The standard solution, therefore, is simply to project forward from existing patterns of population, personal income, capital investment, and so on. This may be as good a rule as any, but it proves to be increasingly unreliable the further one pushes the figures into the future.

A similar problem arises in choosing a method of comparing the benefits accruing in the present with the benefits that might accrue 50 or 100 years hence. The question is answered in practice by choosing a rate of interest by which future benefits can be discounted relative to current benefits. But what rate shall this be? Once again a decision has been made that is a mix of economic and political considerations. The lower the interest rate used to evaluate future benefits of a Corps project, the higher its projected long-term benefit will be. Since Congress sets the interest rate on all public works projects, the rate is clearly a political decision. In fact, the interest rate is a major weapon in the congressional arsenal for regulating the overall flow of federal dollars into public works projects. This may be as it should, but it only adds to the questions about the Corps' benefit-cost calculations.

Finally, there is the problem of deciding what is benefit and what is cost. The Corps has traditionally answered that to impound water behind

14. Krass, "Flood Control," p. 43.

a dam is beneficial because the floodplain can be developed and the water stored and used for residential use, industry, irrigation, or the generation of power. Costs were associated primarily with the acquisition of land and the actual pouring of concrete. The environmentalists, not surprisingly, calculate things differently. Maintaining free-flowing streams, allowing the natural cycle of the ebb and flow of rivers over their banks, and curtailing residential or commercial development in the floodplain are all seen as beneficial. Who is to say which view is correct? Moreover, how can an intelligent dialogue take place about the details of a project when two such opposing world views exist? In truth it is virtually impossible. Thus the debates over benefits and costs that occur between the Corps and their project opponents reduce to a clash of cultural values, despite all the lip service paid to the sanctity of the benefit-cost ratio in judging the worth of a project.

The problems associated with applying economic analysis to complex real world problems have long been known. When agreement exists on ultimate goals, however, or when the opposition is effectively excluded from the decisionmaking process, the method of calculation is trivial. Historically, this was the case for Corps projects. Now, however, when an intense and concerned effort is mounted to derail a project, the biases toward large structural solutions inherent in the Corps' economic calculations become evident, and thus the entire foundation of the project is open to challenge.

Traditional Mode of Decisionmaking

The Corps' traditional method of deciding which projects should be undertaken reflected its close relationship with local beneficiaries and Congress.[15] The idea for a project usually would emerge from local interests who turned to the Corps, sometimes at the Corps' prompting, for urban or agricultural flood protection, river channelization, irrigation water, or hydroelectric power. In practice this meant that the local people would approach their congressman, who in turn would carry a study request to the Public Works committees of the House and Senate. As a

15. A good overview of the steps in the Corps' decision process is outlined in the monograph by Colonel Gerald E. Galloway, "The Decision Process of the Civil Works Function of the U.S. Army Corps of Engineers," U.S. Army War College Military Research Program Paper (June 1974), chap. 3.

courtesy to the congressman, the committees would usually include the request in the annual public works authorization bill. But this was only the first of many hurdles.

Once a project study was authorized—which is distinct from an authorization to construct—the chief of engineers would direct the relevant Corps district office to conduct a preliminary feasibility survey in coordination and cooperation with the local proponents, the general public, and relevant state and federal agencies. Often at this point some form of public hearing would be held at a local school or community hall, with the general public invited to comment. The problem was that the public seldom knew anything about the proposed project or had any concrete ideas about what the Corps should or should not be doing. At this stage the Corps had nothing specific to present except to say that it was conducting the survey study authorized by Congress to gauge the extent of the problem identified—the problem, that is, as defined by the project proponents and the Corps. As might be expected, these meetings seldom drew much of an audience. Yet for the Corps this was part of the procedural compliance with its rules governing open, or public, participation in its decisions.

Upon completion of the survey study the district office would forward its recommendation through the division office to the Board of Engineers for Rivers and Harbors that operated directly under the chief of engineers and was the final in-house review body for all proposed projects. If the benefit-cost ratio for the project was satisfactory, the board would normally recommend approval. Next came the final clearance with other federal and state agencies. Of particular importance at this juncture was the state governor, who would be asked expressly to approve any project located in his state. If all had gone well so far, the chief of engineers would forward the proposal through the secretary of the Army and the President's Office of Management and Budget to Congress. The Public Works committees would then hold hearings on it and numerous other project proposals, and those reviewed favorably would be lumped together in the year's omnibus rivers and harbors authorization bill. At this time, of course, little would be known about the project outside the tight circle of the project proponents, the Corps, and congressional sponsors. Therefore, even at this late date opposing views were seldom recorded. The omnibus bill, if passed and signed by the President, would be the only formal authorization needed by the Corps to begin construction. One hurdle did remain: funding. Yet just getting to this point alone required about two years for an average project.

Following the project authorization, the chief of engineers would request funding from Congress, through the secretary of the Army and the Office of Management and Budget, to undertake "advanced engineering and design" work. This was the crucial stage when the district office decided which of a range of possible approaches to a problem it would adopt and specified exact dollar amounts needed for the task involved. At the conclusion of this stage relevant federal and state agencies were informed of the district's plan, and a second general public meeting was held. Fliers were sent out and the local press was informed of the meeting—until recently called a public hearing—held, again, usually at the local school in the area where the project was to be undertaken. Typically, this post-authorization and design meeting was the first time that those not directly involved in the initiation and planning of the project would hear about specifics. In effect the public was not informed until the major decisions on the project were made, congressional authorization was attained, and the basic design and engineering were completed.

The final stage in launching a project involved the district office asking the chief of engineers to submit a request for construction funds through the secretary of the Army and the Office of Management and Budget to Congress. If funded, construction would begin and project opponents would have little recourse.

This was the usual decisionmaking process before the environmentalists came on the scene at the end of the 1960s. Naturally, throughout the process the principal local proponents, their congressmen, and the Corps were in constant communication, exchanging information and lobbying one another, the Office of Management and Budget, and the Public Works and Appropriations committees of Congress—to the almost total exclusion of real and potential project opponents. It was this fairly closed decisionmaking process that drew the fire of the Corps' critics at the end of the 1960s and early 1970s. In articles in national publications such critics as Elizabeth B. Drew, Supreme Court Justice William O. Douglas, and Congressman Henry S. Reuss argued that despite the procedural mechanisms the Corps followed to attain "public" input, the nature of the agency's decision process facilitated projects determined only by the Corps in conjunction with its development-oriented allies in Congress and the local communities.[16] The most telling critique of all, however, eventually came from one of the Corps' own:

> The traditional way engineers go about planning a public works project leaves little room for the citizen to be heard. Engineers would first define the "problem," then "objectives" or "goals." Finally, they would develop "The Plan" to attain these goals.
>
> Of course, eventually the public gets a look at "The Plan" in public meetings or hearings. Presentation is oral. And a thick study document is available for inspection, should some persistent citizen have the energy to labor through it. Oftentimes, engineers do not show the public alternate plans; and if they do, written copies are not available for public scrutiny. Questioned about alternatives, the planner is likely to answer: "We looked at other ways to solve the problem, but there was little support for any of them."[17]

But this is getting ahead of the story. The point is that the Corps' traditional decisionmaking process, while involving numerous checkpoints, only facilitated direct participation by project proponents and limited consultation with other government agencies.

The Contemporary Challenge

One of the now classic confrontations between the Corps of Engineers and the environmentalists of the 1960s took place over a proposed flood control project along the Sangamon River in Illinois. The case vividly demonstrates that the Corps' economic and engineering criteria could be effectively challenged. This confrontation thus became the blueprint for assaults on the agency throughout the 1960s and into the 1970s. As such, it is worth reviewing briefly.

Decatur, Illinois, is located midstate on the Sangamon River just below and adjacent to the town of Oakley and several miles above Springfield.[18]

16. See Elizabeth B. Drew, "Dam Outrage: The Story of the Army Engineers," *Atlantic Monthly*, April 1970, pp. 51–62; William O. Douglas, "The Public Be Damned," *Playboy*, July 1969, pp. 143, 182–88; and Congressman Henry S. Reuss, "Needed: An About-Face for the Army Corps of Engineers," *Readers' Digest*, November 1971, pp. 129–32.

17. Colonel Howard L. Sargent, Jr., "Fishbowl Planning Immerses Pacific Northwest Citizens in Corps Projects," *Civil Engineering*, vol. 42 (September 1972), p. 54. Colonel Sargent at this time was district engineer of the Seattle District.

18. This narrative draws liberally from Findley, "Planning of a Reservoir Project";

In the early 1950s local civic leaders realized that the city's water supply, Lake Decatur, was filling with silt. An advisory committee was assembled and eventually outlined a plan to the Decatur City Council that would alleviate this condition. The plan called for the construction of a dam and reservoir at Oakley on the upper end of Lake Decatur as the least costly and most beneficial alternative available to the city. Coincidentally, an Oakley reservoir was part of the Corps of Engineers' long-standing plan for providing flood protection along the Sangamon River; it had been shelved just a few years earlier owing to opposition by local farmers who would have lost land to the lake behind the reservoir. For the city of Decatur, however, the dam and reservoir idea was the optimal way of intercepting the sedimentation of Lake Decatur, providing additional water supply for future growth, and preserving the present lake. Initially uncertain about whether they could prevail upon the Corps for assistance, the committee recommended that the following steps be taken: "1) increasing the storage capacity of Lake Decatur by erecting five-foot gates on the crest of the existing dam; 2) acquiring additional land for the eventual construction of another reservoir on Big Creek, a nearby Sangamon tributary; and 3) cooperating with the Corps so long as a possibility existed that it might complete the Oakley project."[19] The seriousness of the committee's intentions was indicated in its conclusion that the Oakley reservoir should be constructed even if it had to be financed through *local* funds, although if the Corps participated, the city would save $5 million of the $6 million required.

Negotiations then proceeded between the Decatur City Council and the Corps. By 1961 the two had agreed on the construction of a single multipurpose dam and reservoir to serve flood control, water supply, and recreational needs. (The Corps' earlier plan called for a series of reservoirs.) The city of Decatur was to pay about $4.6 million of the cost of construction, which was estimated at $29.6 million but eventually escalated to $65 million. Following its final in-house approval, the Corps presented the project to Congress for authorization in 1962. Authorization was urged by two Illinois senators, Paul Douglas and Everett Dirksen, as well as by Decatur's congressman, William Springer, whose name finally

and J. C. Marlin, ed., *Battle for the Sangamon: The Struggle to Save Allerton Park* (Committee on Allerton Park, 1971).

19. Findley, "Planning of a Reservoir Project," p. 5.

came to adorn the project, which was authorized in the Flood Control Act of 1962.

If the Corps and the city of Decatur had moved expeditiously to build the authorized dam and reservoir neither would have been dragged through the heated battle that followed. But during the final design and engineering stage of the project, which occurred between 1962 and 1966, a new feature was added: water quality control. To dilute effluent discharged by the Decatur sewage treatment plant into the Sangamon, the Oakley dam would be increased in size to store an additional 50,000 acre-feet of water for release during dry periods. Given the flat topography of central Illinois, this required extending the reservoir from the originally authorized 10-mile length up the Sangamon to 25 miles, with all the attendant land acquisition and cost requirements.

Farmers in the Sangamon Basin whose land would be inundated were not sanguine about the plan. But fervent and unified opposition did not surface until it was learned that the extended Oakley lake would inundate parts of Allerton Park. The park was a woodland preserve that had been donated to the Board of Trustees of the University of Illinois by Robert Allerton in 1946 on the condition that it be preserved "for educational and research purposes, as a forest, wild and plant-life reserve, as an example of landscape gardening, and as a public park."[20] Under the Corps' new plan 640 acres of the bottomlands would be inundated permanently, and an additional 220 acres would be submerged during high-water periods that could last for 80 days annually.

This drew the University of Illinois into the fray. After a brief showing of opposition, however, the university decided it was not interested in tangling with the host of local, state, and federal proponents of the project. Angered by the apparent timidity of the university administration, three faculty members formed the Committee on Allerton Park in 1967. They marshaled local public support, retained legal assistance, and most important, put together a team of engineers and scientists that could counter the Corps' expertise.

The key to their eventual success, and the factor that made this effort the model for later opposition to water resource projects, was their ability to confront the Corps on its own terms. The university committee's counterproposal for the Sangamon rebutted each point the Corps used to

20. "Trust indenture between Robert Allerton and the Board of Trustees of the University of Illinois, October 14, 1946," par. 1, cited in ibid., p. 8.

justify the project. The committee contended that there was little need
for the promised water supply: "An abundant supply of pure water can be
obtained by Decatur from the Mahomet Valley Aquifer at far less cost
than that from the reservoir." In addition, the nitrate content of Lake
Decatur already exceeded the U.S. Public Health Service's limit, and the
new reservoir would fall prey to the same condition. The recreational benefits were seen as overstated. "With the exception of motor boating and
water skiing, all forms of recreation claimed for the Oakley Project can
be realized without building dams. . . . Within 65 miles of the Oakley
site there are 26,000 acres of public water surface and only 3,500 acres of
public woodland. Over one-third of this woodland is in Allerton Park."
Finally, the high degree of pollution present in Lake Decatur was expected to exist at Oakley. Mudflats and pollutants would make the Oakley
reservoir unfit for swimming and many other activities, and the flood control promised could be achieved more economically. "The Project is expected to reduce annual urban damages by only $14,000. Farmland which
the Corps proposes to protect can be protected at far less cost by using
existing federal crop insurance and/or levees."[21]

Most devastating of all was the committee's recomputation of the
Corps' benefit-cost figures. Its six-point conclusion changed the focus of
the entire controversy:

1. The Corps claims that the benefit-cost (B-C) ratio for the Project is
1.15. This means that in the average year $1.15 in benefits will be returned for
each dollar in costs.
2. The Corps made a mistake in its B-C analysis when it figured the cost
of an alternative water supply for Decatur at an interest rate different than
that used for the project. Correcting this mistake brings the B-C ratio down to
1.05.
3. The Corps made another mistake when it included the greenbelt in
land upon which it claimed reduction benefits. Correction of this error brings
the B-C ratio down to 0.97, meaning that benefits are less than costs.
4. The Corps has based its B-C analysis on an interest rate of 3.25 percent.
The current interest rate for Corps projects is 5.125 percent. Recalculating
the B-C ratio at 5.125 percent and correcting the two mistakes brings the B-C
ratio down to 0.69.
5. The Corps has claimed benefits for swimming and water quality that
will not be realized. The Corps should also have used well water in its B-C

21. All the quotations in this paragraph are from Marlin, *Battle for the Sangamon*,
pp. 1–2.

analysis as the least cost alternative for water supply. Correcting these matters brings the B-C ratio down to 0.49.

6. Considering all the pressing needs facing federal and local governments and the general lack of money in government treasuries, proceeding with the low priority Oakley Project at this time makes no sense. The Project presents planners with an easy way to save $65 million.[22]

Finally, to avoid being placed in the position of fighting something with nothing, the committee concluded its report with what it claimed was a less costly and less ecologically destructive alternative. "Almost all of the benefits claimed for the Oakley Project can be realized by treating the upper Sangamon watershed for erosion control, developing the greenbelt, and using well water for Decatur. The cost of this alternative project would be about $26 million."[23]

With the publication of this report, the Committee on Allerton Park placed the Corps in a defensive posture, to say the least. Virtually all its expertise was neutralized. The Corps had to either provide a convincing rebuttal to the figures and arguments presented by the committee or withdraw from the conflict. The Corps did not withdraw immediately but ruminated about the issues raised against the project for four more years. In 1975, however, the Chicago District designated the Oakley Project "inactive," ostensibly because of its lack of economic justification. For all intents and purposes the project was dead.

The significance of the battle for the Sangamon is that it occurred just as the environmentalists were moving into action nationwide to challenge large-scale dam and channelization projects. It demonstrated to the environmental community, as well as to the Corps and its political allies, that even the powerful Corps of Engineers could be stopped. Moreover, this could be accomplished with seemingly sound economic arguments and without the need to resort to passionate pleas concerning the less tangible values of aesthetics and conservation, although the latter were the actual motives behind the challenge. The effectiveness of using economic and engineering expertise was proved, and the lesson was not lost on that segment of the environmental community hostile to water resource development projects.

Public agencies are always confronted with disgruntled groups who oppose one or another of their projects, and it is easy to believe that the

22. Ibid., p. 2
23. Ibid., p. 3.

Corps regarded the confrontation over Oakley as one of those rare incidents when very intense local groups manage to defeat agency plans. But evidence to the contrary soon began to emerge. Some of the leading controversies that arose in the late 1960s (many of which are still being contested in the courts and elsewhere) are those over the Tocks Island Dam along the Delaware River; the plan to connect the Tennessee and Tombigbee rivers in Mississippi by canal; the unprecedented plan to transform Dallas into a seaport (the Trinity River project); the Cache River channelization project in Arkansas; the Cross-Florida Barge Canal project (temporarily halted by a presidential order); the Meramec Park Dam proposal in Missouri; the Baldwin Channel proposal to make Stockton, California, a supertanker port; the New Melones Dam project along the Stanislaus River in California; and most recently the revived plan to build an "Aswan Dam" for Maine—the Dickey-Lincoln School Lakes proposal.

The scenario is virtually the same in each case. The Corps presents elaborate economic and engineering justifications for its proposals, and its opponents argue just the opposite for economic, social, and aesthetic reasons. As tenacious as the Corps has been in these and other instances, it has not been blind to the new cultural values reflected in society's perception of mammoth public works projects. It has, however, generally considered certain projects as requiring completion—those whose construction had begun before the late 1960s or those backed by strong political pressures. These projects may be open to some modification but not termination. In a real sense they represent a sunk cost for the Corps, given the time and energy that has already been expended on them. Thus the Corps sees itself as locked into them. It also sees them as providing the necessary balance dictated by its multiple-missions orientation.

The New Mission

Strong pressure to maintain the status quo exists in any large organization. The Corps is no exception. By the late 1960s, however, the agency's traditional missions faced substantial public opposition. The equilibrium that had existed between agency and societal values was upset by the demands for citizen involvement in agency decisionmaking and by the new ecological awareness sweeping the country. The Corps found itself in a state of disequilibrium by the late 1960s. Pressures on the agency pulled in opposite directions. Somehow it had to find a satisfactory resolution, a new equilibrium, in order to survive and prosper.

Initial Response

In June 1970 Lieutenant General Frederick J. Clarke, then chief of engineers, responded to critics of the Corps with this announcement: "We will encourage as broad public and private participation as practical in defining environmental objectives and in eliciting viewpoints of what the public wants and expects as well as what it is projected to need."[24] The announcement was interesting not only for what it said about the Corps' new commitment to public participation but because the program was aimed at eliciting the opinions of the public specifically on environmental matters. The chief obviously saw the two issues as related: demand for substantive changes in Corps projects and for more open decisionmaking were coming largely from environmental groups across the country. His announcement accurately reflected the principal locus of discontent.

Skeptics questioning the sincerity of the Corps' commitment to environmental issues and to public participation quickly point out that such public pronouncements are the stock-in-trade of all public agencies. The reference to a new mission may have been stated, but was it a statement merely designed to better public relations for the agency? This interpretation, reflecting as it does the wisdom of students of bureaucracy, is applicable in most instances. Yet the Corps went beyond a passing comment in both its commitment to a new environmental program and its promise of broader public participation in its planning activities.

As a preliminary action aimed at incorporating an environmental ethic within the agency, the chief established an Environmental Advisory Board in 1970 composed of six nationally known leaders on environmental matters. The chief outlined the board's purpose as follows:

a. Examine the Corps' existing and proposed policies, programs, and activities from an environmental point of view, to identify problems and weaknesses and suggest how these can be remedied.

b. Advise on how the Corps can improve working relations with the conservation community and the general public.

24. Quoted in U.S. Department of the Army, Corps of Engineers, Directorate of Civil Works, "Environmental Program," EP 1105-2-500 (June 1973), p. 3.

c. Advise on environmental problems or issues pertinent to specific plans or programs.[25]

The creation of the Environmental Advisory Board was followed in June by a letter from the chief's office to all Corps division engineers emphasizing that environmental matters were not to be treated casually. This issue would require a fundamental redirection in Corps practices and policy, plus an internal reorganization that the chief fully intended to see implemented. These initial actions of the leadership made it fairly clear to personnel at the operating levels of the agency that they would have to take the new issues seriously. However, this strong commitment by the leadership to an environmental mission raised the problem of value conflict. How were agency personnel to view development and conservation (or worse yet, preservation) of water resources as *not* mutually exclusive? How were they in practice to achieve a balance between their traditional missions and the new goal of environmental quality?

The dilemma was answered in part in November 1970 by a set of environmental guidelines containing four objectives for Corps project planning.

a. *To preserve* unique and important ecological, aesthetic, and cultural values of our national heritage.
b. *To conserve* and use wisely the natural resources of our Nation for the benefit of present and future generations.
c. *To enhance*, maintain, and restore the natural and manmade environment in terms of its productivity, variety, spaciousness, beauty, and other measures of quality.
d. *To create* new opportunities for the American people to use and enjoy their environment.[26]

These objectives would be accomplished, theoretically, through a much more elaborate and explicit planning process than had previously been

25. Lt. Gen. Frederick J. Clarke, "Redirection for the Corps: The Recipient's Perspective," *Water Spectrum*, vol. 4, no. 13 (1972), p. 1. The first chairman of the board resigned after one year in protest over what he considered to be the Corps' failure to respond aggressively to environmental issues. This view was not shared, however, by the remaining environmentalists on the board. (Interview with Roland C. Clement, vice-president of the National Audubon Society and chairman of the advisory board, June 18, 1973.)

26. U.S. Department of the Army, Corps of Engineers, Institute for Water Resources, *Environmental Guidelines for the Civil Works Program of the Corps of Engineers*, IWR Report 70-5, November 1970 (GPO, 1971), pp. 5–6.

practiced in designing and outlining agency projects. Every planning study hereafter would begin with a clear statement of the problem and would contain a list of environmental features or conditions that should be protected, preserved, or developed with great care. Corps planners were then to formulate a wide range of structural and, in marked contrast to past practice, nonstructural alternatives. As required under the National Environmental Policy Act of 1969, all environmental effects of each alternative would have to be examined. A preliminary environmental impact statement would have to be prepared at the outset of all studies and updated as often as necessary. Through these mechanisms the chief hoped "to introduce an environmental viewpoint when . . . projects first come under consideration and to receive and accommodate it at every subsequent stage of their development and utilization."[27] Naturally, this would require new expertise, a new sensitivity throughout the agency, and some mechanism—that is, structural and personnel changes—to actually implement this new program outlined by headquarters. The response at the field level is the subject of chapter 3.

Commitment to Public Participation in Decisionmaking

In the months following the chief engineer's initial announcement of the Corps' commitment to open planning, he continued to affirm his pledge. At a week-long public participation training session for selected division and district personnel held in February 1971 that in itself indicated the chief's serious intent, General Clarke reiterated his position.

In the past we have conducted our planning activities with a relatively small percentage of the people who have actually been concerned, primarily federal, state, and local government officials of one kind or another. Today there are, in addition, vast numbers of private citizens who, individually, or in groups and organizations and through their chosen representatives, are not only keenly interested in what we are doing with the Nation's water resources but who want to have a voice and influence in the planning and management of those resources . . . we cannot and must not ignore [these] other voices. . . . I consider public participation of critical importance to the Corps' effectiveness as a public servant. It is . . . an area I won't be satisfied with until we can truly say that the Corps is doing a superb job.[28]

27. Ibid., pp. 11–12.
28. Quoted in B. H. Dodge, "Achieving Public Involvement in the Corps of Engineers: Water Resources Planning," *Water Resources Bulletin*, vol. 9 (June 1973), p. 449.

It is important to point out that these remarks were not made for public consumption but for the Corps' field staff, for those who were being called on to actually implement the new policies.

Shortly thereafter the OCE issued another set of guidelines to remove any lingering doubts about whether the agency was taking open planning seriously. Public participation was to be a continuous, two-way communication process. Its general goal was "to insure that the solutions to water resource problems satisfy the needs and preferences of the people to the maximum degree possible within the bounds of local, state, and federal interests, responsibilities and authorities." More important, through the public participation effort district offices were to specifically "seek a clear consensus among concerned citizens and their official representatives by facilitating the resolution of a controversy." In other words, without first achieving a consensus on a project at the local level, a district dare not recommend it to the chief for construction. Obviously the public participation program was intended to shore up the agency's sagging public image. It was "to build public confidence and trust in Corps' planning and in Corps' planners."[29]

The objectives of the program and its underlying logic were explicitly spelled out in a public participation manual prepared for use within the agency by the Corps' Institute for Water Resources.[30] The institute, which was the agency's research branch in Washington, was then charged with overseeing the implementation of public participation throughout the Corps.

The manual identified three major objectives of an expanded public participation program: public relations, information, and conflict resolution.[31] What, exactly, did these new goals mean to the Corps? What was

29. Quotations in this paragraph are from U.S. Department of the Army, Corps of Engineers, Office of the Chief of Engineers, "Water Resources Policies and Authorities: Public Participation in Water Resources Planning," Engineer Circular 1165-2-100 (May 28, 1971), p. 3.

30. "Remarks by Lieutenant General F. J. Clarke, Chief of Engineers, U.S. Army Short Course on Public Participation in Water Resources Planning, Georgia Institute of Technology, Atlanta, Georgia, 2 February 1971," in Charles W. Dahlgren, "Public Participation in Water Resources Planning: A Multi-Media Course," U.S. Department of the Army, Corps of Engineers, Institute for Water Resources Professional Development Paper 72-1 (April 1972), sec. 4.0 H-A, pp. 1–4.

31. See excerpt from James R. Hanchey, "Effective Public Participation in Federal Water Resource Planning," in Dahlgren, "Public Participation in Water Resources Planning," pp. 1–9. Quotations in the discussion that follows have been taken from these same pages.

perceived as the pay-off to the agency in pursuing an expanded participation effort that promised to be expensive, time-consuming, and frequently frustrating?

First, the public relations objective was seen as an aid in legitimizing the Corps' role in water resource planning. This was crucial because of the agency's deteriorating credibility in the eyes of the public. As noted earlier, it had received a bad press.

Dissatisfaction with its projects was believed to stem in part from certain misperceptions about the agency, especially the failure of the public to understand and appreciate the legal constraints imposed on the agency by Congress and the executive branch. Thus the public needed to be informed about the agency's "true" role. Moreover, the problem of misperception was not unique to the Corps; it was a "manifestation of the more general disparity between the global manner in which citizens perceive community problems and needs, and the compartmentalized structure of programs designed to meet them." This disparity between public expectations and the agency's "real" capacities could be remedied, it was felt, through a concerted effort by engineers in the field to make explicit the agency's legal authorities, responsibilities, operating procedures, and constraints at the outset of every project study.

Part of the public relations objective was also obviously intended to develop confidence and trust. Without trust, all other attempts to communicate with the public would come to nothing. If the engineers were to be believed, they would have to "develop and maintain an image . . . as the most reliable source of information available on water resources issues." This meant more than simply having the necessary expertise: the agency would have to convince the public it was the primary source of truth in the area of water resources. No one pretended this would be easy. The engineers would have to go beyond the bureaucratic practice of revealing only information that supports the agency's preconceived notions about the best plan for the community. Rather, "the agency must demonstrate a willingness to develop information on all aspects of the planning problem *and to share this information with the public even though some of it might be damaging to programs or solutions which the agency favors* [emphasis added]."

The second objective, information gathering, was directed at both the public and the field planners. Each study was now to begin with a proper diagnosis of a community's problems and needs by the district office. No longer could it be taken for granted that Corps planners plus the local chamber of commerce knew what the local problems were. On the contrary, it was noted that "quite frequently water resources projects have been rejected by the public because the planner and the public had a different view of the local problems which needed solution." It followed, therefore, that public participation activities should be designed to afford the planners an opportunity to test their perception of the problem against that of the local community early in the planning process.

Once into the development-of-alternatives stage of a project, consultation with the public would again be necessary to aid the planner in narrowing the range of alternatives to those most likely to be both feasible (justifiable economically and within Corps capabilities) and acceptable to the local community. Such public sessions would also allow the public an early opportunity to suggest alternatives the planner may have overlooked. Not only could this improve the chances of arriving at the best ultimate solution, but it would enhance the likelihood of acceptance of the agency's recommended solution by the public.

To be complete, the information function would include an agency presentation of the implications of the various solutions under consideration. This was considered an exceedingly important step in the planning and public participation effort in that if "the public [is] to make rational value judgments, they must be supplied with not only the alternatives but the future consequences of the selection of each alternative, in as much detail as possible."

The public relations and information objectives were viewed as intrinsically worthwhile but also as the necessary groundwork for the ultimate objective, which was the resolution of conflict over proposed projects. The recommended approach to the entire effort of involving the public was to structure the situation in such a way that a consensus would emerge. Corps planners were told to work toward a process of "cooperative problem solving in which the conflicting parties have the joint interest of reaching a mutually satisfactory solution." This called for honest, frequent, and direct communication, which would enable underlying issues to surface and thus reduce the likelihood of later misunderstanding. Such communication in turn was expected to bring all parties involved to a recognition of and mutual respect for one another's positions and to establish an atmosphere of friendliness and trust that would be conducive to common problem-solving and the minimization of irreconcilable differences.

While the manual acknowledged that creating an atmosphere of co-

operation would not in itself ensure the resolution of an immediate controversy over a proposed project (such other determinants as the "imagi-
nativeness, experience, and flexibility of the parties" were also involved),
obviously it was felt that such an effort would bear long-range benefits for
the agency. Since the earlier relationship between the parties in conflict
strongly affects the course of conflict resolution, it seemed reasonable to
assume that a sincere effort on the part of the agency to encourage comprehensive public participation would leave a positive impression on the
public, despite any specific substantive outcome. This impression could
not help but enhance the Corps' ability to reach agreement with the public
on future studies.

It was also felt that conflict resolution requires avoiding extreme positions, that participants must not see their choices as all or nothing or
feel they must be totally for or against the Corps' recommended plan. By
maintaining open communications, flexibility in searching out alternative
solutions, and candor about the realistic limits of the agency, the dreaded
situation of polarization and conflict could be avoided. This is to say
again that if the public relations and information objectives were achieved,
they would in turn promote conflict resolution. There would thus be
approval of the Corps' recommended projects.

In essence the Corps was attempting to adopt the participatory model
of decisionmaking as it had evolved in the human relations school of social
psychology and organization theory over the past several decades. The
basic premise of the approach, which has been verified in small group experiments mainly in industrial settings, is that all those who must implement and therefore live with an organization's decisions should be included in the decisionmaking process—participatory democracy, in other
words. Moreover, the group leader (management) should encourage the
impartial consideration of all alternatives before reaching a final determination.[32]

These experiments had shown that the process of collective decisionmaking can satisfy the participant's need for self-respect while simultaneously fostering member support for final decisions. The theory is that

32. The participatory model evolved out of the early experimental work of Kurt
Lewin and his colleagues in the 1930s. See Ralph K. White and Ronald Lippitt,
Autocracy and Democracy: An Experimental Inquiry (Harper, 1960). For the views
of a contemporary proponent of the participatory thesis in social psychology, see Rensis
Likert, *The Human Organization: Its Management and Values* (McGraw-Hill, 1967).

the greater the sense of satisfaction with the group or organization that results from participation, the greater the cooperation among members, and therefore the more effective the implementation of group decisions. Through its public participation program, the Corps was consciously trying to adopt this model of participatory decisionmaking.[33] But the Corps is a large public bureaucracy and not a small, well-defined group. Further, participants representing the public's interests in project planning would not be integral members of the organization in any real sense.

Practical Problems of Public Participation

Obviously, trying to graft this participatory model of decisionmaking onto the Corps involved many difficulties that were unforeseen by agency leaders anxious to foster open planning. How successful would participatory decisionmaking be in the environment of Corps project planning? Would participants truly feel they were an integral part of the process? How would these changes substantively affect the agency's planning process? The Corps would have to deal with such questions in the most minute fashion in its new open planning program and would inevitably

33. The Corps was not the first agency to turn to participatory decisionmaking to resolve conflicts. The concept was basic, for example, to the "war on poverty" of the 1960s. But it was unusual for a group of professional engineers to adopt the ideal of interactive consultation with diverse segments of the community, especially segments hostile to them. The agency was encouraged in this direction by the chief of engineers, the Institute for Water Resources (the Corps' think tank), and by consultants from major universities who were knowledgeable in water resource planning and public relations and from whom the institute's personnel took many of their cues. In the frequently cited studies prepared by Corps planners for the Institute for Water Resources and for the National Water Commission in the early 1970s, planners and social psychologists from the School of Natural Resources and from Rensis Likert's Institute for Social Research, both at the University of Michigan, assured the Corps that open planning could readily be applied to the agency's water resource planning. See Katharine P. Warner, *A Statement of the Art Study of Public Participation in Water Resources Planning*, Final Report, prepared for the National Water Commission (U.S. Army Corps of Engineers, July 1971), especially p. 3. The same message appeared in two earlier studies: Thomas E. Borton, Katharine P. Warner, and J. William Wenrich, *The Susquehanna Communication-Participation Study: Selected Approaches to Public Involvement in Water Resources Planning*, IWR Report 70-6, U.S. Department of the Army, Corps of Engineers, Institute for Water Resources (IWR, December 1970); and A. Bruce Bishop, *Public Participation in Water Resources Planning*, IWR Report 70-7, U.S. Department of the Army, Corps of Engineers, Institute for Water Resources (IWR, December 1970), especially pp. 52–54.

be drawn into the kind of endless debate engaged in by democratic theoreticians and practitioners about who should participate and for what ends.[34]

SCOPE OF REPRESENTATION. Surely not all those directly affected by a proposed project would participate in project planning, even if invited to do so.[35] Only a few of the hundreds or possibly thousands of concerned people could be accommodated in any public meeting or similar event. Thus the Corps would have to decide on a criterion for inclusion. Would there be geographical representation whereby each area potentially affected by a project would have a representative? Would there be functional representation for business, agricultural, environmental, and other assorted interests? Who would select the representatives of the units to be included, the Corps or the units themselves? Finally, what about all those who would never choose to participate directly? How would they be represented?

MODE OF PARTICIPATION. The recommended two-way flow of communications envisioned by the chief of engineers seemed to mean that the public would be involved in the planning process at fairly frequent intervals. But could it mean more? Were weekly, monthly, or biannual contacts intended? Would there be massive gatherings similar to the Corps' traditional public hearings, or would participation entail smaller group-

34. For a sample of the extensive literature see Robert A. Alford, *Bureaucracy and Participation* (Rand McNally, 1969); Roger C. Cramton, "The Why, Where, and How of Broadened Public Participation in the Administrative Process," *Georgetown Law Journal*, vol. 60 (February 1972), pp. 525–50; Ernest Gelhorn, "Public Participation in Administrative Proceedings," *Yale Law Journal*, vol. 81 (January 1972), pp. 359–404; Lloyd C. Irland, "Citizen Participation—A Tool for Conflict Management on the Public Lands," *Public Administration Review*, vol. 35 (May-June 1975), pp. 263–69; Charles O. Jones, "The Limits of Public Support: Air Pollution Agency Development," *Public Administration Review*, vol. 32 (September-October 1972), pp. 502–08; Marvin Meade, " 'Participative' Administration—Emerging Reality or Wishful Thinking?" in Dwight Waldo, ed., *Public Administration in a Time of Turbulence* (Chandler, 1971), pp. 169–87; Emmette S. Redford, *Democracy in the Administrative State* (Oxford University Press, 1969); Walter A. Rosenbaum, "The Paradoxes of Public Participation," *Administration and Society*, vol. 8 (1976), pp. 355–82; Philip Selznick, *TVA and the Grass Roots: A Study in the Sociology of Formal Organization* (University of California Press, 1949); and papers in "Symposium on Public Participation in Resource Decisionmaking," *Natural Resources Journal*, vol. 16 (January 1976), pp. 1–236.

35. See James A. Riedel, "Citizen Participation: Myths and Realities," *Public Administration Review*, vol. 32 (May-June 1972), pp. 211–20.

ings and workshops that are more conducive to interaction and extended dialogue?[36] If the latter, would the agency bring all interested factions together at one time or meet separately with each? Would the agency initiate all attempts at participation or in some cases await the public's request or demand? Would other government agencies be integrated into the planning process, or would they be included only through their participation in the public meetings?

DELEGATION OF AUTHORITY. What would be the role of the public representatives? Were they to serve as advisers and consultants at the pleasure of the agency? Or would they have formal veto powers and substantive decisionmaking authority? If so, which powers were to be delegated and which reserved by the agency? If much formal authority was delegated, would this not have dire consequences for the very legitimacy of the agency? How could extensive public participation be reconciled with the role of the bureaucracy as guardian of the public interest? The complex problem of delegation of authority also raises the difficult issue of whether an intensely concerned but numerical minority of citizens should be allowed to determine policy for the entire public.

LOCUS OF FINAL DECISION. Was the decision whether to proceed with a project to be made by the public at large through a popular referendum? Is this what the chief meant by "broad public participation"? Were such decisions to be made by vote of the activists involved in the planning program? Practically speaking, it was unlikely that the Corps would devolve its formal decisionmaking authority to such an extent, but short of doing so, what real influence would the public have on the ultimate decision?

The answers to these questions have far-reaching implications. In the atypical case of unanimity on a course of action, the mode of participation and the problem of delegation of authority are inconsequential. Open planning in this instance is little more than a ritualized method of demonstrating that a consensus exists: it is a legitimizing exercise.[37] More often, however, the proper course of action is debatable and contested; the person or groups having formal authority to veto or act affirmatively are at a

36. See Thomas A. Heberlein, "Some Observations on Alternative Mechanisms for Public Involvement: The Hearing, Public Opinion Poll, the Workshop and the Quasi-Experiment," *Natural Resources Journal*, vol. 16 (January 1976), pp. 197–212.

37. See Robert H. Salisbury, "Research on Political Participation," *American Journal of Political Science*, vol. 19 (May 1975), pp. 326–27.

distinct advantage over those who may simply voice their preference. In these cases the form of participation is no trifling matter to the Corps; to other federal, state, and local agencies that feel certain Corps projects may impinge on their domain; to private interest groups; or to numerous concerned citizens who take an active interest in water resource development. To take an obvious example, when environmentalists adamantly oppose a proposed navigation project, it is of paramount importance to the outcome of the controversy whether they have a formal veto over the agency's actions simply because they have "participated."

One school of thought on public participation argues that when a program allows only for exchanges of information between the agency and the public, or enables citizens to act only in a consulting capacity, it is permitting little more than tokenism.[38] It may have appreciable therapeutic value for those involved, but in reality the citizen has little effect on the agency's actions. To be of value, public participation requires a working partnership, the delegation of powers, and a formal mechanism for citizen control.[39] In this case citizens have the requisite power to force the agency to compromise and to negotiate solutions with all factions of the affected community.

The other school of thought on participation holds to the more traditional view that public agencies are delegated responsibilities by Congress and the President to represent the public interest. They are charged with the public trust and therefore should not relinquish their responsibility to any one segment of the community that may, for whatever reason, take an active part in the agency's decisionmaking process. To do so would not only be an abrogation of their legal responsibilities but a perversion of the system of political representation of which the bureaucracy is an integral part. In this new program the Corps would have to address this issue.

PROGRAM EVALUATION. A subject about which there are many questions but few reliable and systematic answers is that of how participants have

38. For example, see Daniel P. Moynihan, *Maximum Feasible Misunderstanding: Community Action in the War on Poverty* (Free Press, 1969).

39. See Sherry R. Arnstein, "A Ladder of Citizen Participation," *Journal of the American Institute of Planners*, vol. 35 (July 1969), pp. 216–24. A similar distinction is made by the theorist, Carole Pateman, between full, partial, and pseudo participation. Full participation requires all members of the body to have equal power over decisions; partial is when some members have power over decisions while others have only influence; and pseudo is when some members have no power. (*Participation and Democratic Theory* [Cambridge University Press, 1970].)

actually responded to the Corps' public participation effort. Do the literally thousands of citizens who have taken part in the Corps' new planning
programs view the Corps as sincere or sinister? How do they judge the
process? How do they judge the projects that were the subject of their
participation? Can they be neatly divided into Corps opponents (environmentalists) and Corps proponents (the business community)?

Partial answers to these questions are given in chapters 4, 5, and 6
through an examination of five Corps project studies. Not surprisingly, the
extent of public participation, the number of alternatives examined, and
the extent to which social and ecological considerations are weighed in
each case depends on a range of factors, or on what might best be thought
of as constraints that operate at the district level. Those factors include
the mix of developmental, environmental, and other interests that become
actively involved in the planning process; the predispositions of district
personnel (their receptivity to one set of interests over another and their
willingness to innovate); and the separability of the project under consideration from ongoing or other anticipated activity in the water use area.

Separability is especially important because most of the Corps' projects
are related to much broader considerations such as the overall use of an
area's water resources. Thus a determination to build or not to build a dam
or lock and channel at one point along a river invariably has implications
for the commerce within an entire river basin. It may also affect a larger
regional master plan for residential and industrial development. Thus
there are many real world constraints on local Corps offices, and while
directives from Washington can encourage adherence to the spirit as
well as to the letter of new policies, they can seldom ensure it.

CHAPTER THREE

Reorganization: Developing a New Infrastructure

THE CORPS' CONCERN with environmental quality, as enunciated by its leadership and prompted by the National Environmental Policy Act of 1969 (NEPA), had to be effective at the local or field level to be effective at all. Simply announcing new goals on behalf of an agency produces little substantive change if such pronouncements are not followed up by some mechanism for implementing them. Reorganization was seen as that mechanism. During the year following the passage of national environmental legislation, therefore, the Corps was extremely active, reorganizing local and regional offices in an effort to redirect the agency toward greater environmental sensitivity.

Our analysis of this rather substantial reorganization is based on a sample that included interviews and data collection at 11 district (field) offices; 4 division (regional) offices; the Office of the Chief of Engineers (Washington headquarters); the Board of Engineers for Rivers and Harbors; the Waterways Experiment Station in Vicksburg, Mississippi; and the Corps' Institute for Water Resources. We interviewed over 100 people, the majority of whom were agency personnel in district and division offices. The district and division offices were chosen to approximate a geographic and demographic cross section of the Corps and included New York; Philadelphia; Detroit; Vicksburg; Chicago; St. Louis; Baltimore; Norfolk; New Orleans; the New England and San Francisco districts; and the South Pacific, North Central, Lower Mississippi Valley, and North Atlantic divisions.[1]

In open-ended interviews, we directed a few precise questions to each

1. New England is technically an operating division, but in this study it is included in the district data.

respondent, making every effort to reach a cross section of agency personnel. Some interviewees' jobs were directly related to the new environmental mission; others were not. We also spoke with all but one of the
district engineers, the army officers in charge of each of the Corps' local
offices.

The district was selected as the primary unit of analysis for obvious
reasons. In a decentralized organization such as the Corps, the field response can be crucial. It is at the local level that a new policy or program
either succeeds or fails. Thus in this study the local unit is the crucial
variable in analyzing organizational change.

Reorganization at the District Level

The introduction of new programs or new policy in an agency invariably means that a certain amount of reorganization and reorientation will
occur. This process takes one of two forms: entirely new units may be
added or old units may be renamed and their roles redefined. Usually
federal agencies opt for the latter because they must. Limited resources,
personnel ceilings, and other systemic constraints mean that new personnel are brought on board gradually. In the meantime those already in the
organization are assigned to the new tasks, and existing units are given
additional functions.

The field response to new policy also takes this latter form because
field personnel operate within a tight budget. Few uncommitted resources
are available for a new mission. Further, it seems the more reasonable
course of action to move gradually into a new program and to utilize existing resources and personnel.

An example, however, of the creation of a new unit was the establishment of the chief of engineers' Environmental Advisory Board, which
was composed of citizens. Many district offices—an estimated 75 percent
by 1974—followed Washington's lead and instituted citizen advisory
groups.[2] By 1978, however, virtually all the district offices had opted for
informal meetings with interested citizens and organizations and therefore had disbanded any formal boards they may have established.[3] Such

2. Colonel Gerald E. Galloway, "The Decision Process of the Civil Works Function of the Army Corps of Engineers," U.S. Army War College Military Research
Program Paper (June 1974), p. 34.
3. Telephone interview with Colonel John Hill, environmental officer, U.S. Army
Corps of Engineers, June 26, 1978.

boards are frequently created when a quick response to a need is desirable or when an organization lacks a certain kind of expertise. Advisory boards, like consultants, perform at least a dual function: they show that the agency is "doing something," and they may also provide a viewpoint or some knowledge the agency does not have. Though they often perform important functions, advisory boards are not a permanent part of the organization and therefore their establishment may indicate less commitment to new programs than do other types of responses to demands for change. On the other hand, during times when public values and interests are changing rather rapidly the ad hoc approach, as exemplified by the establishment of advisory boards and the use of consultants, may be desirable from the standpoint of organizational flexibility because it permits trade-offs. Agency decisionmakers must assess short-term versus long-term changes in policy and act accordingly.

Emphasis on Planning

The most obvious change in the agency at the district level, however, has been the introduction of an environmental unit—a direct response to critics who objected to the Corps' lack of environmental perspective, its seemingly closed system of decisionmaking, and its failure to engage in more extensive project planning. Since 1970, district offices, which were made responsible for implementing open planning procedures, have typically been organized in one of two ways. If the local office of the Corps has a separate Planning Division, the environmental unit is placed in it; otherwise the unit is in the Engineering Division. The former generally is preferred because the planning function and the environmental task are seen as conceptually related.

The agency adopted the concept of comprehensive, long-range planning on a continuous basis during the late 1960s to meet needs underscored in a Senate report on the civil works program of the Corps.

The rapid and drastic changes in national policies and in water resource development needs in recent years have imposed unprecedented requirements for planning and developing water resources. The current policies, procedures, organization and staffing of the Corps of Engineers are not being fully adjusted to meet these requirements with the speed or in the ways needed to deal effectively with a much-changed and continuously changing water resources environment. . . .

The increase in size and complexity of the civil works program and the need for increasingly efficient use of resources require generation and use of increased knowledge not only in the engineering fields which have had major application in the program but also in the areas of economics, sociology, and other disciplines which are becoming increasingly important in water resource development.[4]

Planning, therefore, was seen as the route to better decisions by coming to terms with rapid change, increased complexity, and new environmental demands.[5]

Though the Corps' intentions are admirable, is "planning" more than a euphemism? Wildavsky has given one answer to this question.

> The injunction to plan (!!) is empty. The key terms associated with it are proverbs or platitudes. Pursue goals! Consider alternatives! Obtain knowledge! Exercise power! Obtain consent! Or be flexible but do not alter your course. Planning stands for unresolved conflicts.[6]

It is hard to escape the conclusion that the planning function in an agency such as the Corps is indeed a little bit of everything. It does stand for unresolved conflicts, especially of an environmental nature. Corps planners are supposed to take initial responsibility for a project study (a pre-authorization survey) and to iron out the problems—a process that is related more to politics and public relations than to technical matters—before submitting a survey report. Planning, planners say, is very different from the straight engineering of the good old days. Now there are many more variables to consider than just technical, engineering, and even economic factors.

However, the recent emphasis on planning, an often vague term used to excess, has encouraged Corps personnel to recognize the complexity and conflicts inherent in water resource policy. It has brought into the agency a multidisciplinary ethos, evidenced in the data presented later in this chapter, and this development is healthy. The Corps no longer holds an unshakable belief in one "best" way, recognizing that there may be more than one way to do things and that project formulation is better when the public is involved. As one planning chief said, "Our projects are better if they please people."

4. *Civil Works Program of the Corps of Engineers: A Report to the Secretary of the Army by the Civil Works Study Board*, Committee Print, Senate Committee on Public Works, 89 Cong. 2 sess. (Government Printing Office, 1966), pp. 5, 7.

5. An alternative explanation given for the shifting emphases in the Corps during the mid-1960s was that the agency was having increasing difficulty in getting approval from state authorities for its projects. It was a period of numerous turndowns. Thus the need for better planning developed.

6. Aaron Wildavsky, "If Planning Is Everything, Maybe It's Nothing," *Policy Sciences*, vol. 4 (1973), p. 146.

Innovation or change in the Corps did not begin in 1970 after the passage of NEPA or with the chief of engineer's statement on environmental activities and public involvement. The process began earlier than that but was given additional impetus by these more recent developments. While the injunction to "consider the environment" can be as vague as the "need for better planning," such statements nevertheless are indicative of changing attitudes and behavior within the agency.

The Corps Environmental Program: A Sample of Organization and Attitudes

Environmental units were instituted in most district offices between 1970 and 1972. Generally they evolved from the Recreation Resources Section of the district office. New personnel were brought in to staff the new unit, and to a greater or lesser extent the type of functions changed from those performed by the former section.

Staffing

Whom did the Corps seek out to staff its new environmental units? What type of expertise did the agency feel was most lacking and therefore most needed? Table 3-1 summarizes the personnel data for early 1974 of the 11 districts sampled and indicates whether the environmental unit in the district office is a branch or a section and whether it is under the Planning Division or the Engineering Division. In those districts having a separate Planning Division (numbers 1, 4, and 10 in the sample) the environmental unit is a branch under planning. It is also a branch in the Engineering Division in four districts and is a section under engineering in the remaining four districts. Since the organizational hierarchy is division-branch-section, one indicator of relative influence may be whether the environmental unit is a branch or a section.[7]

District 11 is divided into two sections in table 3-1 and in succeeding tables because its personnel have attempted to build an interdisciplinary capability and to decentralize or decompartmentalize the environmental function. Thus in this district two principal units—a section in the Engineering Division and a branch in the Construction and Operations Division—are directly involved in environmental work. This is not to say that

---

7. We should stress that in this analysis no *single* indicator is a reliable measure of organizational change or of the integration of environmental concerns into the agency.

Table 3-1. *Personnel Data on Environmental Units in Selected District Offices, 1974*

District, status, and location of environmental unit	Total professional staff		Discipline of chief of environmental unit	Disciplines represented in environmental unit				
	Environmental unit[a]	Planning unit[b]		Total number	Engineering	Biological and physical sciences[c]	Social sciences[d]	Technical writers and editors
District 1 Branch, Planning Division	20	62	Biologist	4	3	10	5	2
District 2 Branch, Engineering Division	19	[e]	Landscape architect	4	3	9	6	1
District 3 Section, Engineering Division	17	48	Landscape architect/ recreational planner	2	0	10	7[f]	0
District 4 Branch, Planning Division	5	20	Landscape architect	2	0	1	4	0
District 5 Branch, Engineering Division	6	25	Economist	2	0	5	1	0
District 6 Section, Engineering Division	8	67	Civil engineer	2	4	4	0	0

District 7 Branch, Engineering Division	10	21	3	Mechanical engineer	4	3	3	0
District 8 Branch, Engineering Division	8	20	3	Civil engineer	4	3	1	0
District 9 Section, Engineering Division	10	50	3	Biologist	2	5	3	0
District 10 Branch, Planning Division	9	54	3	Engineer/water resources planner	2	3	4	0
District 11 Section, Engineering Division[g]	10	34	3	Economist	3	4	3	0
Branch, Construction and Operations Division[h]	10	...	2	Civil engineer	4	6	0	0

a. Includes part-time or temporary professional help.
b. Provided for comparison; includes environmental unit staff.
c. Includes forestry and oceanography as well as the more obvious biological and physical sciences.
d. Includes landscape architects and recreation planners.
e. No comparable unit.
f. Including two engineers, now called planners.
g. Environmental unit works with the Planning Division and handles environmental impact statements.
h. Environmental unit handles the permits program.

other districts may not have done likewise, but district 11 showed less evidence of compartmentalization than did the others.[8] No one interviewed in the other districts, for example, mentioned that environmental activity had produced a reorganization as substantial as that at District 11.

Table 3-1 illustrates the interdisciplinary capability of the environmental units. In most districts a real effort has been made to bring in people other than engineers to do environmentally related work. The trend has been to hire people with expertise in the biological and physical sciences. One environmental branch chief explained his hiring rationale in this manner: "We could have hired more engineers, but the branch can draw on the rest of the district for that. And since the environmental unit works with project managers who are usually engineers, there's no real need to hire more engineers in the environmental branch."

As shown in table 3-1, most districts apparently follow this rationale when staffing their environmental units. The units are strongest in the biological and physical sciences, and the majority of the districts have three or four different specializations represented within the unit.

Strengthening the interdisciplinary capability of resource-managing agencies has been recommended and encouraged by policymakers in the Corps of Engineers and by its outside consultants. For example, in 1973 the Army Engineer Institute for Water Resources considered "the types of disciplines that ought to be represented on the 'interdisciplinary teams' charged with analyzing environmental impacts for water projects," and concluded:

It is impossible to set down a definitive list of disciplines because the "ideal" composition of the team will depend on the types of projects typically examined and the nature of the geographic region involved. For example, a team involved primarily with reservoirs and channelization projects in the midwest would have a different composition from one involved primarily with coastal dredging and beach erosion projects. However, a generally desirable staff composition would involve at least one representative from each of the following areas: water resources engineering, water quality, biology, landscape architecture (or regional planning) and, for lack of a better term, "conservation."[9]

8. District 11, like all the others, has a unit handling the permit program. But the significant difference between this district and the others is that the linkage was not made between the permit program and environmental functions. Interviewees in a number of districts, however, stressed their Flood Plain Management Services unit as indicative of a changed environmental awareness. District 8, especially, has a strong floodplain management program.

9. Leonard Ortelano, ed., "Analyzing the Environmental Impacts of Water Proj-

According to this criterion a staff of at least five persons is desirable, representing the specializations named above. Our survey of Corps district offices indicates that most offices have done well in building up a multidisciplinary staff. The range of disciplines of the chiefs of the environmental units—two biologists, three landscape architects, two economists, and five engineers (one with an advanced degree in water resources planning)—is also significant.

For purposes of comparison, it is interesting to note the Corps' staffing situation before 1970 and the establishment of environmental units, many of which evolved from the older recreation sections. District 1, for example, had a Conservation and Recreation Section with a staff of five: three biologists, one landscape architect, and one civil engineering technician.[10] The composition of this staff was fairly typical of such offices during the last half of the 1960s. Districts 2, 6, 8, and 9 had similar recreation resources sections; two districts had no identifiable recreation or environmental resources units; two other districts had an Environmental Resources Section before 1970; and two districts had units with other names, from which the environmental unit evolved. As one section chief said, "This section has been here forever." But it had been there with a different name.

The significant conclusion to be drawn from these comparative data seems to be that the Corps is becoming more multidisciplinary, concomitant with its historically documented trend toward becoming a multipurpose agency.[11]

Staffing the environmental unit is not without its problems, however. The agency is still an engineering organization run for the most part by military and civilian engineers. At all levels of the organization there is a reluctance to bring in large numbers of people who have nonengineering backgrounds—who are members of the "exotic disciplines," as they are called in the agency—because, new programs notwithstanding, the bulk of the Corps' work is still primarily related to engineering. People with

---

ects," U.S. Department of the Army, Corps of Engineers, Institute for Water Resources, IWR Report 73-3 (IWR, March 1973), p. 10-4.

10. These historical data are drawn from 1967–68 organization charts and from interviews.

11. Though the Corps has always engaged in a number of different types of water resource projects—dredging, dam building, channelization, and so forth—a qualitative change has occurred recently with the addition of such new programs as wastewater management, urban studies, floodplain management, and a greatly expanded permits program.

backgrounds in the biological, physical, and social sciences may be quite helpful and even essential in some instances, but in the end a knowledge of engineering is regarded as the fundamental requirement for planning a good project.

At the district level, staffing is perhaps even more problematic. A planning chief explained his hiring dilemma this way: Personnel slots in his district office are tied to the work load. Where there is a lot of work to be done, there will obviously be a larger staff and vice versa. Since the districts are still unsure about the future of the new environmental program, he said, they are understandably afraid to hire people who are in nonengineering fields. In his district they prefer to hire consultants to do much of the environmental work because consultants are temporary and thus do not tie up the district's scarce resources "forever." The obvious conclusion is that environmental work brings in few dollars to the district.

In hiring specifically for the environmental unit, the situation is further exacerbated in that agency people do not know whether it is better to hire specialists or generalists. This problem is related to the rather indeterminate nature of the environmental program. No one is quite sure what "good environmental planning" is, including Congress, which passed environmental legislation; the agencies, which must implement it; and the courts, which must serve as referees. So agency personnel do not know precisely which disciplines or how many are most relevant to environmental work.

Districts apparently can use one of two approaches to the hiring problem. They can fill the environmental unit with a few good generalists who function largely as brokers and who monitor contracts to private consulting firms hired to do environmental inventories or assessments. Or the unit can be more adequately staffed and the bulk of the environmental work can be done in-house by an interdisciplinary team. Our sample includes districts using both approaches, but obviously if the objective is to reorient the agency or to fully consider environmental concerns, the latter approach is the more desirable. It is also more expensive.

Functions

Section 102 of the National Environmental Policy Act stipulates that every federal agency must prepare an environmental impact statement (EIS) for its major actions. This section is actually a small part of the act, but in implementing the legislation federal agencies have focused on it because of its relative ease of implementation. It is a precisely defined requirement, more readily translated into an agency regulation than other sections of the act. This is not to say that anyone at the outset knew how to prepare an adequate EIS, but compared with acknowledging a general mandate to incorporate environmental concerns into agency decision-making, producing impact statements was relatively easy.

Therefore the essential function of the environmental unit in each district is the preparation of impact statements for both ongoing and new projects. The EIS requirement is really the raison d'être of the environmental units, and it is doubtful whether many district offices would have created a new unit so early were it not for the legislation.

Since much has already been written about the function of the impact statements, their adequacy, and their efficacy as decisionmaking documents, it is unnecessary to dwell on those factors here.[12] A subject receiving little attention, however, is how agency people feel about this new function and what the potential ramifications of NEPA and the environmental mandate are for agency behavior.

It is hardly a measure of anything to know that environmental units prepare impact statements, because these statements are required by law. A more valuable determination is the degree of the environmental units' integration into the decisionmaking processes of the district offices. Those familiar with the environmental issue often wonder if the staffs of environmental units are simply stuck off in corners somewhere writing impact statements. Or worse yet, are they just monitoring the consulting firms that are doing the initial preparation of impact statements? As Kaufman has asked, are they isolated in planning units or confined to advisory roles?[13]

Table 3-2 is an attempt to assess this essentially subjective question by enumerating the functions performed by environmental units. The general proposition is that the more functions a unit engages in the more influential it is. It should be kept in mind that the categorization of functions

12. For a discussion of the adequacy of impact statements, see Richard A. Liroff, *A National Policy for the Environment: NEPA and Its Aftermath* (Indiana University Press, 1976); and papers in "Symposium on Environmental Impact Statements," *Natural Resources Journal,* vol. 16 (April 1976), pp. 243–414.

13. Herbert Kaufman, *The Limits of Organizational Change* (University of Alabama Press, 1971), p. 56.

Table 3-2. *Functions Performed by Environmental Units*

District	Preparation of environmental impact statements (1)	Public involvement program (2)	Frequent public contact and coordination functions (3)	EA/EIS preparation for permits (4)	Plan formulation or project planning (5)	Adviser to district engineer and division chief (6)
1	yes	some	no	yes	some	some
2	yes	yes	some	no	yes	yes
3	yes	some	some	no	no	some
4	yes	some	no	no	no	no
5	yes	yes	some	no	some	some
6	yes	no	some	no	no	some
7	yes	no	no	some	no	no
8	yes	no	no	no	no	no
9	yes	no	no	no	some	no
10	yes	some	some	some	some	some
11A[a]	yes	no	no	no	yes	some
11B[b]	no	no	yes	yes	no	c

EA = environmental assessment; EIS = environmental impact statement.
a. Environmental Section, Engineering Division, District 11.
b. Environmental Branch, Construction and Operations Division, District 11.
c. Data unavailable.

overlaps somewhat (in columns 2 and 3, for example). Further, the "yes," "some," and "no" evaluations are soft, but this type of survey does not lend itself to precise quantification. The evaluation is based essentially on what people (both in the environmental unit and in other parts of the district office) said they did and on what they could be observed doing. A "yes" response implies major responsibility for, or significant involvement in, the particular activity; "some" means limited participation; and "no" means little or no responsibility for the activity.[14]

Running the public involvement program is generally not a primary responsibility of the environmental unit. The planning branch or division usually does this, although in a number of districts someone from the environmental unit attends the public meetings. "In some cases we've actually been on the platform," one environmental branch chief said. Who gets involved—which units of the organization, which individuals, and at what level—is partly a function of personality, but it may also be indicative of the importance attached to the program within the agency. For instance, how much time the commanding officer of the district (the district engineer) spends on this activity varies significantly from attendance at only those public meetings where his presence is mandatory to attendance at as many of the meetings, workshops, and seminars connected with a project study as one person is physically able to manage. The increased number of these sessions is one reason, certainly, for the variation found from district to district, since before the recent expansion of the citizen involvement program, the job of the district engineer was largely defined as "meeting the public."

It probably still is. But it is interesting that many district engineers (as well as other Corps employees) make an implicit distinction between the public involvement program and their "normal" public duties, such as attending luncheons given by local business or professional groups, meeting with local economic interests, coordinating with other governmental bodies, and the like. In other words, the public involvement program is perceived as just one of several channels of communication to the public and generally to a specialized public at that: the environmental interests. Therefore, most district engineers replied in the negative when asked whether they spend much of their time at public hearings, workshops,

14. It should also be noted that many environmental units still have major responsibility for recreation planning. We would say that the majority of these units do recreation studies.

and seminars. Obviously they spend a great deal of their time in meeting with interest groups and in other public relations-related activities and thus often regard the formalized public participation program as just one part of the total effort of reaching the public.

There are exceptions, though, and one district engineer mentioned that he spent most of his office time with his environmental resources staff in dealing with local citizen groups. This district happened to be in an area where environmentalists were particularly active. "Engineering is the least of my concerns," he said. But the norm appears to be to view the new program as serving a particular clientele and not as the single or best way of reaching the public, except in districts where environmental issues are of overriding importance.

Also highly variable is whether the chief of the engineering division involves himself in the expanded citizen involvement effort. Since the chief is the highest ranking civilian employee in the office, his support or lack of it could be viewed as one indicator of the importance attached to the program. Only two or three chiefs of the 11 district offices sampled personally handled this program and made attendance a normal part of their job.

Involvement in the program is also idiosyncratic; one must enjoy working with the public, since it means frequent attendance at meetings or workshops (usually held at night), making oneself accessible to individuals or groups visiting the district offices, answering correspondence, making sure that all interested parties have been made aware of the Corps' plans, and the like. In most cases, therefore, responsibility for the program has devolved upon the planning staff, often with assistance from the environmental unit. The reasons are numerous, but the conclusion seems to be that the agency perceives this effort as one of tapping not *the* public interest but a specialized part of it. Yet it is an important activity inasmuch as public acceptance of a project is crucial; environmental opposition can cause long delays or even halt projects in rare instances.

Frequent public contact and coordination functions (column 3) include contact with private groups, individuals, and other federal and state agencies. Essentially this column of table 3-2 is an attempt to measure the extent of the environmental unit's informal contact and communication with outside groups, as opposed to its participation in the more institutionalized procedures of the public involvement program.

Few people in the environmental units said they spent much of their time in this manner. The outside contacts they do have are primarily with other federal agencies, principally the Environmental Protection Agency and the Bureau of Sports Fisheries and Wildlife, and with state and local environmental agencies. In preparing environmental impact statements, for example, those in the Corps' environmental units will touch base with these agencies and will often request information from them.

Environmentalists within the agency—those in the environmental units —do not, however, see environmental groups and organizations as their allies. They do not solicit information or viewpoints from these groups and have little informal or collegial contact with those outside the agency.

Because environmental groups have been the Corps' most vocal critics, considerable distrust and hostility undoubtedly have built up between the two. With the exception of one or two districts, the prevailing attitude is one of suspicion and frustration. Agency personnel, including those in the environmental units, do not understand what their critics want. "Nothing less than *no* project ever pleases them," one agency spokesman lamented. Another said, "The public is either pro- or anti-project; but *we* have to work with subtle variations in between." This is to say that the agency by definition has a pro-project position.

People in the environmental units are somewhat more sympathetic to the environmentalists' objections but only marginally so. This situation leaves considerable room for improved relations, but it will take both sides to realize this. As it stands now, the relationship between the Corps and environmental groups is still that of adversaries.

Few environmental units handle the Corps' permit responsibilities, a program that has grown significantly in recent years (column 4). The Rivers and Harbors Act of 1899 and subsequent legislation have given the Corps authority to review applications for permits authorizing discharges or deposits into all the navigable waters in the United States and their tributaries. Thus the agency has potential control over industrial and residential development and discharge affecting critical areas such as rivers, streams, oceans, and wetlands. As one chief of a permit section said, "The permit activity of the Corps can be an obstacle to further development; otherwise, the agency is prodevelopment."

Column 5 shows whether the environmental units function as an integral part of the agency's planning process or in a more peripheral manner. This was determined in part by evaluating the role played by the unit's principal product, the environmental impact statement, in the decisionmaking process. All districts complained of the backlog problem that resulted from the Council on Environmental Quality's decision to make NEPA retroactive.[15] Because of this decision, agency personnel had to write impact statements for completed and ongoing projects—a requirement that literally swamped the small staffs of the environmental units for a time. Increasingly, the tendency was to contract out the work and have the environmental unit serve as a conduit to channel funds from the agency to consulting firms and universities for the information that eventually wound up in an EIS.

The Corps' ultimate objective in environmental planning has been to achieve an "integrated planning process" for water resource projects whereby environmental considerations could be raised at the outset of a survey report and integrated into the project plans, as engineering or economic considerations are.[16] Coping with the backlog, however, often prevented agency personnel from effectively participating in new studies and in new project planning. Most of the people in the environmental units looked forward to catching up on the backlog and being free to get in on project planning from the start. By 1978 they were able to do so; the backlog problem had been resolved, and agency personnel could spend considerably more time analyzing the environmental effects of new projects than writing justifications for old ones. At least one significant obstacle to achieving an integrated planning process has therefore been removed, and so we would expect the environmental staffs to be more integrated into the daily work activities of the office than they were in 1974.

Column 6 of table 3-2 shows the extent to which an environmental unit (or its head) functions in a direct advisory capacity to the district engineer or to the chiefs of the engineering and planning units. Two district engineers said that they spoke with the heads of the environmental units "more than with anyone else." Another officer, in his weekly staff meetings with division chiefs, made the "EIS schedule" the number one topic of discussion on his agenda. Most district engineers claimed that they carefully read and reviewed the impact statements written by the environmental staff. One district has an environmental officer as a special assistant

15. The Council on Environmental Quality issues guidelines, which are recorded in the *Federal Register*, for the implementation of NEPA by federal agencies.

16. See C. Grant Ash, "Three-Year Evolution," *Water Spectrum*, vol. 5, no. 4 (1973), pp. 28–35.

to the district engineer. Our general impression, however, is that all but two or three districts adhered to the normal chain of command and communication—district engineer, division chiefs, branch chiefs, section heads. The environmental unit is therefore probably neither more nor less important than the other units occupying the same position in the organizational hierarchy. The increased policy emphasis on environmental considerations has not greatly disrupted the normal functioning of most district offices, although one district engineer quipped: "It must have been dull being a district engineer before NEPA."

Generalizing on the basis of this information on functions performed by the environmental units, there appear to be three basic types of activities the units can perform:

1. They can do substantive research, either reactive or innovative, into environmental questions and problems. Reactive research would consist of procedural compliance with NEPA or the filing of impact statements that have no discernible effect on decisions. Innovative research would include attempting to look at agency projects in a new way and using new approaches to water resource problems.

2. They can serve in an intra-agency advisory capacity, assisting the districts' decisionmakers on environmentally related questions.

3. They can serve as public relations units of the agency, spending considerable time on public contacts, coordination functions, and the like.

Columns 1, 4, and 5 of table 3-2 relate to the research function of the units; columns 5 and 6 to the advisory function; and columns 2 and 3 to the public relations function. These are not mutually exclusive categories, however, and no doubt most units have done all three at one point or another. It is the *degree* to which the unit is involved in research, advice-giving, and public relations that is significant. Therefore, the more effective units are those that (1) do substantive (innovative) research, (2) are involved in at least some of the essential public contacts, and (3) are perceived as necessary advisers to the district engineer and his division chiefs.

Table 3-3 and 3-4 provide information based solely on people's *perceptions* of the role and purpose of the environmental units. Table 3-3 reflects what people in the environmental units said they did or did not do and how they characterized their role in the agency during our interviews. Table 3-4 presents the opinions of Corps personnel in other units of the organization: people in the planning and engineering divisions, primarily, as well as the district engineers, and some people in the permits sections.

Table 3-3. *The Role of Environmental Units as Perceived by Their Staffs*

District	Complying with NEPA and OCE Regulations	Responding to public pressure and changing public values	Acting as service unit for other organizational elements	Being involved in multidiscipline planning	Providing important information to decisionmakers in the district	
					By direct access	By indirect access
1	yes	no	yes	yes	no	yes
2	yes	no	yes	yes	yes	no
3	yes	no	yes	no	no	yes
4	yes	yes	no	no	no	no
5	yes	no	yes	yes	yes	no
6	yes	no	yes	yes	no	no
7	yes	no	yes	no	no	no
8	yes	no	yes	no	yes	no
9	yes	no	yes	yes	no	no
10	yes	no	no	yes	no	yes
11A[a]	yes	yes	no	yes	yes	no
11B[b]	yes	no	no	no	yes	no

a. Environmental Section, Engineering Division, District 11.
b. Environmental Branch, Construction and Operations Division, District 11.

Table 3-4. *The Role of Environmental Units as Perceived by District Staff outside the Units*

District	Essential for compliance to NEPA and engineering regulations[a]	Performs a negative function	Recommends necessary project changes	Provides needed expertise	Represents Corps' changing missions	Participates actively in plan development
1	yes	no	yes	no	yes	no
2	yes	no	no	yes	yes	yes
3	yes	yes	yes	yes	no	no
4	yes	no	yes	no	yes	no
5	yes	yes	yes	yes	no	no
6	yes	yes	yes	no	yes	no
7	yes	yes	yes	no	no	no
8	yes	yes	yes	no	yes	no
9	yes	yes	no	yes	yes	no
10	yes	yes	yes	yes	no	no
11A[b]	yes	no	yes	yes	no	yes
11B[c]	yes	no	no	yes	yes	no

a. Engineering regulations are issued by the Office of the Chief of Engineers.
b. Environmental Section, Engineering Division, District 11.
c. Environmental Branch, Construction and Operations Division, District 11.

Because the sample for each district is relatively small, averaging five or six persons, conclusions based on the sample per district must be viewed as tentative. In the aggregate, however, a composite picture emerges. Impressions from individual districts and divisions frequently reinforced one another. Certain themes were reiterated. The discussion that follows is therefore based on the composite.

As mentioned earlier, virtually everyone sees the principal role of the environmental unit as one of complying with the law and with regulations issued by the Office of the Chief of Engineers (OCE). A typical response to the question of why such a unit had been created was, "NEPA and the necessity to write environmental impact statements for Corps projects." In a few districts people said that they "saw NEPA coming," and thus began to make changes in personnel before the passage of the act, but there is little doubt that the impetus for this reorganization came from outside the agency in the form of increased public concern with environmental quality, which subsequently became codified in NEPA.

This should not necessarily be construed as criticism of the agency. The translation of public opinion and public interests in the political system is generally accomplished in this manner, as most students of American politics will verify. Bureaucracy, Congress, and even the presidency are not especially innovative institutions (although some administrations are more innovative than others). Rather, their role is generally one of responding to changing social and political situations by translating new concerns into policy. Often this process takes a long time; often, too, it is imperfect.[17]

The interesting question, however, and the one most relevant to this study is: to what extent has the agency incorporated environmental concerns into its operations beyond this procedural compliance?

The process of integration is evident, but for numerous reasons it has not progressed as far as some might think. Many people in the environmental units felt that there was still too much compartmentalization or isolation of functions. "Early involvement in project planning," one environmental unit member said, "is still in its infancy in the district."

17. There is not always a one-to-one relationship between new political demands and the subsequent translation of them into policy. See Jeffrey L. Pressman and Aaron B. Wildavsky, *Implementation: How Great Expectations in Washington Are Dashed in Oakland, or, Why It's Amazing that Federal Programs Work at All* (University of California Press, 1973).

District personnel in general felt a need for interdisciplinary planning, but our impression is that few districts have been able to implement this objective to any great extent. It is, after all, a difficult concept as well as a difficult organizational principle; in a basic sense it represents a method of problem-solving and policy implementation radically different from the methods traditionally utilized by bureaucracy.

A number of people in the environmental units perceived their role as that of providing a new viewpoint within the agency, or as being responsible for objective reviews of project planning. That the units frequently must perform in the role of devil's advocate reflects their basic problem within the organization. They are generally regarded as necessary to the agency in light of the shifting emphasis in water resource planning, yet they are frequently seen as performing an essentially negative function. This was revealed in numerous comments during interviews: "the EIS thing slows us down"; "we're in the third year of shutdown on this project"; "we've gone too far in this environmental activity"; "the cheapest way isn't the best way any longer"; and "we don't want to bring on board extremists who want to stop all development."

Thus the environmental mandate has not been welcomed with open arms everywhere in the agency, according to the viewpoints expressed by agency people. Nevertheless, the Corps has performed very well in procedural or structural terms. Most of the districts we visited had what agency consultants considered to be an adequate staff—10 or more people in the unit—with a fairly broad range of disciplines and interests represented. Further, those in the environmental unit were hopeful that the agency was beginning to take "environmental concern" seriously. Their real complaints were that they were overworked and understaffed, due mainly to their backlog problem; that there were as yet no clear guidelines as to what was an "unacceptable environmental effect"; that the team, or interdisciplinary, approach had yet to be fully implemented; and, finally, that most nonengineering positions were essentially dead-ended in the Corps. As one person noted, in order to be promoted beyond a certain GS level one had to revert to a technical (engineering) position.

Table 3-3 shows that those in the environmental units defined their role or purpose primarily in two ways: to comply with NEPA and OCE regulations and to act as a service unit for other elements of the organization. The word "service" cropped up frequently in discussions with staff both in the environmental units and elsewhere in the offices. Thus the environmental function is frequently considered as auxiliary, though necessary, to the principal functions of the agency. As one environmental branch chief said, "Our major work load varies, really, from year-to-year. It varies according to what the current emphasis is in the district."

The last two columns of table 3-3 need to be explained and put into context. The point to be kept in mind is that providing information is a *relative* measure of input to the decisionmaking process. Obviously all units in the agency have access to at least the next higher level in the organization. There is no question about that. Some environmental units, however, appeared to be more influential than their counterparts in other districts. This is to be expected in a highly decentralized organization where districts operate in very different environments. The nature of the work load in the New York District, for example, is very different from that in the Vicksburg District. There may not necessarily be a single "best" organizational style for all units of the agency.

Table 3-4 represents a sort of "scale of influence" when read horizontally: from compliance with the laws and regulations, through "negative" but necessary functions, to providing new and needed expertise or reflecting the Corps' changing missions, to, finally, active participation in plan formulation and development. Again, the district-by-district indicators should be regarded as tentative. In the aggregate, though, the perceptions of those outside the environmental unit cluster around the first three functions in the table. By and large, agency personnel outside the environmental unit see the unit's role as being necessary. There is, however, an undercurrent of frustration with the delays, resources expended, and in some cases the project modifications that are attributed to these new requirements.

Conclusions

The data show that during the Corps' first five years of living with a new environmental awareness substantial reorganization occurred throughout the agency. When the chief of engineers suggested in 1970 that the environmental issue would entail reorganization at local and regional offices as well as at headquarters, the districts and divisions quickly responded. Only one district out of 36 refused to create an environmental unit, holding out for several years but eventually succumbing when a new district engineer was appointed.

Therefore, despite some opposition within the agency to environmental concerns, a considerable effort has been made to create what might be called the infrastructure necessary for the incorporation of this new policy. The Corps has performed very well both in reorganizing and in hiring new personnel with nonengineering backgrounds to meet this new concern. Whereas in 1969 there were approximately 75 "environmentalists" in the entire agency, by 1977 there were 575.[18]

It seems clear that the Corps of Engineers has made a serious and honest effort to cope with environmental considerations, which is no mean feat for a construction-oriented organization with a strong commitment to resource development. The organization's formal structure has also undergone considerable change. The agency is continuing to bring in new personnel, and these younger people generally take the environmental issue seriously. Over time, this should produce considerable change in project design. The agency now at least has the capability for seeking environmentally sound solutions to water resource problems, although it can hardly be expected to do a complete about-face with respect to its long-standing singular commitment to economic development. It can legitimately be expected to be more sensitive to environmental effects but not to entirely abandon its construction mission. After all, public works projects are the source of the agency's budget. The environmental issue by itself does not generate the kind of money that comes from construction and development, nor has it generated the kind of political support essential to making environmental policy coequal with water resource development within the agency.

Whether the kinds of changes that appear to be taking place in Corps project plans as a result of legislative and reorganization efforts will survive the agency's extended project planning period (often from five to seven years) and ultimately be executed (which could take up to another decade) depends on more than pronouncements of new environmental objectives by the chief or even the development of the necessary organizational capabilities. Unless new publics are ensured a central role in the

18. Information obtained from the Office of the Chief of Engineers, U.S. Army Corps of Engineers, Washington, D.C.

agency s decisionmaking process, there is little reason to believe that it will not slip back into its traditional symbiotic relationship with Congress and with those receiving direct and tangible benefits from a project. Thus in the next several chapters we focus on the new range of decisionmaking processes operating at the field level as of the mid-1970s and on what the experience with them reveals about the prospects for long-range organizational change in the Corps of Engineers.

CHAPTER FOUR

Problems of Transition:
Open Planning

IF MEASURED BY the leadership's policy pronouncements and internal reorganization at the field level, the response of the Corps of Army Engineers to the demands for consideration of the environment and for open planning is impressive. But the crucial test of the many changes made was how they affected decisions on specific projects. To begin with, not every district readily adopted the new open planning envisioned by the chief of engineers and set forth in the agency guidelines reviewed in chapter 2. New structures to facilitate open decisions paralleling those for developing environmental impact statements were not developed. Rather, changes were adopted on a project-by-project basis. Evidently the Corps found it easier to reorganize to address technical issues, such as environmental impacts, than to become involved in the potentially all-encompassing open planning. The strategy chosen, therefore, was to let district offices initiate and experiment on their own, with only technical support and much encouragement from the Office of the Chief of Engineers. Presumably the "best" methods that resulted from this strategy would then be adopted agency-wide.

Not only were the more experimental public participation programs to be optional—to the extent that they went beyond the public hearing requirement of the executive guidelines for implementing the National Environmental Policy Act (NEPA) of 1969—but they were intended primarily for new project studies. Thus for projects that had not yet received congressional authorization the order was clear. The Corps' directive issued in May 1971 stated that public participation would be "an integral part of each Plan Survey."[1] But for post-authorization studies, some of which had been on the books for two, three, or even more decades, the directive merely suggests that public participation *"should be considered . . .* whenever there are substantive changes from the authorized plan, new interests are affected or changed conditions warrant such action."[2] The need for public participation was repeated in 1974 in a directive on post-authorization studies, which called for "one or more public meetings or workshops" to ensure consideration of the views of interested parties. Like prior directives, however, this one only suggested that meetings or workshops should be held.[3] Basically, then, the decision to include the public in post-authorization planning was left to the district that initially conceived, then designed, and finally promoted the already authorized project.

For either pre- or post-authorization planning, when a decision about public participation is made there are no provisions for a formal appeal to the courts, the Council on Environmental Quality, or even the higher echelons of the Corps. Informal pressures can be brought to bear, however. The Council on Environmental Quality can advise and admonish, but it rarely does this, having little substantive power. The chief of engineers tried to prod districts to expand their participation programs and had provided assistance to those willing to do so—the Technical Assistance Program, for example. But in the period of our investigation, pressure to include the public was almost exclusively directed at pre-authorization studies. The implication is far-reaching. In the extreme, it could mean that districts could exclude the public as an integral part of their planning for the hundreds of authorized but not yet constructed projects.[4] Whether this will occur depends on the constraints operating at the district level, as illustrated by the two post-authorization studies that will be discussed in this chapter.

We chose to examine these two Corps studies, along with three others

1. U.S. Department of the Army, Corps of Engineers, Office of the Chief of Engineers, "Water Resources Policies and Authorities: Public Participation in Water Resources Planning," Engineer Circular 1165-2-100 (May 28, 1971), p. 3.

2. Ibid., p. 4 (emphasis added).

3. U.S. Department of the Army, Corps of Engineers, Office of the Chief of Engineers, "Engineering and Design: Post-Authorization Studies," Engineer Regulation 1110-2-1150 (June 7, 1974), p. 13.

4. The cost of completing authorized projects was an estimated $16 billion in 1973. See Lieutenant General F. J. Clarke, "A Tenure of Change," *Water Spectrum*, vol. 5, no. 3 (1973), p. 6.

that are presented in chapters 5 and 6, in an attempt to determine the sincerity of the effort to achieve open planning, to judge the substantive results of the effort, and to get some idea of how this first generation of experiments would affect decisionmaking throughout the agency. The criteria for selecting the five project studies were (1) that a major portion of the attempt to involve new publics in decisions affecting them would occur after the chief's announcement of the new era in open planning; (2) that they would represent different geographical regions of the United States; (3) that they would include a dam, a levee, channelization, and wastewater management; and (4) that we could be assured of the cooperation of the district corps office.

The studies selected are listed below in the order of their presentation: Unit L-15 of the Missouri River Levee System, extending from Portage Des Sioux along the Mississippi River downstream to its confluence with the Missouri River just north of St. Louis and up the Missouri to St. Charles; the new lock and connecting channel of the Mississippi River–Gulf Outlet (MR-GO) below New Orleans; the flood control and related water resource problems on the Wildcat and San Pablo creeks, portions of which run through San Pablo and North Richmond in Contra Costa County, California; wastewater management for the Cleveland-Akron metropolitan area and the Three Rivers Watershed area in northern Ohio; and flood control on the Middle Fork of the Snoqualmie River, approximately 20 miles east of Seattle.

Although these studies are for major types of Corps projects, they are not a representative sample of dam building or channelization or flood control activities in any statistical sense. Furthermore, the open planning programs illustrated by each case reflect only the range of alternative decisionmaking approaches being used by the Corps during the period of our field investigations. To capture the breadth of the range, we include extremes: the MR-GO study in which the role of citizens was confined to two large, rancorous public meetings held toward the conclusion of the Corps' post-authorization study; and the Snoqualmie River study, which was conducted in conjunction with the State of Washington's Department of Ecology, and during which a number of citizen groups developed their own comprehensive plans that became part of the final report. Moreover, the mix of studies was biased in favor of those involving experimentation with new forms of open decisionmaking. This should be kept in mind when reviewing the findings.

It is apparent in the two post-authorization studies that follow that the issues of representation, mode of involvement, delegation of authority, and locus of final decision were not carefully thought through in advance. It was also difficult for local Corps decisionmakers to devise a productive way for the public to participate in planning after the planning had been accomplished. This resulted in a rather disjointed, sometimes direction-less participatory process and considerable dissatisfaction with the results.

Project Study I: Taming the Missouri

In 1944 Congress authorized the Missouri River Basin Plan, also called the Pick-Sloan Plan in honor of the key architects of two separate pro-posals, one from the Corps and the other from the Bureau of Reclamation, that were combined. Lewis A. Pick was a colonel in the Missouri River Division of the Corps, and W. Glenn Sloan was assistant director of the Bureau of Reclamation at Billings, Montana.[5] Their plan was a massive multipurpose scheme for flood control, navigation improvements, and the provision of power and irrigation along the Missouri River from its head-waters in Montana, Wyoming, and Colorado, down through the Dakotas, Nebraska, Iowa, Kansas, and Missouri. The heart of the plan was the construction of seven mainstream reservoirs along the upper reaches of the Missouri. The reservoirs were to be supplemented by some 100 lakes and 50 to 60 local projects throughout Nebraska, Iowa, Kansas, and Mis-souri. Finally, the Corps was to build a navigation channel and system of flood protection levees from Sioux City, Iowa, 760 miles downstream to St. Louis. This system was called the Missouri River Levee System.

The formula for funding these projects was spelled out in the Flood Control Act of 1936 and in amendments in 1937 and 1938, which stipu-late that the federal government will assume the total costs for the con-struction and operation of flood control reservoirs and navigation im-provements where benefits are considered to be widespread and in the general public interest.[6] For the more localized protection projects and levees the law calls for the local sponsoring agency (city, county, or state)

5. For an excellent history and evaluation of the plan, see Henry C. Hart, *The Dark Missouri* (University of Wisconsin Press, 1957).

6. See Beatrice Hort Holmes, *A History of Federal Water Resources Programs, 1800–1960*, U.S. Department of Agriculture, Economic Research Service, Miscel-laneous Publication 1233 (USDA, June 1972), p. 20.

to absorb some of the costs; they are to furnish all land easements and rights-of-way, to cover the costs of relocating roads and utilities, and to operate and maintain the project after it is completed. But even for these smaller projects the major share of the costs still falls to the nation's tax-payers. The federal cost of the Pick-Sloan projects completed by the Corps by the mid-1970s was approximately $1.74 billion; an additional $1.5 billion in federal costs was associated with the Corps projects then under construction.[7]

The Corps first completed the six major mainstream reservoirs and the dozens of tributary reservoirs, then turned its attention to flood protection projects and levees.[8] The strategy adopted was to construct flood protection devices at the upper reaches of the Missouri and gradually work downstream. By the mid-1960s the Kansas City District Office (KCD) had turned its attention to the last major undeveloped stretch of the river, that between Kansas City and St. Louis. An important part of the Corps' plan for the lower part of the river is the so-called Unit L-15 levee, a project that became the focus of a controversy in the early 1970s and that will be discussed shortly.

The Corps' structural approach to flood management has led to a seemingly endless cycle of construction. First, flood walls and levees are built to protect private property from a river's flood overflow. But the water must go somewhere, and it usually chooses to go downstream. Communities downstream then demand, and usually receive, protection from the new flooding brought on by the upstream structural flood protections. The effect of upstream flood control has been quite noticeable along the Mississippi River. For example, in 1973 a water flow of 849,000 cubic feet per second generated a crest of 43.23 feet, whereas in 1927 a greater volume of flood water—889,300 cubic feet per second—generated a crest of only 36.10 feet.[9]

The increased flooding caused by levee construction appears to be

7. Letter, Joseph D. Auburg, chief of the Economics Branch, Missouri River Division, Corps of Engineers, to Daniel Mazmanian, May 14, 1974.

8. By the early 1970s, in addition to the 6 mainstream reservoirs and 85 minor reservoirs, 57 local protection projects had been completed and 7 reservoirs and 11 local protection projects were under way. See U.S. Department of the Army, Corps of Engineers, Kansas City District, transcript of public meeting on Unit L-15 of the Missouri River Levee System, Portage Des Sioux, Mo., July 19, 1973, p. 68.

9. Memorandums, Leo A. Drey, chairman of the Environmental Task Force of the East-West Gateway Coordinating Council, to the Board of Directors, ibid., exhibit GG.

aggravated by "wing dikes," which the Corps builds to accommodate navigational interests. As the Environmental Policy Center reported:

Approximately 30 percent of the increase in the intensity of last year's [1973] flood along the middle Mississippi can be attributed to the wing dikes built by the Corps to constrict the river channel and force it to carve out a deeper course for barges. The dikes are built from the shore out into the river and trap silt behind them, forcing the river to cut a deeper channel in the middle. In addition to the environmental and aesthetic damage done by the wing dikes, they dramatically reduce the capacity of the river to carry flood flows.[10]

It has taken decades to construct the great waterworks conceived of by Pick and Sloan, and only recently have the long-term effects of these projects been recognized. This has generated criticism, whether warranted or not, of the defects in the structural approach to flooding and also of those public agencies responsible for using this technique. Environmental groups were the first to speak out, but now even state leaders who have received the greatest direct benefit from the mammoth public works projects are questioning the program. Governor Christopher S. Bond of Missouri is one such critic. In 1973, responding to the Corps' proposed plan for construction of the Unit L-15 levee he stated:

We have spent hundreds of billions of dollars on flood control in this country since 1936, and much of it has been spent in the two major river basins affecting Missouri. Despite these expenditures, however, the floods of last spring, measured at St. Louis, were the smallest in volume yet reached the highest crest of all the major floods since 1844. From this information, it would seem that high levees which deny flooding rivers the natural reservoir of flood plains has contributed to higher crests of the rivers.

Another major consequence of our flood control project has been to increase potential for major disaster and destruction when floods do occur. The construction of high levees and other flood control structures has tended to encourage the commercialization, industrialization and residential development of protected areas. When, as the case of this spring, these major levees are topped, the damages are far greater than would have occurred had the flood control structures not been developed in the flood plains. For these reasons, I do not favor a full-scale industrial levee which would encourage high-density development in the flood plains.[11]

    10. American Rivers Conservation Council and the Environmental Policy Center, "95 Theses" (May 1974), p. 1. Available from EPC, Washington, D.C.
    11. Letter, Governor Christopher Bond to Colonel William R. Needham, district engineer, Kansas City District, August 14, 1973.

Criticism from highly placed public officials cannot be dismissed, since the Corps must rely on the approval of state governors before proceeding with most of its projects.[12]

Unit L-15 of the Missouri River Levee System

The Corps of Engineers, along with people living adjacent to the Missouri River, seldom see either the Pick-Sloan projects or the problems of flooding in quite the same way Governor Bond and many environmental groups see them. The Corps expended considerable energy to get its master plan approved and so far has spent 30 years implementing it on an incremental basis: dam by dam, levee by levee. It is proud of its accomplishments. Mindful of these sunk costs, in the mid-1960s the KCD first informed residents along the Missouri River in the St. Charles area and along the Mississippi in the Portage Des Sioux area that if they wished to form a levee district (later known as the North County, or Unit L-15, Levee District), plans could begin on a flood protection system for their land.[13] The total length of the proposed levee was approximately 44 miles; 25 miles along the Missouri and 19 miles along the Mississippi (see figure 4-1). The proposition sounded irresistible to the people who would be protected. All they had to do was incorporate into a levee district, which the Corps would then formally recognize as the local assuring agency providing the rights-of-way and other assurances required by federal law. The taxpayers of the United States, via the Corps of Engineers, would reward these efforts by funding and building a flood control levee system.

At a minimum, the 37,000 acres of natural floodplain at the confluence of two of the nation's largest rivers would be less susceptible to periodic flooding. Moreover, if the levee were built to protect against the 100-year flood (the largest reasonably probable flood that might occur once in 100 years), or better yet, according to "standard project flood" specifications (providing protection against the largest reasonably probable flood from a storm of the greatest possible magnitude imaginable), the former flood-prone land would then be suitable for residential and industrial develop-

12. The governor of a state must approve a proposed project before it can be submitted to Congress for authorization.
13. It is unclear whether the KCD literally prompted the formation of the Unit L-15 Levee District, although this is the story related by Marvin Meyer, resident of Portage Des Sioux and secretary of the levee district. See KCD, transcript of public meeting, St. Charles, Mo., September 30, 1971, p. 110.

Figure 4-1. *Proposed Unit L-15 of the Missouri River Levee System*

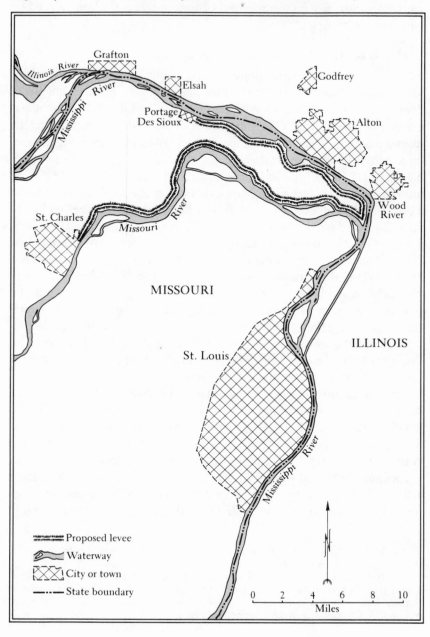

ment. The KCD, obviously aware of these project benefits, began building support for the levee on this basis. In 1967 the Corps announced that "the North County Levee District is or will be experiencing the agricultural-urban transition in the near future. The present trend of industrial development in Unit L-15, . . . with barge, rail, truck, and pipeline transportation facilities and major utilities readily available, would indicate that one-third to one-half of the area will be occupied by industrial facilities within the next 25 to 50 years."[14]

Significantly, a consensus did not exist within the Corps on these projections, however. Some differences of opinion arose between the OCE in Washington and the KCD on the propriety of using long-range projected industrial development as a rationale for building industrial-height levees. The issue was resolved when the district and headquarters agreed to pursue a two-stage construction plan: the construction of an agricultural-height levee designed so that it could easily be raised to urban height if justified by future development.

The First Public Meeting

In 1967 shortly after the incorporation of the North County Levee District, the KCD began a detailed design study of the L-15 levee.[15] Since L-15 was part of the already authorized Missouri River Levee System, the Corps was obliged only to secure annual funding for its post-authorization study, to develop detailed design memorandums, and with these in hand, to return to the appropriations committees of the House and Senate for construction funding. (This fairly typical funding procedure takes from two to three years from the initiation of the advanced, or final, project design to breaking ground for construction.)

The KCD was not oblivious, however, to changing public sentiment toward its waterworks projects. As word of the KCD's renewed interest in

14. KCD, "Missouri River Levee System: Economic Study" (August 1967), in KCD, transcript of public meeting, July 19, 1973, exhibit W. The basic forecast of development remained unchanged as late as May 1970 when the KCD informed Congressman William L. Hungate of Missouri: "Because of its proximity to the St. Louis metropolitan area and the presence of barge, rail, and truck transportation facilities and with major utilities readily available it is expected that the present trend of industrial development will continue and in the next few decades will supplant the existing agricultural character of the area." (Letter, KCD to Hungate, May 8, 1970, in KCD, transcript of public meeting, September 30, 1971, p. 78.)

15. See KCD, transcript of public meeting, July 19, 1973, p. 130.

L-15 spread, local residents outside the levee protection area who felt they would be adversely affected began to form a loose coalition. People living along the Illinois side of the Mississippi River were especially concerned with hydrologic issues. To what extent would a levee on the Missouri side of the river increase the flood crest on their side? They feared the worst. Environmentalists and conservation and wildlife interests saw the levee as fostering rapid industrialization and urbanization of the last remaining large block of agricultural riverfront property close to the St. Louis metropolitan area, as well as exacerbating flood problems downstream. These factions began to insist that the Corps consider what effects the L-15 project would have on a broader geographical area and make the decision to build or not in light of a broad range of alternative uses of land and water resources.

By December 1970 the KCD decided to shelve its levee design, at least temporarily, and to make contact with a cross section of the interests inside and outside the project area. "Because of changed planning criteria and because of changes in environmental awareness around the country," the KCD deemed it appropriate to restudy the L-15 design.[16] A range of alternatives would be considered, from "constructing no levees at all, through several degrees of rural protection, to complete urban standard protection by levees."[17] A "formulation stage" public meeting, customarily held only as part of the pre-authorization planning process, was scheduled for September 1971. The KCD assumed that when the district engineers had further refined the possible alternatives another meeting would be called—a sequel to the pre-authorization "late stage meeting," which comes after detailed studies but before report completion. In taking these traditional pre-authorization steps the KCD believed it would not only be opening its doors to the public but also would be protecting itself against any future accusation by local groups, by the OCE, and especially by the courts that it had not conducted itself in an open and forthright manner.

The illusion that holding public meetings would quell opposition was dispelled on the night of the first public meeting, September 30, 1971, in a high school gymnasium in the small rural town of St. Charles, Missouri. More than 400 people turned out from as far away as Elsah, Wood River, Godfrey, and Alton (towns on the Illinois side of the Mississippi

16. Ibid., p. 68.
17. Circular announcing the public meeting on Unit L-15 at St. Charles, Mo., September 30, 1971.

River) and from metropolitan St. Louis, some 15 miles away. Most came to protest. They distrusted the Corps and its local sponsors, believing that both groups were conspiring to add just another round to the seemingly endless cycle of levee building, urban and industrial development, and the aggravation of downstream flood and sewage conditions.

The mayor of Alton set the tone of the evening in presenting a resolution passed by the Alton City Council opposing the L-15 project "that would periodically threaten, unduly, populated areas never before threatened, destroy a recreation area of rare value to all people of the metropolitan St. Louis area," and "create industrial development in an area ill suited for it and well suited to the use it had already been put." The distaste for industrialization (a theme repeatedly heard that night) was reiterated next by the mayor of Elsah, who argued that construction of "a very long levee to enclose a very narrow point of land between the two rivers" was a "very expensive way of creating more industrial land, much more expensive than would be the case in protecting a single straight riverbank, or certain[ly] than developing land not adjacent to a river, of which there is much in the St. Louis area."[18] A representative of Pride Incorporated of Alton then stepped forward to present a petition signed by 2,400 area residents opposing any further planning or construction of the L-15 levee.

Even the business community of Alton, traditional allies of the Corps and of unrestricted development, found itself on the side of the opposition. The president of the Greater Alton Association of Commerce presented the view of his 650 members politely but firmly. "The Greater Alton Association of Commerce does not in any way wish to impede progress of any type. However, there are times when certain actions, contemplated in the name of progress, are in reality detrimental to those they profess to serve." In view of the controversy over the hydrologic, economic, and environmental effects of the project, the association requested "that a proper and thorough study be conducted by an independent, impartial organization that would answer these and all other questions that have arisen as a result of the proposed L-15 levee."[19]

Hours passed before the St. Charles Enthusiasts for a Natural Environment, the Illinois Prairie Club, the Coalition for the Environment, the Illinois Wildlife Federation, the Mississippi Valley Duck Hunters Asso-

18. KCD, transcript of public meeting, St. Charles, Mo., September 30, 1971, p. 74.
19. Ibid., p. 80.

ciation, the Missouri Audubon Society, the Webster Grove Nature Society, the Sierra Club of Missouri and Western Illinois, the Citizens for a Healthful Environment, the Lewis and Clark Society of America, the Alton Lake Harbor Association, and various and sundry other groups and individuals had registered their opposition. The Corps' sincerity in weighing all views equally and impartially was repeatedly questioned. An unending stream of questions was raised about how specific hydrologic, economic, social, and environmental aspects of the project would affect the interests of each speaker and his constituency.

The strongest defense of the project came from the secretary of the Unit L-15 Levee District, who cataloged the suffering and costs that severe floods had inflicted on the 5,000 people living in the area. He claimed parenthetically that the members of the levee district were considering only an agricultural, and not an urban, levee. The St. Charles County Soil and Water Conservation District also voiced support of the plan, along with a few local residents.

In many ways this first public meeting was typical. True, the opponents were well prepared and well represented, but this is not as uncommon as some assert. One can almost predict in advance those who will turn out to support or to oppose a project, for their interests are usually obvious. Every faction is expected to exaggerate its case, and its views are discounted accordingly. In this sense public meetings are symbolic confrontations, not intended to convert but to convey the intensity of each position and the breadth of its appeal.

The Corps enters the process with its own set of biases and resources, viewing itself as guardian of the federal interest. Yet it usually seeks to perpetuate both its mission and its power by promoting the "do something" construction approach. No one was more aware of this than Colonel Edwin R. Decker, retired former district engineer of the St. Louis District. Colonel Decker, a professional engineer who was intimately familiar with Corps operations, came to the public meeting as a concerned citizen. He could challenge the Corps on its own terms, and did. "I appear here today," he said, "because of a deepseated conviction that the Corps of Engineers levee construction program is passé, and with an even more deeply seated conviction that the Corps of Engineers with its zealous desire to build levees does not tell the people the facts of life."[20] This was

20. Ibid., p. 83.

not the Sierra Club, the Audubon Society, or the Duck Hunters Association speaking, but one of the Corps' own. Decker then ticked off a long list of potentially disastrous hydrologic, economic, land-use, and long-term development implications of the proposed plan. These implications were not purely hypothetical but were drawn from years of experience with similar projects, a half-dozen of which were known to most of those present. No more damaging indictment of the Corps could be imagined.

Decker's appearance was clearly the high point of the evening and was widely reported the next day in the local press. A headline in the *St. Louis Globe-Democrat*, October 1, 1971, announced: "Corps of Engineers' Levee Plan Draws Fire of Ex-Chief." In a subsequent newspaper interview Decker expounded on why the Corps often undertakes projects that in his estimation were wasteful and pointless. "Bureaucratic self-preservation" was his explanation.

Someplace along the line a group of people decide, wouldn't it be nice to have a dam and a reservoir, or a levee, or something.

They form an association like the Meramec Basin Association or the North (St. Charles) County Levee District. The Corps doesn't organize them but it usually helps.

They get their congressman to pass a resolution which goes into the biennial rivers and harbors bill. The Corps probably writes the resolution for them. It calls for a study of the project. The association goes back to Congress every session for more money to keep the project alive. You have to have an appropriation to keep the project going.[21]

The process is endless, he said, with industrial developers, towboat operators, and recreational developers all lining up for a piece of the action. Decker went on to say that the L-15 levee could only be justified if designed to protect industrial development, implying that therefore that must be what the Corps secretly had in mind.

The opposition, representing well over a majority of those who attended the KCD's first public meeting, rested its case.

The Opposition Enters the Planning Process

What to do? Theoretically the KCD could have proceeded with an advanced design for the levee, returned to Congress for construction funding, and then built its levee. But this strategy would surely have prompted

21. E. F. Porter, Jr., "Former Army Engineer Critical of 'Beaver Corps,' " *St. Louis Post-Dispatch*, October 5, 1971.

a lawsuit, moving the controversy to an arena where the opposition might well receive more sympathetic treatment. More important, both the KCD and the OCE shunned the inevitable adverse publicity that accompanies a court confrontation. The idea of dropping the project entirely was also rejected. The path chosen involved experimentation: to actually bring all factions into the planning process so that the "best" solution would evolve from the interaction between the various groups. This, of course, was something quite new for the district—almost revolutionary— but by rejecting the extremes of either proceeding as planned or dropping the project, few options remained. The district's decision proved timely.

By early 1971 the internal reorganization of the Corps was under way. The Corps' Institute for Water Resources (IWR) had just initiated its Technical Assistance Program (TAP) to aid field engineers in their public participation efforts. Four months before the September meeting on L-15 the KCD had requested TAP assistance. The district, however, had not yet determined where such assistance could be used. Although a couple of the district's projects had been proposed in correspondence with the IWR, L-15 was not among them. But by November, when the IWR staff visited the district, L-15 was a burning issue, and it was quickly agreed that this was where the TAP assistance could best be used.

For the staff of IWR, L-15 was an early test case. Could the Corps be changed from within? Could field engineers be persuaded of the efficacy of involving the public, including the opposition, as an integral part of their planning? Moreover, would the Corps abide by the conclusions reached through the public involvement planning process? Could the theories of decentralized yet comprehensive planning then in vogue actually be implemented, even in the oldest of bureaucracies? Finally, could the Corps earn the esteem of the community through involving the public directly in its planning?

To help the project managers implement a more thoroughgoing public participation program, two private consultants were retained. They first recommended asking a number of the groups that had expressed concern over the project at the public meeting, as well as the St. Louis District Corps office, to take an active part in the renewed planning effort. At a meeting hosted by the East-West Gateway Coordinating Council in St. Louis, the representatives of a dozen groups met with six Corps personnel as an ad hoc committee in March 1972. The committee used the transcript of the first public meeting to identify several dozen key questions raised about the proposed project so that a list could be mailed to all those who had attended the first public meeting. The committee then split into five work groups responsible for studying questions of land use, economics, hydraulics, recreation, and environment and for reporting on them. Additional members were added so that each group consisted of from six to nine representatives of both public and private organizations. Through this process the KCD hoped to (1) reach a consensus on the "best" plan; (2) establish the credibility of the Corps' goals, convincing skeptics that the Corps had no vested interest in building a project; and (3) establish the credibility of the Corps' methods of analysis.

On May 25, 1972, all the work groups gathered on the St. Louis campus of the University of Missouri. Then each group held an additional two or three meetings at various locations throughout the metropolitan area. After six months, research on the questions posed in March was by and large completed. The first of two final meetings of the ad hoc study group was held in early September on the campus of Lindenwood College in St. Charles, Missouri. After meeting in groups, all came together for a summary presentation by the KCD. But as the representative of Pride noted, the presentation focused only on the trade-offs associated with each of the structural alternatives and did not mention the nonstructural alternatives. This omission was rectified, however, three months later at Principia College in Elsah, Illinois, during a meeting devoted to nonstructural alternatives.

The Second Public Meeting

After the final work group session the KCD prepared a brochure that summarized the findings of the five groups and was widely circulated. A second large-scale public meeting was then scheduled for July 19, 1973, to present the results of the ad hoc study group to the broader public and to receive their comments. Over 350 people packed into St. Francis Memorial Hall, Portage Des Sioux, to hear the Corps' report.

Unknown to most, the KCD had more in mind that evening than simply to review the pros and cons of each alternative. After a year and a half of restudying and consulting with the work group members, it was now prepared to unveil its preferred plan. Colonel William Needham, district engineer, opened the meeting with a review of the various structural alternatives—the 10-year, 25-year, 50-year, 100-year, and standard project flood levees—and some of the nonstructural alternatives, particularly since these had been proposed by the independent work groups and not by the Corps. The most comprehensive of the nonstructural alternatives, the Great Rivers Recreation Plan, had been developed independently by local planners who simply submitted it to the Corps in March 1973.[22] To compare the nonstructural alternatives, the KCD developed a matrix that displayed the social, economic, and environmental trade-offs. The matrix was considered far more complicated, crude, and judgmental than a benefit-cost ratio. Despite its shortcomings, however, the matrix gave a point value for the environmental, social, and economic effects of all the alternatives. Summing across the three factors the KCD was then able to rank the five levee proposals with the "floodplain regulation," "Great Rivers Recreation," "combination," and "no action" alternatives.

The two extreme levee proposals, the 10-year and the standard project flood levees, were dismissed on economic grounds. The elimination of the latter, the levee most conducive to urban and industrial growth, had to be considered a victory for the project opponents. This left the 25-year, 50-year, and 100-year levees as cost-effective. They were cost-effective, however, by using a low 2.5 percent interest rate to compute the benefit-cost ratios.[23] And since federal flood insurance is available for structures built behind a 100-year-or-more flood protection levee, the likelihood of high-density development had not been completely eliminated. But Colonel Needham, in deferring to the wishes of the work group, countered this possibility:

Now it appears that all of the work groups and most of the members of each of the work groups agree that a levee that would provide protection against 100-year or greater flood would accelerate a change in land use. It would appear that a 100-year levee or higher would lead to urbanization or industrial development. . . . Therefore, it would appear that the 100-year levee is not a desirable alternative.[24]

22. The plan was developed by Robert E. Goetz and Associates, landscape architects and land planners, and Gerwin K. Rohrback, planner. See "Great Rivers Recreation Plan," in KCD, transcript of public meeting, July 19, 1973, exhibit L.

23. Under present law the interest rate used to evaluate a project is that which is in effect at the time a project is authorized, 2.5 percent in this case. On the recommendation of the Office of the Chief of Engineers, the district also computed benefit-cost ratios based on both a 5.5 and a 5.75 percent rate. When these rates were used, none of the structural alternatives were economically justifiable. (See ibid., p. 73; and statement on interest rates by Congressman Paul Findley, ibid., exhibit C, p. 5.)

24. Ibid., p. 77.

Needham then proposed what the KCD thought to be a genuine compromise. Taking the levee with the highest benefit-cost ratio (1.23 to 1) and comparing it with the most promising nonstructural approach from the matrix, he proposed a "combined plan": a 50-year levee in conjunction with the Great Rivers Recreation Area Plan.[25] Some flood protection would be provided for the local residents, although not the 100-year levee they had originally desired. For the environmentalists and those concerned with wildlife, there was the recreation area plan: small amounts of land would be purchased for public ownership within the L-15 area, and most of the rest of the land would remain in its present agricultural or private recreational state. To ensure that the land would continue to be used this way, scenic easements would be sought. To reduce flood loss, some homes would be relocated above flood levels. The westerly panorama enjoyed by the people of Alton and the other affected communities on the Illinois side of the Mississippi would be preserved, although the possibility remained that the flood-stage crest along their side of the river might still increase—a point omitted in the Corps' presentation—but not up to the 10 to 12 inches that might occur if a standard project flood levee were built.

Reaction to the combined plan was mixed. Project proponents were pleased that some protection would be forthcoming but were not complacent about the scenic easement or some of the other provisions in the recreation plan. But since the Corps could not implement the nonstructural aspects of the plan in any event, they were not too serious a threat.

People from Illinois were not at all satisfied. They saw no compromise, only a scheme whereby they would be flooded, but perhaps less so. The Alton Lake Committee and the Greater Alton Association of Commerce demanded that a public meeting be held on the Illinois side of the Mississippi to air the L-15 issue.

Environmental and wildlife enthusiasts recognized that the Corps had lowered its sights appreciably but felt that even a 50-year levee would lock the area into a development cycle. After all, once the 50-year levee was constructed, it would be fairly simple for developers to lobby to have it raised the three or four feet necessary to give 100-year protection. These fears appeared to be confirmed when shortly before the second public meeting the press reported that private developers had awarded a $90,000

25. See letter, Robert E. Goetz to Colonel William Needham, August 16, 1973, ibid., exhibit XXX.

contract for a plan of an inland port facility in St. Charles County consisting of canals linking the Missouri, Mississippi, and Illinois rivers and industrial sites of 50–100 acres.[26] Moreover, the Coalition for the Environment concluded that it was evident that the two parts of the combined plan were incompatible. In effect, "the purpose of the Great Rivers Recreation Area would be nullified by the simultaneous construction of a 50-year levee."[27] For these reasons the environmental and wildlife groups were not content with a partial victory, to wit, a reduction in the height of the levee. They wanted assurance that the area not only would be maintained in its present state but would be enhanced recreationally. With a few recent exceptions, however, the Corps does not have the authority to provide this kind of assurance.[28]

Aftermath

After the public meeting the TAP consultants helped the KCD put together a two-page flyer on the pros and cons of the alternatives under consideration. The flyer was widely disseminated, but there was little additional activity until 1974–75 when the KCD again gave its attention to the cost-effectiveness of the 50-year levee proposal. The district office concluded that the project could be justified under the 2.5 percent rate provided for in the authorizing Pick-Sloan legislation but not under the more contemporary 5.63 percent rate. Furthermore, by this time Corps planners had accepted the argument that even a 50-year agricultural protection levee would inevitably contribute to the cycle of commercial and industrial development, as the project opponents had contended all along. Challenged on the political front and stuck with the 2.5 percent interest rate, the district placed the L-15 study in inactive status in 1975, and a change in this status is not foreseen at present.

For several reasons this was probably the district's only viable option. First, for it to recommend a 50-year levee would go against the agency norm of requesting nothing less than 100-year levees. Second, to forward to Congress a controversial project that could be economically justified

26. See statement by the Sierra Club in KCD, transcript of public meeting, July 19, 1973, exhibit Z, p. 3.

27. Letter, Goetz to Needham, ibid., exhibit XXX.

28. The Water Resources Development and Preservation Act of 1974 authorized two nonstructural projects for the Corps: the Charles River Watershed in Massachusetts and Prairie du Chien in Wisconsin.

at only the 2.5 percent interest rate might well lead to a public airing of the general issue of the interest rates applied to projects authorized decades earlier. And even if Congress sidestepped this issue, it would surely be raised by the President's Office of Management and Budget. Understandably, the Corps has never been anxious to debate its interest rate policy, particularly with respect to older authorized projects.

Regardless of the outcome of the L-15 study in terms of the substantive issues involved, the procedures followed demonstrated that through public meetings, work groups, and a continuing dialogue, a full range of views on a project can be brought to light. The general outline of alternative solutions can be made known to the Corps and to the public. What comes of this knowledge is an entirely different matter. L-15 also shows that, in practice, new modes of public participation were not necessarily going to be restricted to pre-authorization studies. The newer modes of participation, however, were not being implemented automatically as part of the post-authorization planning process but as a sort of last resort response to extremely divisive controversies. Yet by then it may already be too late to arrive at an amicable and widely accepted solution. And just because a congressionally authorized project has become extremely controversial and divisive is no guarantee that a district will respond with the kind of useful public participation program suggested in agency guidelines. The following case clearly illustrates this point.

Project Study II: Centroport U.S.A.

The transshipping of hundreds of thousands of tons of cargo annually down the Mississippi River and its tributaries, as well as receiving cargo arriving from all the nations of the world, makes New Orleans the number one grain port in the United States, number two in foreign commerce, and number three in total quantity of cargo. To accommodate all this traffic the port facilities of New Orleans spread along 25 miles of the Mississippi River, the Inner Harbor Navigational Canal (known as the Industrial Canal), and the Mississippi River-Gulf Outlet channel (see figure 4-2). Thirty-seven thousand people work the port facilities, which constitute Louisiana's largest industrial employer.

The political influence of shippers and related commercial industrialists in New Orleans is commensurate with their preeminent role in the economic life of the community, and the pressure on the New Orleans

Figure 4-2. *Proposed New Lock and Connecting Channel for the Mississippi River–Gulf Outlet*

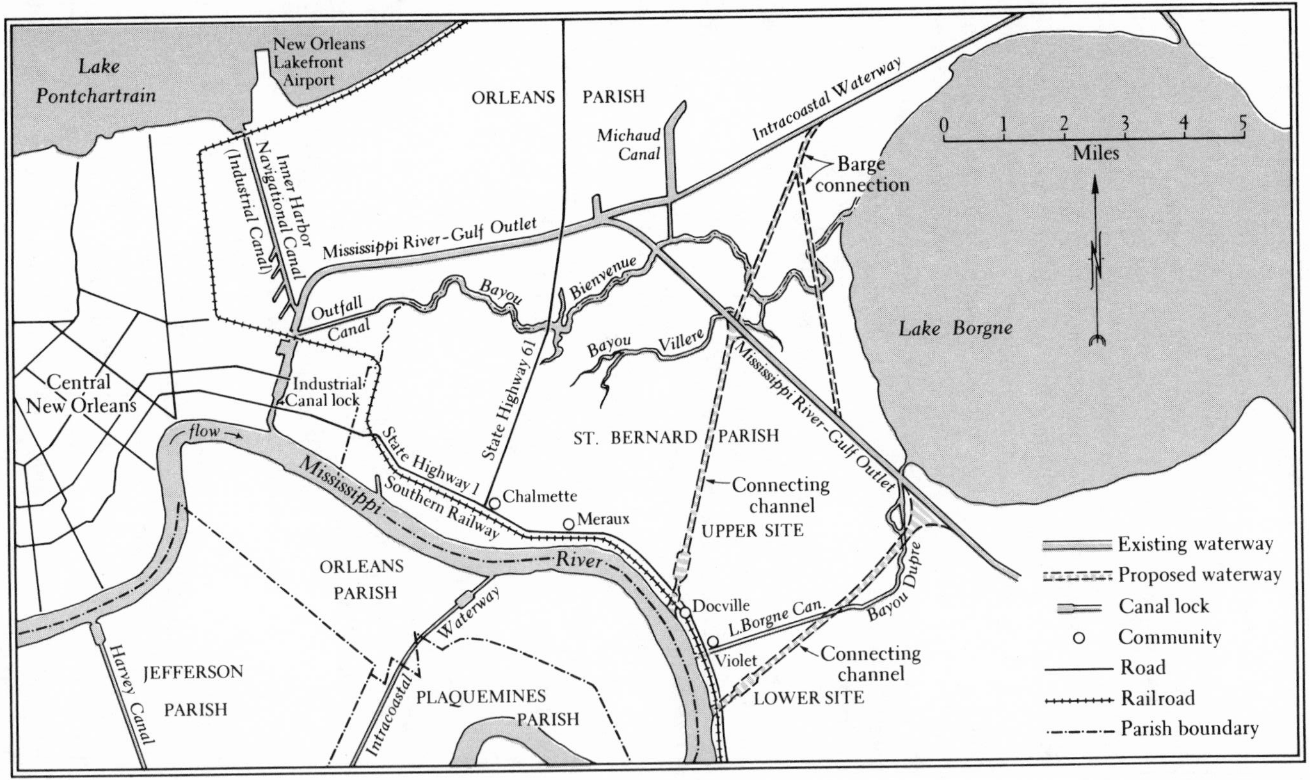

District Office of the Corps of Engineers to accommodate the shippers is understandably great. Indeed, the New Orleans office has often served as the design and construction arm of the shippers.[29]

The public voice of the shippers and related commercial interests is the Board of Commissioners of the Port of New Orleans, commonly known as the Dock Board. The board is a state agency located in New Orleans, and its members are appointed by the governor.[30] Its responsibilities extend to all port activities: it allocates wharf and dock space to both private and public interests, serves as the local assuring agency for federally funded waterway projects throughout the greater New Orleans area, and has a virtual monopoly over the planning and promotion of the port's growth and expansion.

Centroport U.S.A. is the Dock Board's 30-year, $400 million master plan for modernizing the port facilities of New Orleans.[31] The plan, begun after World War II, has evolved into a concerted effort requiring massive commitments of money, land, and human resources to transform New Orleans into the Rotterdam—the largest, most modern port in the world today—of the Western Hemisphere. The projects of several federal, state, and municipal agencies are to be combined in this comprehensive, farsighted plan, which requires a dramatic upgrading and expansion of all port facilities. The plan anticipates the modern docks, storage space, and new methods of handling that will be needed by the container, LASH/Seabee, and giant cargo ships now being constructed and entering world trade and by the even larger vessels being contemplated. These needs, along with those for deep-draft berths, public bulk terminals, rail yards, and barge carrier terminals are being met in large part by shifting the primary port area from the already congested banks of the Mississippi River at New Orleans to an inner tidewater area in the eastern corner of Orleans Parish. In addition, the plan allocates several thousand acres of

29. The symbiotic relationship between the two is suggested by the fact that the district engineers of the New Orleans District often moved into the heirarchy of the Board of Commissioners of the Port of New Orleans upon completing their New Orleans tour of duty with the Corps.

30. In practice the governor appoints the choice of the nominating committee, which is composed of representatives from leading shipping and business enterprises in New Orleans.

31. The discussion of Centroport is drawn largely from Colonel Herbert R. Haar, Jr., "Centroport—for the Year 2000," *Military Engineer*, vol. 65 (January-February 1973), pp. 1–3.

land adjacent to the tidewater port for light and heavy manufacturing. The plan provides for improved access by ship, barge, rail, highway, and air transportation, to carry the threefold increase in general cargo projected for the port by the year 2000. With the development of Centroport, New Orleans will become the leading port in the nation; without it, the city will be unable to remain competitive with the increasingly aggressive southeast Atlantic and Gulf Coast ports. Or so goes the scenario of Centroport proponents.

Between 1958 and 1974 much of the construction has shifted to Centroport's tidewater area, at the juncture of the Industrial Canal and the MR-GO. The initial container terminals and deep-draft berths were begun, and at the Public Bulk Terminal the rail yard and the open storage area were expanded and more handling equipment was added. Manufacturers began to move into the tidewater area surrounding the port facilities.

Much more remains to be done, however. The MR-GO, now maintained by the Corps to a depth of 36 feet, must be widened and excavated to a depth of 55 feet to accommodate the new generation of deep-draft ships.[32] Of the required $400 million investment in dock, terminal, and related facilities, only $50 million had actually been committed as of 1974. Most important of all, much of the scheme hinges on the yet-to-be-built access routes from the river to the inner tidewater area and the Mississippi River–Gulf Outlet. As Colonel Herbert Haar has observed, "The lack of an adequate connection between the two parts of the port [the river and the tidewater area] could delay Centroport's progress and could mean that the wharves along the river would have to be rehabilitated to give much longer service."[33]

At present only one route exists through an antiquated lock at the mouth of the Industrial Canal, in service now for half a century (see figure 4-2). The shippers allege that the lock is already at peak capacity. In 1971, for example, "the lock handled 23,650,000 tons, passing 65,876 vessels which required 13,324 lockages," and a larger, deeper lock is needed to accommodate the projected increase of 1 million tons of cargo a year for the next 50 years.[34]

32. The New Orleans District did a feasibility study of deepening the MR-GO to 55 feet (ibid., p. 2).
33. Ibid., p. 3.
34. Ibid., p. 2.

This eventuality was anticipated in the 1956 act authorizing the construction of the main MR-GO channel and stating that "when economically justified by obsolescence of the existing industrial canal lock, or by increased traffic, replacement of the existing lock or an additional lock with suitable connections is hereby approved to be constructed in the vicinity of Meraux, Louisiana."[35] When initiated by the New Orleans District Office, the new lock study therefore fell into the same category as the L-15 study—post-authorization planning. But the manner in which the district carried out the study, with regard to both public participation and environmental considerations, provides an interesting contrast. The new lock study spanned two rather distinct eras of environmental consciousness, first in 1960 and then in the early 1970s.

The First Public Hearing on the MR-GO Lock and Connecting Channel

In February 1960 the New Orleans District Office held a daylong public hearing at the St. Bernard Parish Courthouse in Chalmette, Louisiana. Over 200 people attended. The district called the meeting to get help in deciding which of the two parish crossings selected by the Corps in consultation with the Dock Board would be most acceptable to the people directly affected—the residents of St. Bernard Parish.[36] Even in 1960, eight years before the main MR-GO was fully operative and bringing traffic into the tidewater area from the coast, the Industrial Canal lock was operating at over 90 percent of its capacity.[37] It was necessary to start planning a new lock immediately. District officials expressed their willingness to entertain alternatives to their two sites, assuming of course that sufficient reason for doing so could be demonstrated. Though it was common knowledge that the district was undertaking the new lock study at the request of the Dock Board, the board felt it necessary to disclaim at the hearing any interest whatsoever in the site location. This disclaimer, which few believed, was contradicted at another point in the hearing by the chairman of the Board of Public Works of the State of Louisiana.[38]

35. 70 Stat. 65.
36. St. Bernard Parish borders New Orleans to the east, extending to the Gulf Coast.
37. U.S. Department of the Army, Corps of Engineers, New Orleans District, transcript of public hearing on the navigation lock of the MR-GO, Chalmette, La., February 1, 1960, p. 18.
38. Ibid., pp. 10, 11.

Colonel G. M. Cookson, district engineer for New Orleans, briefly outlined the two alternatives, noting that they were selected on the basis of navigational and shipping needs and as being the least intrusive on the rapidly expanding St. Bernard community. By 1960 St. Bernard was the fastest growing parish in Louisiana. The Upper Site alternative shown in figure 4-2 extended from Docville on the Mississippi River, approximately eight miles below the Industrial Canal, running along a north-by-northeast course for five miles across St. Bernard Parish, then connecting with the MR-GO below the easternmost tip of the planned Centroport. The Lower Site alternative began another mile or so downriver, just below Violet, again cutting northerly across to the MR-GO. Both routes would bisect the parish, leaving much of its land area and at least 10 percent of its residents below the channel.

The Dock Board and representatives of commercial and navigational interests came to the meeting to endorse one or another of the site locations. The influential shipowners and river pilots were in agreement on the preferred crossing, as the chairman of the Waterways Development Committee of the Chamber of Commerce of New Orleans and the River Region informed the audience: "In determining the most feasible location we called together officials of the steamship organizations [and the] association of river pilots who are thoroughly familiar with the river conditions at these locations, and it was the unanimous opinion of these people that the site would be at the Upper Site."[39]

As they listened to these endorsements, the residents of St. Bernard could barely contain themselves. They had not assumed that a new lock and connecting channel were foregone conclusions or that the gathering was simply an exercise in site selection between the two alternatives being offered them by the Corps. They had come to express their anger at the cavalier manner in which the Dock Board and the district had treated them. Moreover, they felt that whether a lock and channel were to be built within their parish was for them to decide. This meant that their own Port Authority, Planning Commission, or Police Jury (the governing body of the parish) would have to be designated the assuring agency, and not the intruder, the New Orleans Dock Board.

The debate over jurisdictional control reflected a long-standing con-

39. Ibid., p. 18.

troversy. Not one of the nine members of the Dock Board was from St. Bernard, yet as the State of Louisiana's designated assuring agency, the board had broad powers over the economic life of the parish. The outcome of the controversy over the location of the MR-GO, for instance, served to vividly remind the people of St. Bernard what the lack of representation meant. Despite local opposition the MR-GO was located so that 70 miles of it cut through the parish. Many local residents felt that the Dock Board acquired the right-of-way in a very heavy-handed fashion. As a local attorney recounted:

> The Dock Board, as you remember, some few months ago held a hearing as to what they were going to do for the parish on the MR-GO—they held it right here in the same room. And what happened? The meeting was quickly discontinued because they were getting too much opposition for that Gulf channel, and then they came back and threw it down our throats and told us that they had deadlines to meet and if we didn't agree to give them the ground they were going into court and take it away from us—that's what they did— that's what they intended to do here.[40]

Local self-determination—political power—was the issue. Who was to have control over the lives and property of the people of St. Bernard? Local elected public officials or the regional New Orleans Dock Board?

Objections were also raised about the cost-sharing provisions of the plan. Addressing the local people, Judge Leander H. Perez, district attorney for St. Bernard and the neighboring Plaquemines Parish, wryly observed: "I can imagine you people voting bond issues on yourselves to build a bridge over a seaway [the proposed new connecting channel] constructed by the Federal Government when it is fundamentally an obligation of the Federal Government to take care of its waterways."[41] This waterway, it should be remembered, would only serve to speed traffic to the port of New Orleans, not to benefit the people of the parish in any way. Of course, the St. Bernard citizens would have a nice view of ships cruising down the channel.

Faced with the outpouring of local opposition at its public hearing, the Corps retreated to its New Orleans office. The plan for the new lock

40. Ibid., p. 40.
41. Ibid., p. 17. Under law the federal government cannot fund the bridges that would be required as part of the plan, and the state made it explicit that it had no intention of doing so. Thus if a bridge were built, the local government would have to fund it.

was shelved, and for the next several years attention turned once again to the completion of the main MR-GO channel.

Getting Nowhere Fast

For the remainder of the decade the Dock Board and the New Orleans District Office continued to examine alternative strategies for providing access to the tidewater area without bisecting St. Bernard with a ship lock and channel. Since much of the waterway traffic was barge traffic and would continue to be with the coming generation of containerized ships, in 1961 the Corps compiled figures that would justify a design study for a barge lock, rather than one for ships. Although the envisioned lock and channel would be located at the same Lower Site suggested in the ship lock proposal, the Corps hoped that because the channel would be only 12 feet deep, it would be more acceptable to the community. But the idea was rejected by higher Corps authorities when they determined that no authorization existed for a barge lock or even for the preparation of a survey that would lead to its authorization. They so informed the Dock Board and the idea was dropped.[42]

By 1964 the Dock Board concluded that if it were to get the desired new lock it would have to forgo hopes for a channel in St. Bernard. Thus it requested the district office to consider simply modernizing the lock at the mouth of the Industrial Canal.[43] By 1966 the Corps had produced a preliminary report in which it proposed a new ship lock 375 feet upstream from the existing one. This proposal might have been the basis for a timely resolution of the issue: the shippers would have a new lock, if not the second access route into the tidewater they preferred, and since St. Bernard Parish would be unaffected, the proposal should have sailed through unopposed. Subsequent soil investigations, however, revealed unexpectedly poor foundation conditions. Given current technology, it was infeasible to locate a new lock any closer than 750 feet upstream of the existing lock. This created serious problems for the Dock Board.

Since the Dock Board was responsible for attaining rights-of-way and

42. New Orleans District, transcript of public meeting on the MR-GO new lock and connecting channel and high-level bridges, New Orleans, November 29, 1972, vol. 1., p. 6.

43. Letter, Board of Commissioners of the Port of New Orleans to the New Orleans District Office, November 13, 1964.

for relocating any houses, businesses, and utilities that would be displaced by construction, it conducted a study of the effects of locating a lock 750 feet from the existing lock. Its conclusion was that the social and economic consequences would be traumatic. Ten marine-oriented businesses and a dozen others would have to be relocated, along with 989 families in 673 dwellings, some 4,000 people in all. Three vehicular bridges and one railroad bridge would have to be replaced, and utilities and pipelines woud have to be rerouted. The cost of all this to the assuring agent, that is, the State of Louisiana, was estimated at over $220 million. This was more than the federal government's entire costs for building the lock and channel, estimated then at $131 million. It was unlikely that the state legislature would fund the project at this price, so in August 1969 the Dock Board withdrew its support of the Industrial Canal plan.[44]

Meanwhile the main channel of the MR-GO was in full operation, and the bottleneck at the existing lock was continuing to cost the ship and barge operators precious time and millions of dollars in forgone business. The shipping industry grew increasingly apprehensive. In turn, the pressure on the Corps to build something mounted. The district office returned to its 1960 plan and approached the established political leadership of St. Bernard Parish to win support for building a new channel across St. Bernard Parish.[45] The issue had come full circle.

The Second Round of Planning

In 1969 a series of private meetings were held between St. Bernard officials, the district office, the Dock Board, and the Tidewater Development Association (TDA) in an attempt to reach an accord on a site for the new lock.[46] The meetings went reasonably well and by December the prevailing assumption, at least of the district office, the Dock Board, and the TDA was that apart from ironing out a few details, the Lower Site crossing would not be opposed by St. Bernard's political leadership. The

44. New Orleans District, transcript of public meeting, November 29, 1972, vol. 1, p. 6.

45. Herbert R. Haar, Jr., "MR-GO—New Ship Lock: Sequence of Events" (typewritten memorandum; n.d.).

46. TDA is an ad hoc committee of New Orleans business interests that was initially incorporated just after World War II with the sole purpose of marshaling support for the MR-GO. It dissolved once the channel was under construction but was revitalized in 1968 to provide backing for the new lock and connecting channel.

district office was ready to go ahead with a public meeting to present alternative sites to residents of the parish, although it actually had only one in mind.

Nevertheless, the issues to be resolved were far from trivial and had long been matters of contention. How would the costs be allocated between the federal government, state government, and local residents—not only those for the lock and channel but the appreciable incidental costs associated with the construction, acquisition, and maintenance of the project? Who was to have jurisdiction over the lock and channel, the Dock Board or the St. Bernard Port Authority? If the Dock Board retained jurisdiction, what kind of representation on the board would be granted to St. Bernard Parish? A new issue had also come to the fore—provisions for hurricane and flood protection—and would remain paramount in the minds of St. Bernard residents throughout all the machinations of the 1969–74 period. This issue and that of environmentalism was yet to be raised publicly.

The plan for the MR-GO authorized in 1956 made no provisions for hurricane levee protection. It was solely a navigation project, or so the engineers who designed it thought. Not that anyone was unaware that the New Orleans area is more prone to hurricanes and floods than all the rest of the nation, but levee protections have customarily been treated separately from navigation projects by the federal government. For example, the federal government usually requires a local contribution of 30 percent of the costs of hurricane protection levees, whereas it bears the total cost of navigation projects. But what if a navigation project exacerbates an existing hurricane flood potential? What if the MR-GO's 500-foot-wide channel provided a straight path from the gulf into the delta, thus inundating the lands along its banks?

The question was posed early on in reports and hearings but received little attention until hurricanes struck—Betsy in 1965 and Camille four years later.[47] The extensive flooding caused by both sparked yet another unresolved controversy over the contribution of the MR-GO to the severity of the flooding and the obligations of the federal government to come to the aid of the people of St. Bernard. The position of the St. Bernard Planning Commission, most of the elected officials of the parish, and an overwhelming proportion of the citizenry was that the MR-GO did fun-

47. See New Orleans District, transcript of public hearing, February 1, 1960, p. 48.

nel tidal swells up into the parish, thus adding measurably to the flooding, and would continue to do so. They contended that since the MR-GO is a federal waterway, it is the federal government's responsibility to provide them with complete flood levee protection. In essence, they believe the government is obligated to compensate the local population for the Corps' poor initial design of the channel. A satisfactory resolution of the issue of levee flood protection became one of the major preconditions of any serious consideration of a new lock and connecting channel crossing. In dollar terms this meant that the federal government would have to absorb St. Bernard's 30 percent share of levee costs all along the MR-GO levee protection system then under construction, which in 1972 had already cost the parish several million dollars and was projected to cost many times that amount in the coming years.[48]

The issue placed the Corps in a difficult position. It had no authority to absorb levee protection costs as part of the MR-GO or to include more than the 70 percent federal share allowed under law in any future authorization request. Funding aside, the district office adamantly denied that the MR-GO had contributed in even the slightest way to the flooding of St. Bernard caused by Betsy and Camille. It saw the issue of levee protection simply as the ransom being asked for the new lock and connecting channel.

To lay the groundwork for the district office's upcoming public meeting, TDA began a fairly intensive publicity campaign in 1969 to inform the citizens of St. Bernard of the "benefits" that would accompany the construction of a crossing through their parish.[49] Residents were skeptical. The promise of 10,000 new jobs for the parish in port and industrial development, with an annual payroll of $80 million, was one of the least supportable and most often criticized of the alleged benefits. The MR-GO had existed for 10 years, yet not a single port facility or industry had located along its banks in St. Bernard Parish. And considering the projected growth of the nearby Centroport, there was no reason to believe the situation would change materially with the addition of another five miles of channel.

48. Ibid., November 29, 1972, vol. 1, p. 65.
49. For example, a booklet, *Important Information about the Proposed Ship Lock*, was prepared and widely distributed by the TDA in 1970. A flyer, "This Is Important to You," was mailed at the same time to all registered voters in the metropolitan New Orleans area.

Just before the district office announced its public meeting, then scheduled for September 1970, the political leaders of St. Bernard balked. They had not received sufficient satisfaction in their private negotiations with the development interests, and as word of the plans for a parish crossing spread, vocal citizen opposition began to emerge. At this juncture the local political leaders broke off private negotiations and decided to oppose *any* channel through the parish. Communicating through their congressman, F. Edward Hébert, they asked that the public hearing be postponed so that they could study the matter further. The hearing was rescheduled for early summer in 1971, the first of a series of postponements requested by St. Bernard officials.[50] Then, on August 25, 1970, the St. Bernard Planning Commission unanimously passed a motion opposing the construction of a new channel and lock anywhere in the parish. A week later the Police Jury did likewise. But the following month the jury sent an unsigned memorandum to the district office listing demands that must be met before the connecting channel would even be considered. The bill of particulars included concern about bridges, levees, and jurisdiction, as well as the project's overall effect on St. Bernard.[51]

NEPA and the New Lock

By 1970 the people of St. Bernard had found an ally in the environmentalists—primarily the Audubon Society and the newly formed Ecology Center of New Orleans—who had just begun to take the offensive against government agencies, including the Corps. At the same time, St. Bernard officials acquired a new legal weapon: the National Environmental Policy Act of 1969. Henceforth, the new lock was opposed, among other reasons, as a serious threat to the wetlands of the parish. Drawing upon local university talent and professional environmental planners, the Police Jury commissioned extensive economic and environmental studies to consider both the need for a new ship lock and channel and their potential effect on the parish. Meanwhile, the jury's legal council began to amass the case histories of similar controversies with the Corps that had been litigated under NEPA.[52]

50. The officials renewed their request for postponement as the summer of 1971 approached, and the meeting was moved to April 1972 and then to November.
51. See Haar, "MR-GO—New Ship Lock," p. 3.
52. An injunction against further planning of the new lock and connecting channel by the Corps had already been sought under NEPA, but the government's motion

The discord between the Dock Board and the Police Jury reached its peak in the spring of 1972 when the jury declined an invitation to lunch with the Dock Board in New Orleans on the grounds that the growing visibility of the issue and the intense reactions of the jury's constituents precluded any meeting with the board behind closed doors. Instead, the jury extended an invitation to the board to come to Chalmette for an open meeting. The board was outraged. Its members were not about to venture into St. Bernard in order to be made into public spectacles.[53] The district office, meanwhile, held steadfast. It would proceed with its planned public meeting, giving all concerned the opportunity to express themselves, and would then press on with the advanced design of the Lower Site crossing.

The Public Meeting

In an atmosphere so highly charged and with both sides seemingly intransigent, what could be expected of the public meeting? The lineup of forces was known well in advance. Opposition to a St. Bernard crossing would come from the citizens and political leaders of the parish, a number of environmental organizations, and a small number of local shallow-draft barge interests (who thought they could arrange a barge-only lock and channel compromise). Proponents would include the remainder of the shallow-draft interests, the Dock Board, Congressman Hébert, the district office, the governor and various state agencies of Louisiana, the mayor of New Orleans, and shipping interests.

Each side lived up to expectations. No sooner had the district office announced the time and place of the meeting than a controversy arose. Because of pressure from the Dock Board, the meeting was scheduled to be held in New Orleans, a decision that immediately drew fire from St. Bernard officials who insisted that it be held in the area affected. The district office compromised by scheduling two days of meetings, the first in New Orleans and the second in St. Bernard.

The morning of November 29, 1972, 700 people gathered at the Naval and Marine Corps Reserve Training Center in New Orleans to thrash out

to dismiss, based on the premature nature of the suit was granted on October 18, 1972. Mississippi River–Gulf Outlet, *George F. Lopez, Nolan Lapeyrouse, Claude Alphonso, and August B. Robin* v. *Corps of Engineers, Stanley Resor, and Frederick Clarke,* U.S. District Court, Louisiana, Civil No. 72-785 (not published).

53. Interview with Dock Board officials, February 22, 1974.

the many issues of the new lock project. Colonel Richard L. Hunt, New Orleans district engineer opened the meeting with a lengthy presentation of the background of the study and of the economic, social, environmental, and engineering reasons for preferring the Lower Site over all the others. But as soon became evident, many of the people of St. Bernard had not come to listen attentively or even to debate.

Congressman Hébert proclaimed once again his unswerving support of the project, reminding the citizens of St. Bernard:

I have helped obtain a number of improvements in the project that is under consideration by the Corps. The Federal Government has agreed to build proper levees, and importantly, to maintain these levees on both sides of the project. At the 1960 hearing, these important considerations were not included as Federal contributions. It was not clear then who would build and maintain the levees. To me, there is no question but that this must be at Federal cost, and the Federal Government has now accepted this responsibility. . . . This is what I insisted on 12 years ago; this is what I insist on this morning. I do not change overnight like a chameleon. . . .

A most significant step was taken when the Dock Board agreed by official action to turn the project over to St. Bernard Parish for development after its completion. This means—hear me well—this means that the New Orleans Dock Board, as we popularly know it, will have nothing to do with any control over any of the land on either side of the project. It will withdraw as the Assuring Agency. This offers St. Bernard Parish the opportunity to plan and develop considerable acreage for industrial and commercial use, creating many good jobs and payrolls.[54]

This bill of particulars, these so-called concessions, had been heard by the people of the parish many times before. What stood out in their minds was not that adverse effects of the project were being mitigated but that their congressman had the gall to come before hundreds of them and reiterate his allegiance to the MR-GO and the shipping and commercial interests of New Orleans, rather than to the citizens of St. Bernard. (New Orleans, however, provides more than four-fifths of the votes in the congressional district Hébert represented.) Before Hébert could continue, pandemonium broke loose. His next sentence was interrupted with catcalls and boos, followed by a parade of demonstrators marching around the meeting room.[55]

54. New Orleans District, transcript of public meeting, November 29, 1972, vol. 1, p. 23.
55. Even after a lifetime of Louisiana politics, this was too much for Hébert. He

It was well into the evening before all those who came to praise, condemn, and raise questions about the project were heard. The project unquestionably had appreciable political backing as indicated by the next speaker, James E. Fitzmorris, Jr., lieutenant governor of Louisiana, who read a statement from Governor Edwin W. Edwards. The governor's position was unequivocal. "I am firmly convinced that the information to be presented today will clearly establish that Louisiana and, in particular, the New Orleans area must have a new lock facility in order to maintain its position as a leader in the world of shipping markets and intercontinental port facilities." Moreover, it was his position that the new lock could not be located on the Industrial Canal. "Every attempt was made to utilize the Industrial Canal area for the new lock. But this appears to be impossible. The cost to the state would be astronomical and far beyond what any government could in good conscience approve as long as reasonable alternatives existed." Of course, this left only one alternative, a St. Bernard crossing. Or, as the governor put it: "Faced with these conditions we are forced to seek another, more practical location. I am aware that this alternative is one that the people of St. Bernard Parish are fearful of. But I reiterate my pledge that their interests will be safeguarded. *This I personally promise.*"[56]

The Dock Board too was insisting on the St. Bernard crossing. Its president, Richard B. Montgomery, Jr., stated:

It is the unanimous opinion of the Board that the new ship-barge lock project that is under discussion today is of paramount importance to the future of the Port of New Orleans if it is to continue to grow and prosper and remain the No. 2 port in the nation. A ship-barge lock is a must to provide the port access to the tidewater area where we expect to take advantage of large backup areas required for modern cargo handling and to move approximately half of our future operations by the year 2000.

The Board is unanimously strong in its convictions that this new lock must be a ship-barge lock and should be built in the vicinity of the Violet Canal [the Lower Site].[57]

In presenting their case, the opponents to a St. Bernard crossing did

claimed to have never seen such a disruptive and discourteous crowd and said that he would never again participate in such public meetings. (Interview, February 1, 1974.) In 1976 he retired from office.

56. New Orleans District, transcript of public meeting, November 29, 1972, vol. 1, p. 28.

57. Ibid., November 21, 1972, vol. 1, p. 70.

not have the backing of the federal government, the state, or the leading economic interests of the region. They were supported by the hundreds of intensely concerned citizens attending the meeting, a petition signed by 18,000 people of St. Bernard Parish, all of St. Bernard's local political officials, and the lengthy professional, economic, and ecological reports that the Police Jury had earlier commissioned.[58]

With these reports in hand, the state senator from St. Bernard, Samuel B. Nunez, Jr., was able to rebut many of the major arguments of the proponents. He first tackled the alleged economic benefits to the parish: "Many communities in this nation have now exploded the myth that economic expansion solely for the sake of economic expansion is beneficial. Many areas will no longer accept at face value the advantages and promises of more jobs and large payrolls." It was even problematic whether such commerce would ever develop. He asked the audience, "How many jobs did the Gulf Outlet bring to you people in St. Bernard?" "None" was the reply. "How many contractors got work on the Gulf Outlet? Very few. . . . In short, gentlemen, it is no longer possible to buy one's way into a community simply by promises of economic expansion. It is very obvious to me that our sense of values is changing."[59]

He then turned to the Corps' fairly sanguine estimation of the environmental impact of a new lock channel.

I think that we must recognize that wetlands are regarded as state and federal resources, and we are about to destroy them. The wetlands are caught in a vise whose jaws are closing in from both the north and the south. On the north we have the ambitious plan advocated by the proponents of the Centroport project, including the cut. On the south we have the pressure to be exerted by the Superport [the new deep water port being located along the Gulf Coast]. The wetlands are caught in the middle and are rapidly disappearing.

In all, Nunez raised over 20 specific points relevant to the assumptions underlying the Corps' environmental and economic analyses, citing such things as the Corps' shortsightedness, its disregard for the social goals and values of people in the parish, and its disregard for the Army chief

58. The number of signatures on the petition, which had been placed inside the polling booths on election day, was impressive. The report by the jury was not only lengthy—300 pages of material were submitted for the record—but added new data on the environmental effects of the proposed project.

59. This and succeeding remarks by Nunez are from New Orleans District, transcript of public meeting, November 21, 1972, vol. 1, pp. 31–37.

of engineer's own wetlands policy. He asserted that the district office was "deliberately encouraging the establishing of a large population [in] an area which is constantly threatened by hurricanes and floods," based on the presumption that "we can get them out when the time comes." He, for one, would not stand by idly and let this happen. His closing remarks prompted applause and a standing ovation.

The district office eventually replied to Nunez and others with facts and figures of its own. But neither the people of St. Bernard nor their political leaders would budge. They were little impressed by the promises of Congressman Hébert, the district office, the Dock Board, the TDA, and the governor that no crossing would be started until a vehicular bridge and highway connection were completed. Nor did they see much in the Dock Board's promise to turn over the operation of the new lock and connecting channel to St. Bernard authorities upon completion. Their cause had become a crusade. They would not relent at any price; promises of bridges, roads, jurisdiction, Dock Board representation, wetlands mitigation, or flood protection would not sway them. Or so they said.

The same array of interests, and most of the same persons—with the notable exception of Congressman Hébert, who said he would never again submit himself to such abuse—again confronted one another 10 days later at the St. Bernard Civic Auditorium in Chalmette. The district office remained determined to listen to each and every person who had anything at all to say and was not deterred by heckling or outbursts from the audience. Accomplishing an almost herculean feat, it kept the meeting open from 10 A.M. on Saturday, December 9, to after 1 A.M. on Sunday morning. There is little question that a public forum was maintained; a more open meeting cannot be imagined. But for the people of St. Bernard, who had been excluded for so long from the decisionmaking process of the district office, a single public meeting was little compensation. They believed the Corps held the public meeting only because it was legally obliged to do so, not because it welcomed their views or sympathized with their position. Mutual suspicion was the order of both the day and night.

Aftermath

If the public meeting served no other end, it vividly demonstrated the breadth and intensity of the opposition to this project. Furthermore, St. Bernard officials had been so unequivocal and outspoken that in effect they had crossed the Rubicon. In the months following the public meeting they therefore continued to update their environmental studies and prepared their legal brief.[60] Proponents of the Lower Site crossing similarly had exhausted most of their options. They could either return to the Industrial Canal site or face a protracted legal and political battle with St. Bernard over the lower crossing. As for the district office, it was back to the drawing board.

After eight months of soul-searching and reviewing some 14 alternative sites, the district office reduced the most promising sites to four, at two locations. Two of the alternative designs were again at the lower site; the other two were modifications of the old Industrial Canal site design. As the district office interim report in 1973 candidly acknowledged, these were substantial modifications indeed.

Since the public meetings, great engineering effort has been expended in an attempt to significantly reduce the required rights-of-way and the resulting socioeconomic impact of the 1969 IHNC [Inner Harbor Navigational Canal] plan. This has been largely achieved. This newfound capability stems from the use of new construction techniques, the application of which was not obvious as recently as August 1969.[61]

Instead of displacing almost 700 dwellings, 4,000 people, and many businesses, as required in the 1969 design, only 889 people in 157 dwellings and 11 canal-side businesses would need to be relocated.[62] The nonfederal costs of the two locations had also drawn much closer. The two Lower Site designs would require a nonfederal outlay of from $75 million to $90 million, whereas the Industrial Canal designs were now estimated at $111 million—half of the 1969 nonfederal estimated costs of that alternative.

The interim report indicated that a shift back to the Industrial Canal site was conceivable. In the eyes of district office officials the Industrial Canal and the Lower Site were competitive. By opting for the Industrial Canal site the 57,000 people of St. Bernard Parish could of course be placated, at an added cost to the Dock Board of about $25 million. This is not a trifling amount, but it was far less than the estimated annual $31 million loss for every year that the opening of a new lock is delayed.[63]

60. Interviews with members of the St. Bernard Police Jury and Planning Commission, February 22, 1974.
61. Form letter, New Orleans District Office to interested individuals and groups to report on site selection, August 17, 1973, p. 4.
62. Ibid., p. 8.
63. The loss figure is based on July 1973 price levels, ibid., p. 7.

On the other hand, such figures did not take into account the important yet somewhat intangible cost of refurbishing the Industrial Canal,
a cost that is seldom mentioned publicly. If the old lock was to be re-
furbished, it was unlikely that a new route would ever be laid across St.
Bernard to the tidewater area. To the extent that the future development
of Centroport depended on such a second access route, the adverse effects
of the decision would be felt for decades to come, not only in New Orleans
but in St. Bernard as well.

The new route across St. Bernard was important to the shipping interests; thus despite vociferous opposition to the Lower Site channel on both
ecological and social grounds, this site was the one the district finally
recommended to the OCE in its site selection report of March 1975.
After sitting on the recommendation for over a year, the OCE finally approved it in August 1976. Since this was a post-authorization study, all
that remained was for the Corps to secure congressional funding and
move into the final design and construction stages. Traditionally, at least,
that was all that remained. But newly elected President Jimmy Carter
decided to conduct a sweeping reevaluation of all major federal water
resource projects to assess their possible social and ecological effects and
their financial soundness. Years of controversy had made the MR-GO
new lock and connecting channel of obvious interest, and in this instance
the President concluded that the Corps was wrong. He made it quite
clear in a directive to the agency that the Corps could replace the old
lock but could not dig a channel across St. Bernard.

The project should be modified to eliminate consideration of the new channel
location. Further study should be carried out to determine whether repair or
replacement is needed of the existing lock at the existing site. If replacement
and expansion are deemed necessary, special care should be taken to minimize dislocation and disruption of residents near the site.[64]

The district engineers and planners of the project were taken aback.
Disregarding their years of study and their final professional judgment, the
President had stepped in at the last minute and reversed their decision.
Since this action was unprecedented, the engineers' reaction was not too
surprising. What is surprising, however, is that within a year the engi-
neers were well on their way toward developing a method of replacing

64. Jimmy Carter, "Statement on Water Resources," press release, Office of the
White House Press Secretary, April 18, 1977, p. 20.

the existing lock on the very site of the present one, a possibility they had considered unfeasible earlier. Furthermore, it appears that the replacement lock will cause a minimum of disruption to the surrounding urban community.

What does the evolution of this study reveal about the Corps' new era of open planning? Since the restudy of the Lower Site began in 1970, district officials have maintained that it was a post-authorization study and that thus the agency's new public participation guidelines were not applicable. When pressed on the issue, they resorted to the argument that the public participation guidelines suggest but do not require any public consultation in post-authorization planning. The public meeting held by the district office in 1972, the project opponents were informed, was held only through the good graces of the district officials because they wanted to hear all sides of the controversy. They refused to go beyond a single large public meeting. Finally, there is no indication that the OCE ever made a serious effort to persuade the district to interpret differently either the chief's intentions or the agency's public participation regulations; that is, to insist on a more meaningful and open public participation program and to ensure that all major differences were reconciled.

Conclusions

The limits of public participation as traditionally practiced in planning Corps projects is vividly illustrated in the study of the MR-GO lock and connecting channel. The large-scale public hearings held by the New Orleans District at best accomplished only the chief's goals of information-gathering. They did not contribute to establishing the legitimacy of the Corps as a neutral and dedicated public servant or to the mediation of conflict between competing local interests.

Parenthetically, the substantive outcome of a more thorough public participation program might have been no different from that reached. That is, the result of extensive consultation, workshops, and the like, and the sincere neutrality of the district office might also have led to the abandonment of the new channel proposal and a return to the idea of simply modernizing the Industrial Canal lock. Reaching this conclusion through a participation process, however, might well have won respect for the Corps from a majority of the citizenry, if not all the shippers, and praise and recognition for the chief of engineers.

Nevertheless, as the L-15 study shows, an extensive public participation effort cannot assure that all three of the chief's objectives—information-gathering, legitimization, and conflict resolution—can be completely met in any public participation program. It is a tool, and nothing more than that. After its initial hesitance, the Kansas City District went to appreciable lengths to involve the public in large-scale meetings and workshops and through individual consultations. In so doing, it overcame some but not all of the public's initial trepidation. In the end it was unable to mediate the conflict between contending local interests, though it was able to win the respect of most of the participants in the planning process.

How well did the New Orleans and Kansas City district offices resolve the issues of representation, modes of involvement, delegation of authority, and locus of final decisions that were raised by the chief's policy of open planning? It is evident that the New Orleans District viewed its study of the new lock and connecting channel as exempt from the new policy. It adhered to the traditional practice of holding large public hearings and made little effort to expand the scope of participation beyond the public officials, other government agencies, and affected economic interests on the usual mailing lists.

The mode of involvement, the post-authorization public hearing, was also traditional. Authority was not delegated to any new decisionmaking body, and the issue of whether any group or individual other than the district office should make the final decision on the project was never entertained.

The L-15 study provides a notable contrast. The KCD considered itself responsible for reaching out to as wide a group as possible through the use of traditional mailing lists and the sign-up sheets from earlier public hearings on the project, and through initiating contact with groups that expressed an interest in the levee proposal, whether they favored or opposed it. This may not have provided exhaustive representation, but it was thorough.

The use of study groups to focus on various aspects of the project was an innovation for the KCD. These groups went well beyond the traditional public hearing, bringing together the contending factions to work together on specific problem areas.

An issue never confronted directly during the L-15 study was the extent to which authority was being delegated to the study groups or would be delegated to the public in general. To what degree did the district intend to share its powers? Avoiding direct consideration of this question did not solve the problem, for the participants were forever concerned with the utility and meaning of their efforts. The KCD made it clear that it would not be bound in any formal way by the decisions of the study groups or wishes of any of the citizen groups. But the fact that the study groups were convened and that the public was continually encouraged to contribute to the planning process surely implied, at least to the participants, that they would share in making the decision. Otherwise the exercise would have been pure tokenism, which would only have exacerbated the issue of the Corps' legitimacy and integrity. The issue of decisionmaking, however, was left ambiguous. Perhaps that was the optimal strategy. We can only surmise from the outcome—the district's tentative compromise proposal and then inaction—that citizen input was indeed taken seriously and that some power was shared. But the final decisionmaking authority clearly remained with the Corps. That the agency decided on inaction implies nonetheless that widespread acceptance is a crucial ingredient in proceeding with a project.

The importance of the separability of a project is highlighted in both cases. The L-15 proposal was only one part of the Pick-Sloan master plan. If the Corps were to accept the argument of the L-15 opponents that levees are inherently bad flood control devices, causing worse flooding downstream and encouraging unwanted development in open spaces, it could jeopardize similar projects, both in the Pick-Sloan Plan and, more important, elsewhere throughout Corps operations. Since the use of structural flood control techniques is so much a part of the Corps' traditional thinking and practice, this result would be viewed as catastrophic.

The proposal for the MR-GO lock and connecting channel was unique in itself. But at least one part (possibly both) of the proposal was required for the ultimate success of Centroport and in turn the viability of the MR-GO (which the Corps spent a decade building). Thus the Corps and private industry had already committed enormous energy and resources to expanding the shipping facilities in and about New Orleans and were not prepared to accept the "do nothing" preference of the project opponents.

CHAPTER FIVE

Open Planning Made Easier:
Involving the Public
in New Projects

BOTH PRACTICAL CONSIDERATIONS and the legal and formal requirements discussed in chapter 2 have made more extensive public participation in agency decisions a necessary part of Corps planning studies for
projects that have not yet received congressional authorization. Thus
adverse local reaction to pre-authorization project studies may well present
a more serious threat to the agency than in the case of post-authorization
studies.

The chief of engineers and members of the Public Works committees
of Congress become perturbed when a project proposal is forwarded to
Washington for approval before a consensus has been reached at the
local level. Like Congressman Hébert, they obviously dislike being cast
in the role of arbiters or proponents in hotly disputed local matters or to
be put in the position of authorizing a project that has a good chance
of ending up in protracted litigation. This in effect compels Corps districts to reach an accord on all controversial issues before submitting a
plan, and they can only do so by means of extensive consultation and
coordination with all contending interests, both inside and outside government. The sooner these interests are included in the planning process,
the less likely it is that unanticipated opposition will arise after the district
has become committed to a plan.

Within this new framework, a number of Corps districts have experi-
mented with novel modes of public participation. The three projects
examined in this and the following chapter have been innovative and in
some ways have been quite successful. Indeed, they have been chosen for

Figure 5-1. *Wildcat and San Pablo Creeks, Contra Costa County, California*

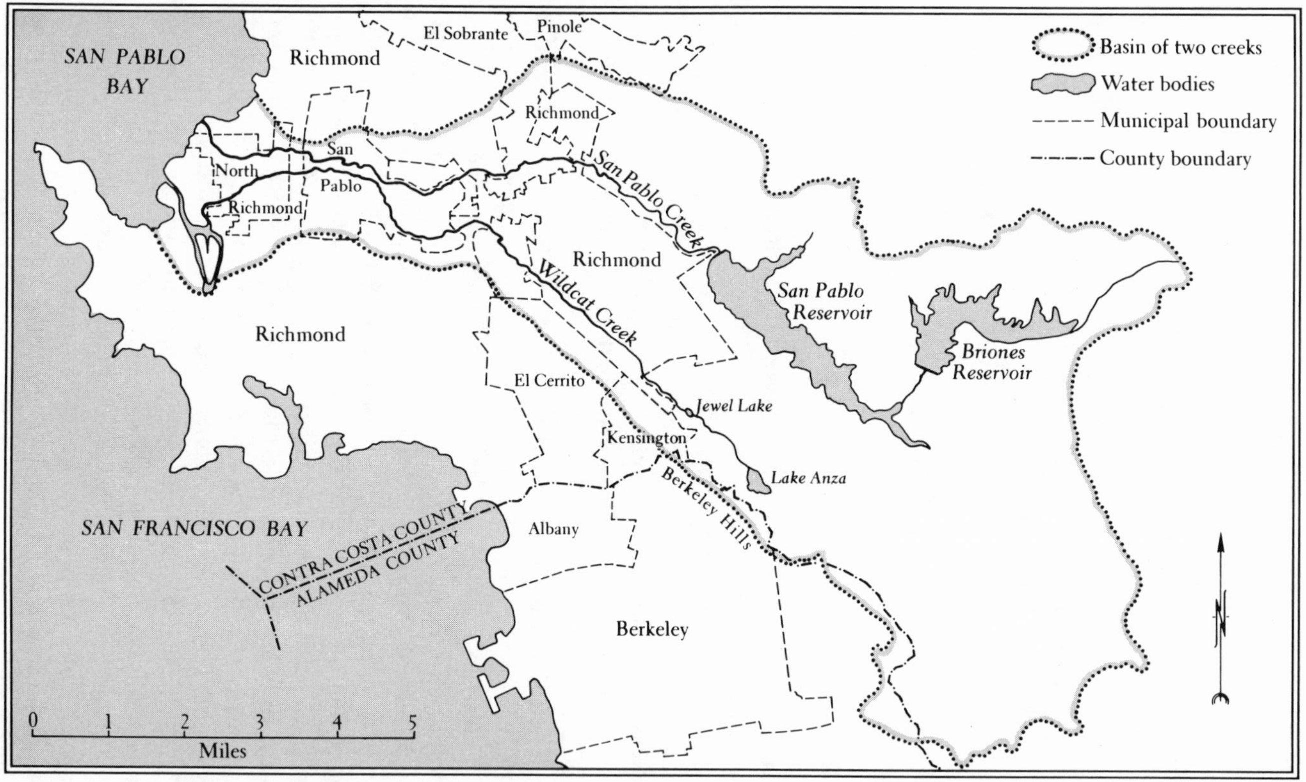

Legend:
- Basin of two creeks
- Water bodies
- Municipal boundary
- County boundary

SAN PABLO BAY

Richmond

El Sobrante

Pinole

Richmond

San Pablo

North Richmond

Richmond

San Pablo Creek

San Pablo Reservoir

Briones Reservoir

Richmond

Wildcat Creek

Jewel Lake

Lake Anza

El Cerrito

Kensington

Berkeley Hills

Albany

Berkeley

SAN FRANCISCO BAY

CONTRA COSTA COUNTY
ALAMEDA COUNTY

Miles
0   1   2   3   4   5

discussion because they illustrate positive accomplishments in the area of public participation in agency decisionmaking.

But satisfying the demands for greater participation, as noted, has posed dilemmas for the Corps. A negative aspect is that bringing numerous new groups into the planning process can result in either a "do nothing" recommendation or an alternative that the Corps itself cannot implement. Some see the implications of a broader participation program as ominous; the Corps may be forced out of business as a major "concrete-pouring" public works agency. Although this seems an unrealistic prospect, agency personnel evince great concern about it. Citizen involvement in project studies IV and V reviewed below reveals that agency fears are to some extent well grounded.

Project Study III: Flood Control on Wildcat and San Pablo Creeks—A California Showpiece

The Wildcat and San Pablo creeks study undertaken by the San Francisco District (SFD) Corps of Engineers seems almost too good to be true. It represents ideal intergovernmental and community-government cooperation in bringing together diverse interests to reach an amicable solution to a vexing problem affecting an economically depressed section of a major metropolitan area. This cooperation was undoubtedly facilitated in part by the pluralistic nature of political power in the community. No faction or interest—industry, commerce, the local poverty organizations, or the environmentalists—dominated. The outcome was also greatly facilitated by the positive attitude and earnest efforts of the SFD.

The adjoining basins of the Wildcat and San Pablo creeks are situated just northeast of Berkeley, California, and east of San Francisco Bay.[1] Both creeks originate in the Berkeley Hills–San Pablo Ridge area and flow northwest through sparsely populated hills and valleys, then due west through the cities of Richmond, El Sobrante, and San Pablo and the community of North Richmond (see figure 5-1). From there they spread across flatlands and salt marshes, emptying eventually into San Pablo

1. Information about the two basins is drawn primarily from U.S. Department of the Army, Corps of Engineers, San Francisco District, "Wildcat and San Pablo Creeks, Contra Costa County, California: Feasibility Report for Water Resources Development" (August 1973).

Bay, which in turn empties into San Francisco Bay. Wildcat Creek extends along a narrow 11-mile watershed, draining about 7,000 acres (approximately 11 square miles), and San Pablo Creek runs some 17 miles, draining about 27,000 acres (42 square miles). The two streams run roughly parallel courses, coming within 500 feet of each other in the city of San Pablo. They share a common floodplain from that point on into San Pablo Bay.

The city of San Pablo was only a small hamlet until World War II when its population increased to 18,000. By 1970 it had reached 21,500. The section of the city within the floodplain is predominantly middle class and residential, with some supporting commercial enterprises. North Richmond, an unincorporated community located on flatlands adjacent to San Pablo Bay, is almost totally a product of the wartime shipbuilding boom that lured many workers to the area. The shipbuilding industry has since declined, leaving behind a population of some 6,000 low-income, mostly black, residents housed in inexpensive dwellings.

Man's encroachments on the floodplain of the two creeks predictably have resulted in a chronic flooding problem. Inundation of the lower reaches of the basin occurs almost annually, and in some years more than once. Over the years landfilling and the construction of light industry and houses have impinged on already inadequate channels, especially along Wildcat Creek. During the winter the creeks can rise rapidly and overflow within 24 hours after the outset of a storm. North Richmond is usually the hardest hit; mud and water often remain on the streets of this relatively poor community throughout the rainy season.

Extensive damage was caused by the floods of 1955, 1958, and 1962, and significant overflows occurred again in 1970 and 1973. The 1958 flood spread over 825 acres, causing an estimated $429,000 in losses due to inundation and erosion. In the Flood Control Act of 1960 Congress authorized a survey report on flood control and allied problems along Wildcat and San Pablo creeks.

North Richmond was already in a state of decay, with low property values and no signs of a resurgence of growth and development, and appeared to the agency to be a poor place to invest federal flood protection dollars. (The Corps has been criticized for biasing its benefit-cost criteria in favor of affluent areas.) Thus shortly after initiating the survey investigation in 1965, it concluded that on the basis of primary flood control benefits alone neither multipurpose reservoirs nor channel improvements and levees were economically justifiable. The Corps then discontinued its study of the two-creek basin and set it aside in 1968.[2]

North Richmond's Model Cities Program

Just as the Corps shelved the North Richmond study, another agency of the federal government was taking steps to reverse the community's bleak prospects. In April 1967 the Department of Housing and Urban Development (HUD) awarded a Model Cities planning grant for North Richmond to Contra Costa County. The prospect of a comprehensive plan for municipal revitalization inspired guarded optimism about the future of the community for the first time in memory.

From the summer of 1967 to that of 1968 the Model Cities staff, together with city and county officials, developed the Comprehensive Plan for North Richmond, which outlined goals for the community in nine areas: environmental protection, housing, education, health, social services, crime and delinquency prevention, manpower, economic development, and recreation and culture. Flood control, storm drainage, and recreation along the Wildcat and San Pablo creeks were crucial aspects of the plan.

The goals of environmental protection, better housing, adequate health care, economic development, and increased recreational opportunities all hinged on an adequate flood control program. Without it there was little likelihood that the community could ever become attractive and thriving. In its report on the feasibility of developing the water resources of the area, the Corps concluded: "Without flood protection the most likely result for the community is that the intervention of Model Cities in North Richmond will have only marginal effects."[3]

HUD tentatively indicated that it would underwrite a major first step of the Model Cities plan by approving a 90 percent grant for a storm drainage system for North Richmond. But the grant would be conditional on assurances that flood protection would also be provided, a measure HUD felt was needed to protect its investment. At this juncture, in

---

2. U.S. Department of the Army, Corps of Engineers, San Francisco District, transcript of public meeting on flood control and allied purposes for Wildcat and San Pablo creeks, Contra Costa County, Calif., held in San Pablo, Calif., May 31, 1973, p. 6.

3. SFD, "Wildcat and San Pablo Creeks Feasibility Report," p. C-5.

June 1968, the Model Cities staff asked the Corps to reopen its study of the flood problems of Wildcat and San Pablo creeks. The Corps in turn asked the Model Cities staff to prepare projected land-use and development data for the Corps to use as justification for reexamining the position it had taken earlier on the feasibility of a federal flood control program. The data were provided, and the Corps became a part of the redevelopment effort. Model Cities also commissioned a private research group to study the connection between flooding and the social and economic blight of North Richmond.[4]

Detailed plans for the Model Cities area were then facilitated by a HUD 701 planning grant sought by Contra Costa County at the prompting of the Model Cities staff. The County Board of Supervisors also established the Joint Agency Committee for Development of the North Richmond–San Pablo Bay Area in February 1970 to administer the anticipated grant. The 701 grant was awarded in July, and the North Richmond–San Pablo Bay study was completed by the Joint Agency Committee in September 1971. It was quickly adopted in principle by the Contra Costa County Board of Supervisors. Once again storm drainage and flood protection were pinpointed as primary needs, which if met, would pave the way for the solution of a wide variety of other problems.

In 1970 Contra Costa County formally applied for a grant-in-aid from HUD to correct the drainage problem and to provide flood control for North Richmond. The grant requested funds for an expanded storm drainage system, channel improvements on Wildcat Creek, and levees to protect against tidal floods. HUD agreed to partially fund the project. It would assist with storm drainage but not flood protection, which was to be left to someone else (presumably the Corps of Engineers). After local officials promised to secure the necessary flood protection, HUD approved the grant-in-aid in 1971. In 1972, $2.3 million was appropriated by HUD for the construction of storm drainage, and in 1973 construction finally was under way.[5]

The Corps' Wildcat and San Pablo creeks study was in effect an extension of the Model Cities and Contra Costa County planning efforts. The Corps was invited to participate because it had both formal authority over federal flood control projects and the technical expertise necessary

4. INTASA, "Relationship of Proposed Flood Control Project and Model Cities Objectives for Community Development in North Richmond" (Menlo Park, Calif., June 1971).

5. SFD, transcript of public meeting, May 31, 1973, p. 19.

to implement them. The particulars regarding what kind of protection system and at what price remained unresolved, however.

Congress appropriated funds in late 1970 for the San Francisco District to reopen its survey study of Wildcat and San Pablo creeks. The scope of the study had broadened appreciably from the initial emphasis on flood protection to include the Model Cities objectives of "social well-being of the people and environmental quality in the Model Cities neighborhood and in the City of San Pablo, as well as the regional effect the project would have on the economic development of the adjacent communities."[6] The Corps' view was that localized flood control improvements were "a catalyst and an integral part of solving other urban problems."[7] In fact, the restudy would represent a new orientation for the Corps. The primary design criteria were that San Pablo Creek be disturbed as little as possible and that Wildcat Creek be enhanced with recreation facilities and improved environmental quality.[8] From the outset, then, the Corps closely coordinated its planning effort with those of the Model Cities program and other local agencies and set out to design a system that intruded on the landscape only minimally. This was *not* to be a massive cement-pouring operation.

Efforts were made throughout the planning process to confer with local and state officials as well as organized community interests. First, the range of alternatives, from reservoirs, channelization, and levees to flood-proofing and nonstructural devices, was outlined. Then the Corps scheduled a series of informal meetings and work sessions from August through October 1971 to keep all concerned parties informed of the Corps' plans and to give them an opportunity at this early stage to suggest additional avenues of investigation that might be pursued. Two of the sessions were held with the residents of North Richmond, who expressed their approval of flood control as well as skepticism that it could ever be realized. There had been talk of flood control for years, by the Corps and others, with no tangible results. Many local residents remained skeptical throughout the planning process. The East Bay Trail Council asked the SFD to present the Corps' plans for trail systems along the stream basins. The San Pablo City Council wanted to know about cost-sharing features

6. John Breaden, project engineer for the Wildcat–San Pablo Creek study, "Presentation on Wildcat and San Pablo Creeks Survey Study for Water Management Math Modeling Seminar" (May 10, 1972), p. 4.

7. Ibid., p. 1.

8. SFD, "Wildcat and San Pablo Creeks Feasibility Report," p. F-2.

at its meeting with the SFD. The industrial and commercial interests and Richmond's Waterfront Development Committee wanted to be assured that areas zoned for industrial use would remain so. The Planning and Recreation Departments of both Richmond and San Pablo wanted to be assured that the flood protection plan meshed with the East Bay Regional Parks Master Plan. And a meeting with water resource agencies in Sacramento cleared the way for the formal review by the governor that would be required before the plan could be forwarded to Congress.

In general the outline presented by the SFD to each of these groups of a multipurpose flood protection system with recreational areas and wildlife and salt marsh protections was well received. Details had yet to be worked out, but by being open-minded and making an early effort to get in touch with all interests, the Corps established rapport with the community and earned its trust, owing in no small part to the efforts of the district engineer then running the SFD. Even conservation and environmental groups supported the SFD's efforts and believed that it was doing an exemplary job. From the outset, then, an atmosphere of mutual respect was established, despite the skepticism of a few individuals. The SFD was receptive to the environmental groups' ideas for environmental and wildlife protection, and in turn the environmentalists did not adopt the immutable anti-channelization, anti-levee, anti-structural approach that their stereotype would lead one to expect. As long as the SFD remained sincere about its multipurpose objectives, the environmentalists would accept the structural features of the project as necessary evils and as the price for environmental and recreational features. This was no love feast, but the environmentalists believed they were giving the Corps a chance to prove itself.

Through the dozen or so small meetings and workshop sessions, the SFD informed local officials and leaders of its activities and attained at least tentative approval of its plans. It still had to make a similar effort to get the cooperation of the broader public. The first step in this direction was the preparation and circulation of a public information pamphlet in December 1971 that summarized the evolution of the study and presented the seven flood protection alternatives then under consideration.[9] The pamphlet was reasonably concise and informative, and was intended for a general audience.

9. U.S. Department of the Army, Corps of Engineers, San Francisco District, "Public Information Pamphlet for Flood Control and Allied Purposes on Wildcat and San Pablo Creeks, Contra Costa County, California" (December 1971).

Proposed Alternatives

The first alternative entailed a multipurpose reservoir to prevent flooding in the two stream basins during heavy rains. The cost of the project was estimated at $33 million, all of which would be absorbed by federal taxpayers.

The next two alternatives combined channel improvements through San Pablo and North Richmond and two diversions of Wildcat Creek into San Pablo Creek, one within the city of San Pablo and the second at the boundary of San Pablo and North Richmond. Both included a nature study pool, a freshwater fishing impoundment, and a saltwater swimming lagoon, and all these "improvements" terminated before the salt marshes. The cost of each alternative was $12.5 million, with 50 percent of the costs being nonfederal.

The fourth alternative included a channelized floodway, nature study area, freshwater fish impoundment, and a swimming lagoon and also terminated at the salt marshes. But the diversion of Wildcat Creek was dropped. This alternative would also cost $12.5 million, with a federal share of approximately 50 percent.

The fifth alternative called for a phased channel improvement, beginning with the construction of an earth trapezoidal channel on Wildcat Creek in North Richmond. All existing and future development of the area north of Wildcat Creek and west of the Southern Pacific Railroad tracks (running along the eastern boundary of North Richmond) would then be controlled by building codes to guard against potential damage by flooding. Flood-proofing would be required for all existing and new structures to an elevation of the flood design. New structures with working or living areas below the flood design would not be permitted. The federal government would assume 80 percent of the estimated $9 million cost of this alternative.

Last was the "no action" alternative. Neither structural nor nonstructural measures would be taken to alleviate flood damage.

Public Meetings

Notification of the reexamination study, set for January 19, 1972, was sent with the public information pamphlet.[10] The result of the meeting was almost a foregone conclusion, since the groundwork had been laid

10. Another public meeting had been held during the initial study in 1965, which was before the period of our investigation.

throughout the previous summer and fall in the smaller sessions with community leaders, who were not expected to present any opposition. Over 150 people turned out at Dover Elementary School in San Pablo on the night of January 19 to applaud the Corps' efforts, to inquire about details, and in a number of instances, to express a preference for one or another of the alternatives identified in the public information pamphlet. But most of the meeting was devoted to a general round of self-congratulations by HUD, local officials, and the environmentalists for working so well together, particularly in conjunction with the Corps, to bring about a flood protection program. This was a rare phenomenon, as the HUD spokesman noted:

Perhaps most of you are not aware of how unusual this meeting and this project are. At the local level you see two cities and a county working in concert toward a common objective. . . . Even more surprising, however, is the cooperation which has taken place at the federal level. Neither HUD nor the Corps can point with pride to their past record for intergovernmental cooperation. Each of us was accustomed to working in isolation toward objectives which were, more often than not, at cross-purposes.[11]

The environmentalists, too, saw this as a highly commendable effort. In commending the Corps on its thorough examination of the alternatives for flood control, the spokesman of the Save San Francisco Bay Association said: "The study reliably reflects the concern of Save San Francisco Bay Association that the environmental value of the Bay be preserved and enhanced as much as possible."[12]

By the time the meeting was over it was fairly evident which of the flood protection schemes was preferred. No one who voiced a preference for a specific alternative mentioned plans one or five. The director of the North Richmond Model Cities program supported plans three and four, as did the chairman of the Model Neighborhood Citizen's Board and the Board of the San Pablo Sanitary District. Alternative three received a partial endorsement from a local nursery. The Golden Gate Chapter of the National Audubon Society saw alternative two as offering the "maximum advantage for natural amenities—both educational and aesthetic."[13] But the overwhelming vote of the environmental and conservation groups

11. Julian A. Fitzhugh, program manager, HUD San Francisco Area Office. See SFD, transcript of public hearing on water resources development of San Pablo and Wildcat creeks, held at San Pablo, Calif., January 19, 1972, p. 22.

12. Ibid., p. 70.

13. Ibid., exhibit C-C.

went to alternative four, which appeared to offer something to everyone. The California Native Plant Society, the Contra Costa Shoreline Parks Committee, the San Francisco Bay Chapter of the Sierra Club, the Point Pinole Committee, HUSCICON (Humanities, Science and Conservation), the West Contra Costa Conservation League, and the Save San Francisco Bay Association all endorsed this plan.

On the basis of economic considerations and the response at this meeting, the Corps subsequently narrowed its investigation to alternatives three and four. In consultation with the Contra Costa Flood Control District, the East Bay Regional Parks, the planning departments of San Pablo and Richmond, and the Model Cities staff, it then selected four as the best overall plan. Alternative four combined some five miles of channel improvements on both creeks—providing 100-year protection—with trails, recreational facilities, and the preservation of open spaces, all of which resulted in a benefit-cost ratio for the project of 1.7 (based on a 5.5 percent interest rate).

In May 1973 the SFD held another public meeting in San Pablo to present its final choice to the public and to ensure that its report accurately reflected the views of the local residents and all other interested parties. The meeting was purely perfunctory; for all intents and purposes the issue had been decided. Less than 100 people attended. The SFD's more detailed presentation of plan four met with universal approval. A spokesman for Congressman Jerome R. Waldie, who represented Contra Costa, read into the record his endorsement of the project and commended the Corps for its fine study. Similar praise followed from HUD, the Contra Costa County supervisors, the city of Richmond, Model Cities, local residents, the Richmond Youth Advisory Commission, the East Bay Regional Park District, the Contra Costa Shoreline Park Committee, and so on.

When questions were raised about the hydraulics involved or about the economic and social effects of the project, they were very efficiently handled by Colonel James L. Lammie, the district engineer of the SFD. He either addressed them directly or promised that they would be addressed in the detailed planning that would be required in the design phase following congressional authorization of the project.

Project Implementation

Thirteen years elapsed between the authorization and the completion of the Wildcat and San Pablo creeks flood control study. And this was only the pre-authorization stage. Following the May public meeting, in August 1973, the SFD compiled a feasibility report on the plan for review by the South Pacific Division Office of the Corps. Having been approved there, it was next sent to the Corps Board of Engineers for Rivers and Harbors, where it was again approved. Meanwhile an environmental impact statement was developed for the project and local and state cooperation was secured. In 1975 the recommendation received its final in-house clearance from the Office of the Chief of Engineers. From there it went to the secretary of the army and the Office of Management and Budget. With approvals from both, it was finally forwarded to Congress, which in June 1976 authorized the project for construction at an estimated total cost of $19 million, half of which is to be borne by the Corps and half by local and state agencies.

This did not mean that construction could begin, however. Because approval had required three years, the district's first task after receiving authorization was to do a Phase I study—in effect, returning to the field to determine if the project still had support. The Phase I study went smoothly for the SFD, which then received the needed funding and formal local assurances and moved into Phase II, the final engineering design stage. The work schedule in 1978 called for actual construction to begin in 1980.

Conclusions

Once the SFD decided to cooperate with the North Richmond Model Cities staff and other local planning agencies, serving as their design and implementation arm, all went reasonably well. The area affected by the plan for flood protection was geographically circumscribed, and the resolution of flood problems did not require coordination with distant political units or other population centers. Almost everyone perceived the problem in the same light and agreed on its solution. In this context the Corps' task was relatively easy. Nevertheless, the procedures adopted by the SFD in consulting with community leaders and the broader public were critical factors in establishing the agency's credibility and assuring the acceptance of the district's recommended plan.

But a laudable program of public participation in planning, such as that for the Wildcat and San Pablo creeks flood control study, does not in itself guarantee acceptance of a Corps plan. Although a good public participation program should help resolve some outstanding points of contention and lead to compromise, the acceptance of a plan primarily depends on the degree of the intensity of conflicts in a given community. Some issues are irreconcilable, as in the case of St. Bernard Parish, whose residents adamantly opposed any bisecting of their parish for the Mississippi River–Gulf Outlet new lock and connecting channel. In such situations no amount of goodwill or outreach on the part of the Corps will bring about a happy solution.

Urban Wastewater Management

The discussion thus far illustrates how the Corps responded to widespread criticism of its operations in a number of ways. It took seriously the environmental quality issue by establishing an Environmental Advisory Board, reorganizing itself district by district, bringing in new personnel, and conducting extensive environmental surveys pertaining to its activities. The agency also greatly expanded its citizen involvement effort, investing substantial sums of money, time, and energy in order to reach out to the public.

In yet another manner, however, the Corps responded to the charge that it was solely a pork-barrel, construction-oriented agency. Adopting a totally new kind of program untainted by such criticisms, the Corps set out to prove its superior engineering-planning capability and its real concern for the public interest by enthusiastically gearing up to solve urban wastewater problems.

By the late 1960s wastewater management had become a problem of staggering proportions facing virtually every major American community. Industrial wastes, municipal sewage, and storm-water runoff all were contributing to the rapidly growing pollution of the nation's waterways. Urbanization and industrialization were obviously major causes of the waterway pollution. Two hundred years of Corps construction activities had not helped either, but recognizing a water problem in desperate need of a solution, the agency became a proponent of cleaning up the nation's rivers.

The Beginnings of the Program

In 1969 the General Accounting Office released a report on several major rivers in the United States.[14] Even though $5.4 billion had been

14. See U.S. General Accounting Office, Office of the Comptroller General, *Examination into the Effectiveness of the Construction Grant Program for Abating, Controlling, and Preventing Water Pollution* (GAO, November 3, 1969).

spent at various levels of government for the construction of waste treatment plants during the previous 12 years, America's rivers had deteriorated
to possibly the lowest point ever. This resulted in part because the billions
of dollars had been spent for the construction of inadequate primary and
secondary treatment facilities. The former are designed to screen out and
settle large solid chunks; the latter, through biological processes, remove
80–90 percent of the oxygen-demanding organic waste. These treatments,
however, leave virtually untouched other serious pollutants such as nitro-
gen, phosphorus, and toxic trace elements (mercury, arsenic, cadmium,
lead, chromium, cobalt, and zinc).[15] Consequently the conventional response to water pollution—building more and bigger primary and secondary treatment plants—had been criticized by both a new breed of wastewater management engineer and by environmentalists. Primary and secondary treatment plants were charged with being inefficient in operation
and, most damning, ineffective in achieving an acceptable degree of water
quality. The critics' position was that wastewater must be viewed as part
of a total water cycle and that what are considered pollutants in lakes and
free-flowing streams should be treated as resources out of place. Pollutants
therefore must be rechanneled and recycled back into their natural productive role.

The Federal Water Quality Administration (FWQA) in the Department of the Interior had been made responsible for the federal wastewater management program. At the end of 1970 this responsibility was
transferred to the Environmental Protection Agency (EPA). Apparently,
however, either before or after this move neither the FWQA nor the EPA
were successful at perceiving the wastewater problem in a systems, or total
water cycle, manner. Even with the strongly worded mandates contained
in the Federal Water Pollution Control Act Amendments of 1972, which
charged the EPA with overseeing all basin wastewater management plans,
by the mid-1970s the agency had accomplished less than expected.

Into this void and confusion came the Corps, fully aware of the possibility of introducing an innovative wastewater recycling technology, demonstrating a capability for comprehensive urban planning, and thus coun-
teracting its anti-environment, anti-people image. In its classic "do something" manner, the Corps marshaled its resources and immediately
launched a new program in comprehensive wastewater management.[16]

15. See P. G. Hunt, "Overland Flow," *Water Spectrum*, vol. 5, no. 4 (1973), pp.
16–21.
16. For an overview of the problem and of the projected role for the Corps, see

New engineering talent was hastily recruited and consultants were used liberally. Funds were appropriated and new programs begun. One commentator wrote that no one could

accuse these planners of thinking small or of trifling with serious problems. Alternative systems [of wastewater management] seriously considered would cost up to $12 billion for a single metropolitan area, and the financial implications on a national basis are staggering. However, these enormous costs are fairly realistic for what they are expected to achieve, which is the substantial elimination of pollution in the rivers of these heavily developed areas, until the year 2020.[17]

A major part of the Corps' new program was a bold and imaginative large-scale adaptation of land-treatment technology that requires spraying partially treated wastewater over plots of agricultural land and allowing the water to filter through the soil. In this process, nutrients and other water pollutants (viruses and bacteria) are absorbed by the plants and soil, and the purified water becomes part of the groundwater reservoir. Under appropriate soil and plant life conditions, and with proper application of the waste, the system can even increase crop production. Where the water supply is primarily derived from groundwater reservoirs, falling water tables may be slowed or even halted. The net result—assuming all the necessary conditions are met—is an ecologically sound system of wastewater recycling that produces both an increase in reusable water and the elimination of the need for chemical fertilization of the treated croplands. It had been endorsed by Barry Commoner. In one stroke the agency could thus become the savior of America's pollution-clogged rivers, lakes, and cities as well as the sweetheart of the environmental movement.

The program's chief architect was John R. Sheaffer, who had been the leading figure behind the comprehensive land-treatment program adopted by Muskegon County, Michigan, in the late 1960s.[18] The program was a

---

David J. Allee and Burnham H. Dodge, *The Role of the U.S. Army Corps of Engineers in Water Quality Management,* U.S. Department of the Army, Corps of Engineers, Institute for Water Resources, Report 71-1 (IWR, October 1970).

17. William Whipple, Jr., "Corps of Engineers Plans Regional Water Quality Programs," *Civil Engineering,* vol. 42 (March 1972), p. 37.

18. Dr. Sheaffer was a research associate at the University of Chicago Center for Urban Studies, which was approached in the summer of 1968 by the Muskegon County Planning Commission for assistance in designing an integrated water resource program. A contract was let to Sheaffer and associates by the commission to prepare a water resource policy for the county. The commission was pleased with the results and this led in 1969 to Scheaffer's far-reaching proposal for "a land disposal/spray

signal break with past water pollution practices and thrust both Sheaffer and Muskegon County into the national limelight. An EPA study explained the program as follows:

Whereas previous wastewater management efforts in Muskegon County applied minimal treatment to sewage before discharging wastewater into natural water bodies, the Sheaffer program dictated the principle that effluents should not be released to the natural water bodies at all. Instead, secondary-treated wastewater should be placed upon the land, using the natural properties of the soil to assimilate waste material from the secondary-treated effluent—after which this treated effluent would be discharged into water courses.[19]

The process was expected to remove 98–99 percent of the biochemical oxygen demand, 98 percent of the total phosphates, and 85 percent of the nitrates from the wastewater.[20] Thus as most other communities across the nation bogged down in endless debates over technology, funding, and the uncertain implications of anticipated federal legislation for their own water pollution control program, Muskegon moved ahead decisively.

Land treatment, of course, is nothing new. But the Muskegon project was at the time the largest ever proposed in the United States.[21] To service the 157,000 county residents, the system would ultimately require 10,000 acres of land, of which 6,000 would be utilized for direct spray irrigation. More than 200 families would have to be relocated. Moreover, the county would eventually find itself in the business of growing corn, potatoes, alfalfa, and other crops on its treated sites (a somewhat awkward position for government in a private enterprise economy). Dr. Sheaffer played a key role in winning approval for the project from the county, state, and federal authorities, and through an extensive publicity campaign, from the people of Muskegon. He was instrumental in negotiating the initial federal Research Development and Demonstration Grant for the project with the Federal Water Quality Administration, and for clearing the way for local funding.[22] In the short span of two years he became

irrigation system for wastewater treatment as a county-wide answer for the 1973 [Lake Michigan Enforcement Conference] deadline for 80 percent phosphorus removal and secondary treatment." (Richard E. Foglesong and Judson W. Starr, *Land Disposal of Wastewater: A Land Use Case Study*, U.S. Environmental Protection Agency, Region V [EPA, November 1972], pp. 10–11.)

19. Ibid., p. 11.
20. Bauer Engineering, Inc., "Muskegon County Wastewater Management System #1: Basis of Design" (March 1971).
21. The largest such system outside the United States is in Melbourne, Australia, which uses a land disposal–spray irrigation system to serve a population of 2.5 million.
22. See Foglesong and Starr, *Land Disposal of Wastewater*, pp. 12–19.

the leading national spokesman for both the land treatment concept and the Muskegon project.

The project had won acclaim in both professional and political circles and had received certification and multiple sources of government funding; thus it is understandable why the Corps saw the land treatment technology as innovative, environmentally sound, and politically marketable. The idea, as well as its most noted architect, were immediately adopted by the Corps. In 1970 Sheaffer was appointed to the post of scientific adviser to Secretary of the Army Robert F. Froehlke. He was to be the driving force behind the Corps' new mission of providing planning and engineering and construction expertise for water pollution control projects throughout the nation's urban areas. He was to sell land treatment technology, not only to the public, but to the Corps' field staff.

Other comprehensive wastewater management plans were also examined, but at least during the early stages of the new program, land treatment remained foremost for Sheaffer and for the Corps. This drew criticism from the Corps' rival, EPA, and its sympathizers in the Office of Management and Budget, as indicated by the unofficial conclusion in a review of the Corps' wastewater management studies in March 1972 that "the Corps' studies placed too much emphasis upon land disposal alternatives as compared with the alternative for conventional tertiary treatment, which [was] given a 'wink and a promise.' "[23] But the Corps was not easily ruffled by the EPA, especially since during the initial stage (1971–72) of its wastewater management studies it had achieved such a favorable in-house review, as well as the congratulations of Congress and environmentalists.

Before turning to an examination of one of these studies, a word is in order on the eventual development of the Corps' urban area wastewater management program, which was officially launched in early 1971 with much fanfare. It began with five pilot wastewater management studies that were to "set forth, for local, State and Federal consideration, a range of choices for managing the wastewater in each area that could improve water quality and be compatible with programs for total water management and total resource management use."[24]

The following areas were selected for the pilot studies: the Merrimack Basin (Massachusetts and New Hampshire), San Francisco, Detroit–

23. Ibid., p. 60.
24. U.S. Department of the Army, "Interim Report of the Secretary of the Army on the Pilot Wastewater Management Program" (August 1971), p. 2.

Southeastern Michigan, Cleveland-Akron, and Chicago–Northwest Indiana. After the Office of Management and Budget approved the studies in late 1970, the initial pilot studies were authorized in March 1971 by Congress, which allowed the redirection of funds appropriated for other studies.

The die was cast. Within a year after the pilot studies were under way, the Corps returned to Congress with the proposition that wastewater treatment, based on the experiences of the pilot program, could not be dealt with properly apart from other aspects of urban water resource needs.[25] Thus the agency unveiled a plan for an entire series of comprehensive urban water resource studies. In support of what was to become the Corps' Urban Studies Program, the agency argued in early 1972 that in its pilot wastewater management studies

the primary mission of the Corps of Engineers is to formulate an alternative system for effectively dealing with the wastewater problem—yet, during the course of planning, opportunities have suggested themselves for solutions to problems of solid waste disposal, the proper location of power generation facilities so as to minimize negative environmental effects, and maintenance of open space between urban populations.[26]

The agency, however, was careful to disclaim any responsibility at that time for choosing the *appropriate* solution to the problems of solid waste disposal, powerplant siting, and recreational open space. It only hoped to identify alternative solutions that could be considered by the appropriate local, state, and federal officials.

Congress was very responsive to the Corps' request for support for its new multipurpose, urban-centered program, and within a period of two years urban studies became a major part of the agency's planning activities. For fiscal year 1973, funds were provided at the agency's request for nine comprehensive urban studies. Throughout the year seven more were added through resolutions by the House and Senate Appropriations committees or by administrative action. Finally, in the budget for fiscal year 1974 the program was expanded to 29 comprehensive urban studies across

25. This section is adapted from Daniel A. Mazmanian and Mordecai Lee, "Tradition Be Damned! The Army Corps of Engineers is Changing," *Public Administration Review*, vol. 35 (March-April 1975), pp. 166–72.

26. "The Urban Studies Program of the Army Corps of Engineers," Report Prepared by the Department of the Army in Support of the FY 1973 Budget (February 1972), p. 5.

the nation. In the course of only two or three years the Urban Studies Program had grown to a point where it accounted for one-third of the general investigation funds appropriated to the Corps' Planning Division. Open planning was one of the key elements in the pilot wastewater management studies and in their successors, the comprehensive urban studies.

Project Study IV: Wastewater Management in the Cleveland-Akron and Three Rivers Watershed Areas

The Three Rivers Watershed area consists of the drainage basins of the Chagrin, Cuyahoga, and Rocky rivers of northern Ohio, all of which empty into Lake Erie (see figure 5-2). The combined basins cover 1,500 square miles, of which approximately 23 percent is urbanized, and support a population of 2.5 million. The major urban centers are the industrial city of Cleveland, which is located along the shore of Lake Erie (all three rivers pass through the metropolitan area), and Akron, located approximately 40 miles south of Cleveland along the Cuyahoga River.

One of the most infamous cases of water pollution in the nation is that of the Cuyahoga River, popularly known as "the river that burns." This unfortunate river serves as a receptacle for not only municipal sewage and agricultural runoff but also the industrial waste from the rubber industry of Akron and the metal and chemical industries of Cleveland. According to the Corps study, which was completed in 1973, pollution in the lower 11 miles of the river was so great that the EPA had classed the Cuyahoga as "the third dirtiest river in the United States."[27]

Improving the quality of the Cuyahoga had been attempted for a number of years, not only as an end in itself, but as a major step in reversing the decay of Lake Erie. The State of Ohio recognized the need for a comprehensive approach to its problems of water pollution in the late 1950s and provided enabling legislation in the 1960s. By the early 1970s it began the planning of a program of wastewater management for the Cuyahoga and the adjoining Chagrin and Rocky River basins, which are part of the Northeast Ohio Water Development Plan. The federal government meanwhile began its own investigation. Under section 108 of the

27. U.S. Department of the Army, Corps of Engineers, Buffalo District "Cleveland-Akron Metropolitan and Three Rivers Watershed Areas Wastewater Management Study: Summary Report" (August 1973), p. 61.

Figure 5-2. *The Three Rivers Watershed Area in Ohio*

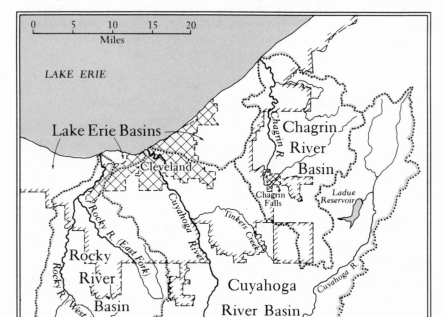

Rivers and Harbors Act of 1970 (84 Stat. 1820) the Corps of Engineers
was authorized to study measures to improve and restore the environmental quality of the Cuyahoga River Basin.

The waters of the Chagrin and Rocky rivers are of far better quality
than those of the Cuyahoga, though both are polluted with either poorly
treated or untreated domestic wastes that contain some mildly toxic
materials and have coliform bacteria counts that exceed state stream

quality standards. Stretches along the rivers below the existing waste-water treatment facilities also contain sludge deposits and have relatively low levels of dissolved oxygen.

The problem of water pollution in the three rivers area presented a major challenge to the Corps of Engineers. The need for a comprehensive, coordinated, and long-range solution was obvious; there was appreciable local, state, and national interest in the condition of the three rivers and in the closely related problem of Lake Erie. Preliminary examinations by the State of Ohio and by the Corps had already laid the groundwork for analysis, and therefore it was not surprising that the Corps chose the Three Rivers Watershed area for one of its five pilot wastewater management studies. The study alone was to cost $2 million, require two years for completion, and result in proposals to meet federal requirements at an estimated $17 billion to $20 billion in construction and operating costs over a 50-year period.

Feasibility Study

The study funds redirected by Congress for the pilot program in March 1971 were only for feasibility studies, that is, for general overview studies that would become the basis for funding a more comprehensive survey study. Districts undertake feasibility studies to provide a rough approximation for the Office of the Chief of Engineers and Congress of the magnitude of the problem, to examine the broad strategies available for solving the problem, to focus on those strategies that appear most appropriate for the study area, and finally, to provide survey study cost estimates. Feasibility studies are the basis on which an in-house decision is made to proceed with a request to Congress for funds for a full-scale survey study. They are basically Corps documents; the general public is not necessarily consulted at this stage.[28]

The Corps office in charge of the Cleveland-Akron and Three Rivers Watershed areas study, the Buffalo District, made no attempt during the feasibility study to keep its intentions from the public. Although the district held no public meetings, it published and mailed a brochure, *Wastewater Study*, to approximately 1,000 federal, state, and local officials and to the media and interested groups and citizens who were on the district's

28. All five of the pilot program's feasibility studies were completed in a little over four months. With them in hand, the chief of engineers returned to Congress and won authority for a more comprehensive study.

general mailing list. (This mailing list grew to include over 2,000 persons by the end of the study.) The idea of a comprehensive wastewater management program was well received by a cross section of interests in the three rivers area. But as word of the district's plan to include a land treatment alternative in its feasibility study spread, strong opposition emerged from those in the rural regions of North Central Ohio. This area is outside of the Three Rivers Watershed area, but it happened to be where the Buffalo District believed a single, massive land treatment–spray irrigation site could best be located.

Of all the technical, economic, and social issues that were to surface throughout the two years of the study, that of the rural residents' antagonism toward the selection of a land-treatment site remained the overriding point of contention. Ultimately their unyielding opposition became the Corps' nemesis, preventing it from making the three rivers area an example of its ability to achieve a new and environmentally sound water pollution control technology. The opposition also restrained the Corps' leap into urban wastewater management elsewhere in the nation.

Public Participation

Public participation and public information activities were a central feature of the pilot wastewater management program. From the outset the Corps realized that it would have to overcome skepticism concerning its motives and its experience. Urban studies constituted a new enterprise for the Corps, which did not have much of a reputation as an "engineering consultant" to local and state governments, let alone to the EPA, to whom it would now often have to defer.

An equally difficult task was to persuade professional wastewater management engineers—at least those outside the environmental community —and the general public of the efficacy of land treatment and wastewater recycling. Particularly in rural communities, where the urban waste was to be spray-treated, the indigenous population would have to be clearly shown the benefits of such a program. Rural residents who farmed the land saw the sludge to be spread over it, not so much as a potent source of inexpensive fertilizer, but only as sewage that city dwellers were trying to dump on them. One of the residents of north central Ohio made a typical comment: "We have enough garbage disposal problems of our own without having to also deal with Cleveland's." Another noted: "If the fertilizer is good for crops, set up a plant so farmers and such can use it as they have need."[29] In short, the Corps' success in wastewater management would depend on both the openness of its planning process and its substantive proposals. As the pilot study progressed, it became evident that the planning process was time-consuming, laborious, and costly, but when all was said and done, it was the easier of the two tasks.

The Buffalo District initiated its study with a concerted effort to touch base with as many groups and individuals as possible. First, agency personnel were made available to describe and discuss the survey study. They also served to channel public opinion back to the district office. A special effort was made to reach professional groups, the university community, chambers of commerce, local officials, and environmental organizations. Second, close coordination and cooperation were maintained with the State of Ohio, primarily through its Department of Natural Resources and its Environmental Protection Agency. Third, the district published and disseminated a range of materials designed for both the casual and the more sophisticated reader.

Finally, in the 18 months from January 1972 through June 1973 the Buffalo District conducted over 60 public meetings, seminars, and workshops throughout the three rivers area and the two potential sludge deposit sites in the north central farming counties of Ohio and the strip-mined counties in eastern Ohio. These meetings, along with the array of written materials and media interviews with Corps personnel, generated some 200 articles in over 45 Ohio newspapers.[30] In all, thousands of people had an opportunity to read about the study or to question the Corps directly about it and to express their reservations and preferences throughout the planning process. Most observers inside and outside the Corps agree that the public participation efforts of the Buffalo District were the most extensive and most successful of those of all the pilot wastewater management studies.

The Use of Published Materials

Besides meeting with the public, the district distributed numerous published progress reports on its study, usually before the public meetings.

29. These and similar comments were scrawled across the items on open planning in the questionnaire we sent to participants in the wastewater management study in late 1973 or were enclosed in separate letters.

30. Buffalo District, "Cleveland-Akron Wastewater Management Study," app. 8, p. 6.

In addition to the first brochure circulated during the feasibility stage of the study, a second brochure, *The Cuyahoga: We've Only Just Begun,* was developed in conjunction with the State of Ohio and distributed before the two public meetings held in January 1972 to consider the comprehensive survey study. It reviewed the findings of the feasibility study and laid out the methods, goals, and timetable of the survey study. A 25-page booklet distributed before the formulation-stage meetings of December 1972 summarized the three technologies of wastewater management under consideration and the relative advantages of each. It also included a brief description of the 12 alternatives being examined, along with some simple illustrations of each. Comparison of the alternatives was facilitated by a chart that listed the water quality objectives of each plan, as well as the number of advanced waste treatment facilities, the acres of land needed for land treatment, the facilities for handling sludge, the storm-water treatment methods, and the average annual costs. The vast majority of the participants thus had an opportunity to examine in advance of the public meetings the Corps' proposals and tentative conclusions. They might disagree with what they read (as many did), but none could claim to have been kept in the dark about the alternatives under consideration.

The pre–public meeting publications were useful as general status reports on the survey study, but they did not provide a useful forum for the Corps to enter the debate among professionals over wastewater management technologies, nor did they allow for news notes or for handling responses to the unending stream of inquiries about the study. To handle these needs the Buffalo District created the "Purewater Press," a newsletter sent to all affected federal, state, and local agencies and to the 2,000 people whose names eventually found their way onto the study mailing list. The first issue in April 1972, for example, was devoted primarily to introducing the reader to the land-treatment method of wastewater management.

Public Meetings and Their Results

The two large public meetings, one in Akron and one in Cleveland, called in January 1972 at the outset of the survey study satisfied the Corps' formal requirement for an "initial" public meeting. The district presented slides and the representatives of various citizen groups made statements and asked questions. By December 1972 a variety of alternatives for dealing with the problems of wastewater management had been probed. Tentative site selections had been made for treatment plants and, in the case of land treatment, for spray irrigation. The Corps satisfied its requirement for formulation-stage meetings by presenting the dozen plans under consideration at public meetings in Akron, Cleveland, and Chagrin Falls. The meetings were publicized in advance by radio announcements and a special edition of the "Purewater Press" and permitted the Buffalo District to explain the evolution of its study, to present estimated costs and land requirements of various alternatives, and to outline the pros and cons of the three technologies of wastewater treatment under consideration: biological, physical-chemical, and land treatment. At the culmination of the survey study in June 1973, a series of "final-stage" public meetings were held; two inside the three rivers area, one in the agricultural area of north central Ohio, and one in the strip-mined area of eastern Ohio.

All the while, less formal and more narrowly focused seminars and workshops were held for a wide range of interested groups: the Chamber of Commerce of Mansfield, of Akron, and of Bucyrus; the Sierra Club; the Ohio Farm Bureau; the Goodyear Tire and Rubber Company; the Cleveland University Consortium; the Ohio Environmental Council; and various chapters of the League of Women Voters. These sessions were devoted to answering questions related to each group's special interests and to communicating their needs and viewpoints to the Corps. In a number of instances, the sessions also served as an opportunity to correct misunderstandings about the nature of the study and about land treatment technology. To say the least, these speaking engagements became a full-time activity and were divided among 10 persons. The district office, however, claimed that this time was well spent, since the meetings were the major mechanism for establishing the Corps' credibility and for informing and educating the interested public. The small workshops were considered especially worthwhile. They were pronounced the "most successful," and thus were rated "the top public involvement method in the study effort."[31]

After weighing both public input and technical analyses, by March 1973 the Buffalo District had pared down the alternatives to three basic plans. These were compiled in a 200-page draft report and made available on a limited basis, going mainly to state and local officials, significant

31. Ibid.

interest groups, and some particularly active citizens. A short summary of the draft report was distributed more widely, and the final public meetings held in June 1973 focused on the three alternatives.

The Corps had three explicit objectives in mind in undertaking the three rivers wastewater management study: (1) to design a system that could accommodate the projected wastewater load for the year 1990, with contingencies for meeting that of 2020; (2) to design a system that could handle pollution from municipal, industrial, and storm-water runoff (but not rural runoff); and (3) to attain the most likely future water quality standards of the State of Ohio, as well as to meet by 1985 the zero-discharge standard required by the Federal Water Pollution Control Act Amendments of 1972.[32]

The implicit objectives of the Corps, it appears in retrospect, were to demonstrate the technical feasibility of a large-scale land treatment system and the superiority of this system over other alternatives and to enlarge or rebuild public confidence—especially that of the environmentalists—in the Corps' ability to act on behalf of the public interest. It was only partially successful in attaining these objectives, however.

The Corps' leanings toward the large land treatment systems was downplayed somewhat during the formulation stage of the survey study, when a full range of 12 alternatives were being discussed. But the agency's preference emerged again in the final survey report and in the final public meeting. Plan A-I of the final report outlined the plant requirements of the biological and physical-chemical treatments specified, not by the Corps, but by the state in its Northeast Ohio Water Development Plan for water quality.[33] The plan called for 26 municipal plants; 23 would be biological, and the rest would utilize physical-chemical treatment. Eight of the 26 plants were already in operation, and construction of the others had been

32. Although the five pilot studies were under way before the passage of the amendments, it was fairly evident that the latter would specify a zero-discharge criterion, and therefore this standard was adopted for the pilot studies. The Buffalo District also assumed that the State of Ohio would adopt the water quality standards accepted by the Ohio Pollution Control Board for the Mahoning River Basin. These were therefore used as the state-level standards for the three rivers study. See ibid., "Summary Report," pp. 21–22. The state's actual standards are contained in Ohio Environmental Protection Agency, "Water Quality Standards," EP-1 (July 27, 1973), as modified by the U.S. EPA. See "Navigable Waters of State of Ohio: Proposed Water Quality Standards," Federal Register, vol. 39 (May 3, 1974), pp. 15505–07.

33. The description of the three plans is drawn from Buffalo District, "Wastewater Management Study: Summary Report," chap. 7.

planned to meet the State of Ohio's water quality standards and the criteria for 1977 and 1983 of the Federal Water Pollution Control Act Amendments. Plan A-II, a slight modification of Plan A-I, could meet the zero-discharge standard required by 1985.

At the other extreme, the Corps unveiled a comprehensive land treatment system (Plan C). Although the Corps disclaimed being committed to the land treatment alternative, this is where it put its money. With this alternative, the Corps stood to gain the most from the environmentalists and to win the greatest recognition as an innovative planner. These motives, of course, were behind the pilot program in 1970, and they changed little, if any, by the time the Cleveland-Akron and Three Rivers Watershed areas study was completed. To emphasize the chief of engineer's continuing interest in seeing that the districts did not veer from this path, Dr. Sheaffer played an active role in guiding district planners and even met with groups in the community in the early stages of the study. It was not unheard of for interested parties to get in touch with Sheaffer directly or with the Wastewater Task Force in the chief's office when they had questions about the three rivers study.

The Corps' contention that the comprehensive land treatment plan was the most economical and most technologically advanced alternative met with little challenge at the meeting. Its guiding principle of providing the maximum reuse of treated wastewater was applauded. The problem was how the principle could best be put into operation. Plan C called for a transmission tunnel to convey wastewater and storm-water runoff from the Cleveland metropolitan area 100 miles southwest to a 183-square-mile tract of agricultural land in north central Ohio. Other small sites within the three rivers area would also be used for land treatment. When fully implemented, the land treatment system would treat 81 percent of the municipal and industrial waste and 74 percent of the urban storm-water runoff for Cleveland, Akron, and the Three Rivers Watershed area. Sixty-nine percent of the municipal and industrial waste and 55 percent of the storm-water runoff would be dispersed over the single site in north central Ohio. Of the remaining storm water, half (23 percent of the total) would be treated by an advanced biological treatment plant and the rest would be handled at municipal land treatment facilities or undergo separate storm-water land treatment.

The implications of Plan C, especially for residents of the 183-square-mile treatment site, were enormous. Their property rights, methods of farming, physical landscape, indeed their entire life-style, would be affected by the Corps' land treatment operation. Yet this was the most economical and ecologically sound technology for wastewater management for the three rivers area.

The less impressive, less efficient, and more costly but also more politically acceptable plan in the final report was Plan B. It combined advanced biological, physical-chemical, and land treatment technologies, and its most important attribute was that all aspects of the plan were within the three rivers area. The plan included nine of the large municipal plants in Plan A-I, and also provided for 22 municipal aerated lagoon–land treatment systems, 39 advanced storm-water runoff treatment plants, and 46 separate storm-water land treatment sites to handle the remaining wastewater.

Ecologically speaking, Plan B is only half a program, and from the Corps' standpoint, it may be even less. That a so-called combined plan was necessary clearly illustrates the difficulty of attempting the Muskegon experiment elsewhere in the United States. There is simply too much resistance by rural interests to a land treatment approach, no matter how environmentally sound it is. Thus the direct benefits to the Corps in terms of winning new construction projects remain uncertain.

Following the final meetings of June 1973, the Buffalo District prepared a summary report of the study and compiled an exhaustive report on the history of the study, the recommended plans, consultant reports, and public participation in nine appendixes that were released in August 1973.[34]

Unlike the usual Corps survey study, this one did not conclude with a specific recommendation for action. Instead, it outlined the three major alternative solutions, plans A-I and II, B, and C, and their respective technological, economic, and social-political costs and benefits for use by the State of Ohio in deciding how best to meet the federal government's water quality standards as well as its own.

Resistance to New Technology

The response to the three alternatives outlined in the report was consistent with public reaction throughout the study. Such advocates of cleaning up the three rivers and Lake Erie as the Three Rivers Group of

34. Appendixes 1–9, ibid., run thousands of pages and are the product of both consultant and district office activities.

Northeast Ohio, the Lake Erie Committee, and the State of Ohio's Department of Natural Resources all favored the comprehensive land treatment approach in theory. Their view was expressed in June 1973 by Mrs.
Henrik Kylin of the League of Women Voters' Lake Erie Basin Committee, who said that the league had been "greatly impressed" by "the
modern concepts of land treatment with wastewater of secondary purity
. . . because they are methods of recycling nutrients and conserving costly
chemicals while reaching highest levels of wastewater quality." Yet Mrs.
Kylin, along with all the other enthusiasts of land treatment realized that
the question at hand was not one of the best available technology but of
political feasibility. What course would lead most readily to cleaning up
the rivers and the lake? Thus, she concluded, "After considering the
costs, the probability of acceptance by the public, and the institutional
problems presented by the many counties and municipalities involved, we
favor Plan B."[35]

The astute judgment of the League of Women Voters was attested to
the next day at the public meeting in Willard, located in the heart of the
land treatment site proposed in Plan C. Over 300 citizens attended from
throughout the neighboring counties, four times more than at any of the
other three final public meetings. They were not outwardly hostile or
antagonistic toward the Corps, but they were firm: their land would not
be used to dispose of Cleveland's sewage. Colonel Robert Moore, district
engineer for Buffalo District, went to Willard fully anticipating this
reaction. Thus in asking those in attendance to register, he gave this reason: "to dictate for posterity in the records how many people were at these
public meetings, and obviously the number of people at a public meeting
in an area when one of the plans affects you and you are opposed to it.
That headcount becomes critical to your opposition."[36]

The three-hour meeting entailed an unending stream of opposition to
Plan C. One local farmer and trustee of Vernon Township said he was
"100 percent against this thing," adding, "I don't think it will work, and
let Cleveland have it. We have plenty of our own problems right here at
home." The spokesman for the Mansfield Area Chamber of Commerce

35. Buffalo District, "Wastewater Management Study," app. 8, attachment 12,
transcript of final public meeting on Cleveland-Akron Wastewater Management
Study, held in Newbury, Ohio, June 5, 1973, exhibit 2.
36. Buffalo District, transcript of final public meeting held in Willard, Ohio,
June 6, 1973, p. 26.

reiterated the stand of his colleagues. "Tonight I am here to repeat our previous position in which we are fully committed and have taken a firm position against the treatment of wastewater transported from the Cleveland-Akron area to the North Central Ohio area. . . . Plan C is not in the best interest of this area." The area's congressmen, Delbert L. Latta, Tennyson Guyer, and John M. Ashbrook, though not present, made it perfectly clear in communications to Colonel Moore that they opposed "any plan that would transport Cleveland effluent to the North Central Ohio area."[37]

Even the State Department of Natural Resources and the EPA, both of which had worked with the Corps throughout the planning process and supposedly had championed ecologically sound programs, backed off from Plan C, assuring those at the meeting that they would not consider "alternative C . . . as one of the viable alternatives, unless the public in the Three Rivers Watershed area and the North Central Area requests the State to consider it among the alternatives." The state, however, wished to "give support to proposals utilizing sludges for strip-mined land reclamation" and proposed that "a first year trial of sludge disposal in Harrison County be pursued, based upon local acceptance."[38] This proposal was well received when it was repeated at the public meeting held two days later in the strip-mined area of eastern Ohio.

Aftermath

In opposing land treatment, the rural residents of the north central counties raised numerous questions about how the sludge would be transported; the possibility that the aerated lagoons that would be used to treat raw sewage might generate odors; the possible contamination of the soil by heavy metals or nutrient buildup; the application rates of the sludge; the kind of crops that are best suited for treated soil; potential flooding in local rivers due to the introduction of water supply from the three rivers basin; the potential for contamination of groundwater by the effluent flows; and who would own the properties involved. These were all important concerns of the local residents, and the Corps answered each to the satisfaction of most people. But opposition to the site selection remained.

Rightly or wrongly, the Corps concluded that the crux of the issue was

37. Statements in this paragraph are from ibid., pp. 51, 59.
38. Ibid., p. 39.

not one of economics or of technology, or even of politics, but rather one of rural antipathy toward urban society. The overriding concern of the rural residents who attended the meeting was, "Why should we suffer for the Cleveland-Akron area?"[39] The Corps had no quick reply. It perceived land treatment as a program offering mutual benefits, not one of burdening rural residents with urban waste. Ultimately the Corps' response was to call for the "education of all concerned people" in the basin as well as in north central Ohio so that they would understand the advantages of land treatment technology and accept it.[40] On this note the Corps terminated its study, leaving further investigations and decisions to its former allies, the State of Ohio and the EPA, both of whom had deserted the Corps' sinking ship during the protracted fray. It must be noted, however, that despite the demise of the land treatment alternative in this and other cases, the overall program—the Corps' Urban Studies Program —is faring very well.

39. The Corps became all the more convinced that this was the true motive behind the opposition when the north central counties began considering a land treatment program for their own wastewater toward the end of the survey study.

40. Buffalo District, "Cleveland-Akron Wastewater Management Study," app. 8, p. 31.

CHAPTER SIX

The Total Immersion Approach
to Open Planning

THE SINGLE CORPS district to require an elaborate program of broad participation in all its planning studies is the Seattle District, which has achieved the active involvement of a variety of interest groups through a continual exchange of views and information in workshops, public meetings, and the preparation of study brochures. Such "fishbowl" planning, as it is called, combines procedures used in other districts—for example, the close coordination with other agencies and local governments that characterized the San Francisco District's Wildcat and San Pablo Creeks study; the Kansas City District's use of work groups in the L-15 study; and the exhaustive public consultation and publications achieved by the Buffalo District during its Cleveland-Akron and Three Rivers Watershed study. Why the fishbowl program was adopted and how well it has fared is illustrated in the controversy surrounding the Corps' proposed dam and reservoir for the Middle Fork of the Snoqualmie River in northwestern Washington.

Project Study V: Flood Control on the Middle Fork of the Snoqualmie River

In general, the controversy, which began in the late 1960s, pits recreationists, conservationists, and the governor of Washington against local developers, many property owners within the Snoqualmie River basin, and the Corps of Engineers. At the same time, the seemingly mutual objective of environmentalists and farmers is to preserve the greenbelt nature of the basin, but their strategies for achieving this objective have turned out to be diametrically opposed. The environmentalists are against

132

the construction of a dam and reservoir on the Middle Fork because it would destroy the last remaining free-flowing and unspoiled wild river in the region. They also believe that the mitigation of flooding in the basin will without doubt lead to the commercialization and urbanization of the last greenbelt and recreational area on the fringe of the Seattle metropolitan area. Proponents of the project counter that property owners and farmers in the basin will be able to fend off the encroachment of the expanding metropolitan community and maintain the open space character of the land *only* if the farmland is provided with relief from floods and protected from speculative buying through zoning for agricultural use. Otherwise, rising property values and in turn rising property taxes will compel residents of the basin to sell their holdings to subdividers and speculators.

Finally, the controversy brings to the fore one of the most tenacious problems associated with virtually every Corps flood management study. Despite extensive efforts to include new publics in the agency's planning process, to encourage the presentation of new information, and to respond to changing social values, the Army engineers seem unable to overcome their traditional, almost instinctive, affinity for structural alternatives. Thus they did not approach the issue of flooding on the Middle Fork of the Snoqualmie River as impartial technicians weighing the costs and benefits of both structural and nonstructural alternatives. Rather, their intention was to build dams and reservoirs. Public pressure alone forced the Corps to change its proposal for a dam and reservoir on the Middle Fork *and* a dam and powerhouse on the North Fork to "only" a proposal for a dam on the Middle Fork (planning the North Fork dam was deferred for further study), to an even more compromised plan today. Moreover, it was left to the initiative of aroused citizens to propose most of the nonstructural alternatives to a dam or dams.

Characteristics of the Snoqualmie River Basin

Originating at a 6,000-foot elevation on the western slope of the Cascade Mountains, the Snoqualmie River drains nearly 700 square miles of the southeastern, or upper part, of the Snohomish River basin in northwestern Washington.[1] The basin is mountainous along the eastern bound-

1. The description of the basin is from U.S. Department of the Army, Corps of Engineers, Seattle District, *Snoqualmie River, Washington: Report on Flood Control and Other Improvements* (October 1969), vol. 1, chap. 2.

Figure 6-1. *The Snoqualmie and Snohomish River Basins in Washington*

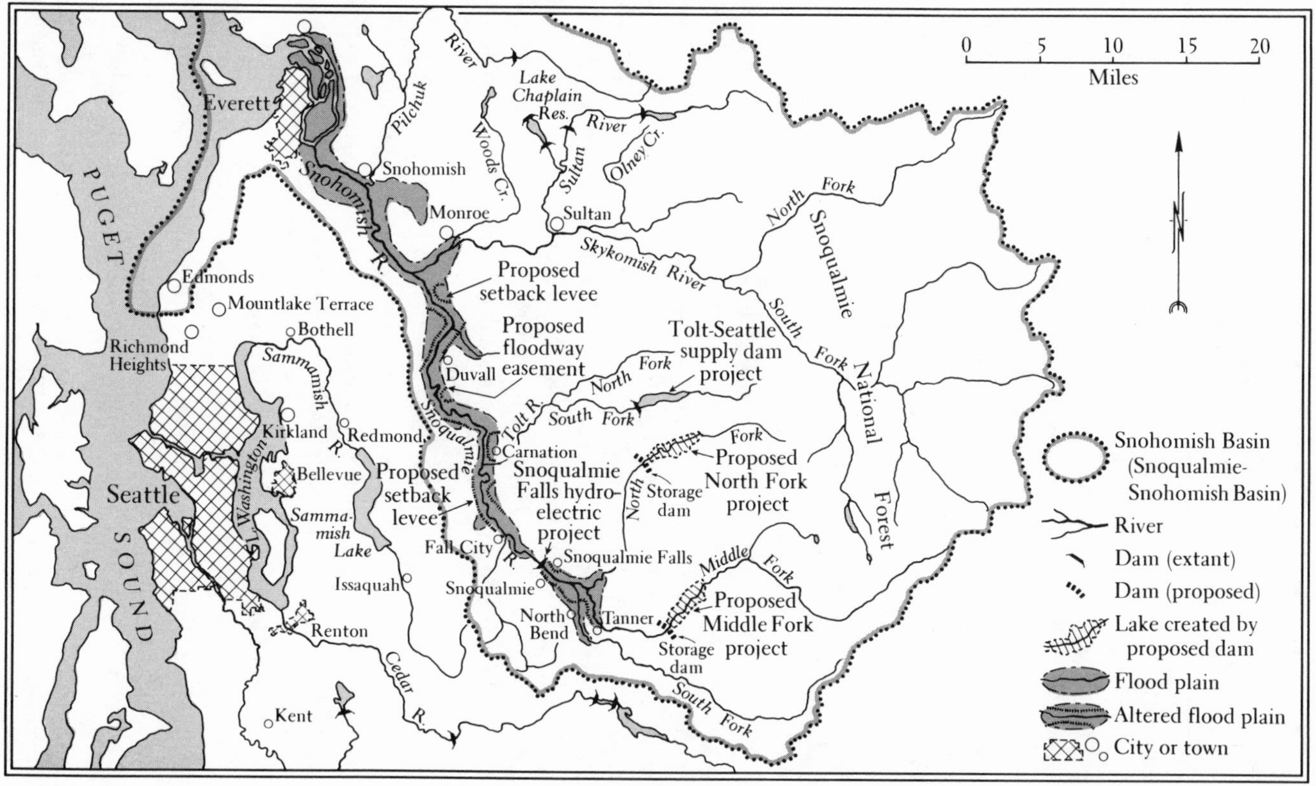

Legend:
- Snohomish Basin (Snoqualmie-Snohomish Basin)
- River
- Dam (extant)
- Dam (proposed)
- Lake created by proposed dam
- Flood plain
- Altered flood plain
- City or town

Miles: 0 5 10 15 20

Snoqualmie National Forest

North Fork
Snoqualmie
South Fork
Skykomish River
Tolt-Seattle supply dam project
North Fork
South Fork
Middle Fork
Fork
Proposed North Fork project
Proposed Middle Fork project
Storage project dam
Snoqualmie Falls hydro-electric project
North Bend
Tanner
South Fork

Proposed setback levee
Proposed floodway
Duvall easement
Carnation
Snoqualmie Falls
Fall City
Snoqualmie
Proposed setback levee

Lake Chaplain Res.
Sultan
Quincy Cr.
Sultan
Woods Cr.
River
Pilchuck
Monroe
Snohomish
Snohomish R.

Everett
Edmonds
Mountlake Terrace
Bothell
Sammamish R.
Kirkland
Redmond
Bellevue
Samma-mish
Lake Washington
Issaquah
Sammamish Lake
Cedar R.
Renton
Kent

Richmond Heights
Seattle

PUGET SOUND

ary and has rolling hills in the western portion. The three forks of the river—the North, Middle, and South—all flow generally westward to a junction downstream from the town of North Bend, forming the Snoqualmie River proper (figure 6-1). Shortly thereafter the river drops 268 feet over Snoqualmie Falls and flows northwesterly through the small communities of Fall City, Carnation, and Duvall, joining the Snohomish River near Monroe. It then empties into Puget Sound at Everett. The drainage area upstream from the falls is commonly known as the Upper Valley, and the 40-mile stretch from below the falls to the Snohomish River is known as the Lower Valley.

The mean annual precipitation for the basin is 92 inches, with about 75 percent occurring from October through March. Thus the basin typically experiences extensive winter flooding, followed by lighter spring floods. It is these floods, so far unchecked by man, that have kept the basin in its essentially agricultural and relatively undeveloped state.

The Snoqualmie River basin has many outstanding natural features that make it a prime recreational area. The floodplain is the last remaining open space on the outer limits of the heavily populated Seattle metropolitan area. Its natural recreational attractions are the waterfall and the upper reaches of the river that provide clear mountain streams running through heavily forested areas. Stream fishing and canoeing can be enjoyed in a near-wilderness setting. As the Seattle District has recognized, "The rugged topography and scenic attractions within the basin are valuable environmental resources within an hour's driving time of the Seattle-Tacoma metropolitan area."[2]

The basin, however, is not in a rustic or wilderness state but supports thriving agricultural, dairy, and lumbering enterprises, as well as some manufacturing in North Bend. Increasingly, it has become a favorite retreat for the nearby urban dwellers as well. The estimated population of the entire Snohomish basin in 1969 was 214,000, while the adjacent Seattle metropolitan area boasted a population of 1.5 million.

Seattle District's Proposed Plan

Although flood management along the Snoqualmie River had been discussed for decades, the most recent debate over the need for a dam and reservoir began after a major storm in the western Cascade Mountains in

2. Ibid., p. 67.

1959 caused flooding along the Snoqualmie, Skykomish, and Snohomish rivers. The storm produced flood stages in a relatively short period of time and substantial overbank flooding, causing great damage to residences, agricultural lands, utilities, and levees. The disastrous effects of the flood on residents living on the floodplain prompted the Washington State Legislative Council to seek federal assistance in developing a long-range flood management program for the basin. Some combination of structural flood protection devices, including a dam, was implied in the request.[3]

Resolutions adopted in 1960 by the Senate and House Public Works committees authorized the Corps to study means of providing federal flood protection assistance. Over the next nine years the Corps, in consultation with local King County officials, devised a plan for flood protection that included a dam and reservoir on the Middle Fork and a dam and powerhouse on the North Fork of the Snoqualmie River. The Corps held public hearings in 1961 and again in 1967, and the study was concluded in 1969.[4] The hearings were essentially gatherings of friends and neighbors and were dominated by the Corps and proponents of the plan. By 1967 most of the plan had been completed and since it had received little opposition in the meetings, the Seattle District anticipated minimal resistance to it. Conditions changed rapidly in the late 1960s and early 1970s, however.

Recreationists and conservationists did not become involved in the project study in its early stages because they lacked broad-based organizational support for their position and thus felt they would be impotent in a confrontation with the Corps. (The Corps' greatest work load is in the North Pacific States.) The Sierra Club was following the evolution of the study with some displeasure, but it was not a potent political force in the Seattle area at that time.[5] But in 1968 the passage of a $100 million transit, park, and open spaces bond issue by the people of the Seattle area activated the environmental movement. Opposition to the Middle Fork dam and the fight to preserve the Snoqualmie River basin as

3. Peter Tice Finden, "Analysis of Flood Management Alternatives Proposed for the Snoqualmie River Basin and the Related Public Study" (master's thesis, University of Washington, 1973), p. 15.

4. Ibid.

5. Interview on January 23, 1974, with Brock Evans, who served as Northwest regional vice-president of the Sierra Club from 1967 to 1972.

the last greenbelt adjacent to the metropolitan area soon became the issue of the environmentalists.

It is important to remember that Congress had not authorized the construction of flood control devices in 1960, only a project study. The Seattle District, like any other Corps district involved in a study, would have to obtain many approvals before its proposal could actually be implemented, including that of the North Pacific Division of the Corps; the Board of Engineers for Rivers and Harbors (BERH) in Washington, D.C.; the Office of the Chief of Engineers (OCE); the governor; the secretary of the army; and the Office of Management and Budget. Only then could the Corps ask Congress for the authority to begin construction.

By December 1969 the report of the district office on flood management on the Snoqualmie River had been approved by the division and submitted to the BERH and the OCE. The local and regional offices recommended to the BERH and OCE that the construction of a multipurpose dam and powerhouse be started immediately on the North Fork. The district stated its position as follows:

The storage in these projects *would control floods in sufficient degree to allow urban and suburban use of the valleys* in the vicinity of Snoqualmie Falls and the town of North Bend [the Upper Valley]. Downstream from Snoqualmie Falls, flood control would be sufficient to reduce flood damages to farms and roads and permit reasonable agricultural returns. The downstream flood plain below Snoqualmie Falls could be managed within the limits of flood protection provided thereby retaining its attractive environmental qualities. By these means, about 15,000 acres of flood prone land would be preserved for open space and agriculture. Also, the increased production from these lands would partially compensate for the loss of agricultural production resulting from continuing *loss of agricultural lands* in the basin to urbanization and industrialization. Recreation facilities on the reservoirs would serve the increasing demands of the adjacent metropolitan areas. The enhancement of fisheries both in the reservoir and downstream would provide additional sports fishing. Low flow augmentation from reservoir releases would increase the commercial production of fish. Power output and water supply from the North Fork project would serve growing demands of the area.[6]

Using 1969 prices, the estimated first cost of the proposed plan was approximately $49 million. The cost to the federal taxpayers was $46.3

6. Seattle District, *Snoqualmie River*, pp. 42–43 (emphasis added).

million for construction and $94,000 annually for operations, mainte-
nance, and major replacements. At an interest rate of 4⅞ percent and an
evaluation period of 100 years, the benefit-cost ratio was 1.8–1.

The Seattle District recommended land-use zoning, which would re-
strict development on the floodplain, as a means of minimizing future
flood damage to property. This recommendation, however, was offered as
a suggestion to the local people, not as part of the federally funded program, since land-use regulations come under the purview of state and local
governments. Critics of the plan have argued that the suggested restric-
tion of development on the floodplain through zoning directly contradicted the district's basic commitment to the development of the basin;
almost 50 percent of the benefits attributed to flood control in the proposal
would result from protecting future residential development.[7]

Alternative flood management solutions examined but rejected by the
district included levee and channel improvements along the Snoqualmie
River below Snoqualmie Falls. These would speed the floodwaters past
the farmlands along the Snoqualmie but would cause increased damage
downstream along the unprotected portions of the Snohomish River.[8]
A diversion of floodflow from the Snoqualmie River and the Sammamish
River basin to Puget Sound was ruled out as too costly. Floodplain evacuation was eliminated as unfeasible, given the level of investment in properties already situated on the floodplain, and the construction of single-
purpose flood control storage sites could only be partially justified by
benefit-cost criteria.

The BERH Review

The Seattle District chose an inappropriate time to forward its recommendation to the BERH for review. By late 1969 the Sierra Club, League
of Women Voters, Audubon Society, Washington Kayak Club, Alpine
Lakes Protection Society, and various other groups had informally banded
together to become a potent force behind the cause of wilderness and
recreation protection in the Northwest. Possibly even more important,

7. Statement of David G. Knibb, chairman of the Seattle Chapter of the Alpine
Lakes Protection Society, in U.S. Department of the Army, Corps of Engineers, Seattle
District, transcript of public meeting on the Middle Fork project, Snoqualmie River,
Wash., held at North Bend, Wash., March 6, 1970, p. 134.
8. Curiously, the problem of downstream flooding associated with the construction
of levees seemed to have escaped the Corps engineers involved in the L-15 study discussed in chapter 5.

however, the movement had become a national one by this time; both Congress and the President were becoming sensitized to the environmental issue.

When the Seattle District submitted its recommendation to the BERH, it also circulated a public notice (required with the submission of all studies) stating that until mid-February 1970 the BERH would afford interested parties an opportunity to furnish additional information about the proposal. Opponents of the dam and reservoir capitalized on this opportunity and flooded the BERH with letters. Because of the large response, the BERH extended the time allowed for comment for another month. Then, given the controversial nature of the proposal and the interest in the environment prevailing in Washington, D.C., the BERH made an unusual request by asking the Seattle District to hold another public hearing on the proposal so that BERH members could attend. The importance of this unprecedented move by the Corps' own review board was not lost on either proponents or opponents of the project.

The format of this unusual hearing was arranged by the Seattle District. Brock Evans, the Northwest regional vice-president of the Sierra Club, was invited to take a half hour to present the views of the opponents. Scott Wallace, long-time resident of the Snoqualmie Valley, a King County commissioner, a member of the Valley Greenbelt Association, and one of the leading spokesmen for the dam and reservoir, was invited to take equal time to present the views of the proponents. Otherwise, the hearing would be open to anyone who wished to speak. The district attempted to structure the hearing so that the Corps would appear to be impartial. In fact, however, the Seattle District was obviously partial to the dam proposal.

The Public Hearing

The hearing, held at a county park recreation center in North Bend on the evening of March 6, 1970, and attended by over 1,000 people, served to emphasize the broad public concern about the project and how severely the issue had polarized the community. It also provided the first point-by-point account of the opponents' arguments.

Those opposing the construction of the Middle Fork dam and reservoir revealed their prime concern: the preservation of the Snoqualmie Valley as an agricultural greenbelt. Eleanor Lee, president of the Puget Sound League of Women Voters, argued, for example: "Regardless of the

Corps' very good intentions, the feeling of security provided by the dam is bound to increase the pressure for more intensive use of land in the flood plain." Furthermore, the "proposal will encourage land-use development inconsistent with the current Comprehensive Land-Use Plan of King County, which shows Snoqualmie Valley in agriculture/flood plain use except for established communities. The proposal is also inconsistent with the Open Space Agreement accepted by members of the Puget Sound Governmental Conference."⁹

Opponents repeatedly referred to the rapid urban and industrial development that had occurred in the nearby Green River Valley after the construction of the Howard A. Hanson Dam. Joan Thomas of the Washington Environmental Council cited a similar occurrence in the Sammamish basin, where in 1963 a modest flood control project was initiated to protect farmers from flooding. "The land was zoned agricultural land, it was open space, and the project went ahead. . . . So what happened after the project was completed? The price of land, which had been selling for about $2,000 an acre, is now an average of $10,000 an acre, and are the farmers getting out of the land? Yes, they are, if there's any land left, it's becoming industrial, developed for industry."¹⁰

Brock Evans's approach was to marshal a string of professionals to lay before the BERH the technical deficiencies of the proposal being made by the district engineers. Earnest Gayden, a professor of urban planning at the University of Washington, pointed out that the Seattle District had calculated as a benefit the projected urban development that would occur on the floodplain but had failed to include as a cost the losses that would result from withdrawing the land from good agricultural use. "If one takes the population projections which are used to justify this kind of project, then one must also take into account the needs of this same future population for milk, meat, and good local produce."¹¹ William B. Beyers of the University of Washington questioned the district's computation of recreational benefits for the project, finding them highly arbitrary and overstated.

An issue arising over every Corps project is the extent to which the project will produce net national benefits. This goes to the heart of the

9. Seattle District, transcript of public hearing, March 6, 1970, pp. 46–47.
10. Ibid., p. 65.
11. Ibid., p. 75.

problem with benefit-cost ratios, which are supposed to index these local, regional, and national benefits. Gardner Brown, Jr., an economist at the University of Washington, questioned the legitimacy of using land enhancements in the valley resulting from the project as net national benefits.

For years, the Corps has argued that flood control brings about a more intensive use of the flood plain. "More intensive" naturally means more economic activity which gives rise to land enhancement benefits, and in this case amounting to $118,000 annually over fifty years proposed for the Middle Fork project. These benefits should not be claimed in general because they are not national benefits. Additional growth due to the flood control aspects of the projects represents a relocation of economic activity from elsewhere in the economy. It may be a regional benefit; it is not a national benefit.[12]

If one accepts Brown's reasoning, then the project benefits cannot be included as part of a project's national economic benefits. Yet this was the main reason for asking federal taxpayers to pay the lion's share of the costs of the dam, as it is in most of the Corps' dam projects. Referring to a number of other alleged overstatements of benefits, Brown concluded that a more realistic benefit-cost ratio would be 0.9, about half of that estimated by the Seattle District.

Jerry Parker, associated with Urban Planning in Seattle, was the last of Brock Evans's panel of experts to speak. He focused on the position taken by the Corps and the local proponents that the greenbelt nature of the Snoqualmie Valley could be sustained and even enhanced by the dam. This position, he argued, contradicted the Corps' own calculations that the project "can only be justified over a 50-year period when you assume the intense growth of the flood plain and the residential use."[13]

The frustrations and anxieties of the proponents of the project continued to mount as they listened to this presentation by a host of professionals. Local proponents saw these professionals as outsiders who had no vested interest in the valley, who did not have to live through the agonizing floods, who had not been around during the previous decade when all the details of the proposal were being hammered out, and who were attempting to undermine a project the local proponents wanted very much.

12. Ibid., p. 85.
13. Ibid., p. 93.

Kirk Smith, Scott Wallace's first speaker and owner of a small publishing firm in Fall City, lashed out:

We think that the people who are going to be most affected by the Snoqualmie River are the people who live here and none of the [previous] speakers or anyone else, I suspect, is really going to propose that we move the towns of North Bend and Snoqualmie off this river, for up to now I've heard no proposal protecting the thousands of people who live in those towns. I am impressed by our own state officials who come out and tell us that they don't think this dam is a good idea, even though that may not be their special interest. Bert Cole, God bless him, he's a Democrat, thinks the hills should be built on, and that's fine. Much against the will of the people who live there, he's already proposed the leases of state land for an explosives factory at Preston. Mr. Levy, our county councilman, and God bless him, he's a Democrat too, says don't move too fast, let's take a few months and maybe a few years, because it would be worth that not to let the Lower Valley go industrial.

I submit it might be worth more to have something on Snoqualmie to stop heavy water in the event of a disaster or potential flood to save people and their homes and their institutions.[14]

Commenting on the opposition's expert testimony, he continued, "As far as I'm concerned, Mr. Evans and the university folk can argue with the experts of the Army Corps of Engineers as long as they wish—go to it—but I would like to see an answer to a need of people in the Snoqualmie Valley, and that's why I am the most firm supporter of the Middle Fork Dam."[15]

The proponents' central theme, aside from assailing the character and motives of the academics and the conservationists, was that the project would *guarantee* the preservation of the basin as an agricultural greenbelt—an objective repeated time and again—and not the reverse. Sympathetic consideration should be given to the people who had to bear the cost of flood damage.

Richard Zemp, North Bend planning commissioner, said that proponents were "aware that environmental hysteria" was causing "dizziness" to characterize "the majority of otherwise sensible people." Nonetheless, he felt compelled to argue that the environmentalists were simply confused, that in fact the proposed project was the best means to the ends espoused by them, and that they didn't realize that correcting "the bad effects of nature, for instance flooding," could serve a positive end. He

14. Ibid., p. 96.
15. Ibid., p. 98.

also said that the proposed project was "the best method of preserving the existing environment in Snoqualmie and Snohomish Basin, and the existing environment is the present social and economic culture long established in the Snoqualmie Valley."[16] The choice, therefore, was not between development and the greenbelt; it was between rampant flooding, the destruction of homes and property, and declining agricultural profitability on the one hand, and the preservation of the Middle Fork as a free-flowing river on the other hand.

Richard Holt, a North Bend attorney, agreed with many others that a compromise solution was possible and that if the dam, which had been proposed for valid reasons and in the expectation of many benefits, were built, strong legislation could "preserve the things that the Sierra Club and the other people are talking about."[17]

The problem, of course, was that zoning legislation did not yet exist. Opponents therefore felt that it would be folly to go ahead with the construction of the dam before they had ironclad legal guarantees that further development of the floodplain would be prohibited. Once the dam was constructed, property values in the basin would inevitably soar; the owners then would resist any agricultural zoning or land-use restrictions that in effect would deny them a great windfall profit.[18]

In summarizing the frustration of the opposition George B. Yount, a resident of Snohomish County, stated:

My view at least is that the citizen is really getting the short end of the stick here. He's gone to the polls and expressed his views to save the open space [the 1968 bond issue] and he is met by a government agency unwilling to heed the vote. An aroused citizenry sees the rape of the land they love and protest in books, periodicals, and television, in the streets, and even at hearings such as this. Your answer is that it isn't in the best interest for all concerned. It is for the economy. My answer is that this project not only benefits too few, but it is a sacrifice too great for the public to bear.[19]

After more than six hours of nonstop presentations, all 70 persons who had anything to say had been heard. A wealth of information had been presented in support of both positions, although not necessarily in a

16. Ibid., pp. 101–02.
17. Ibid., p. 114.
18. Fifty percent of the floodplain was in the hands of 5 percent of its residents (ibid., p. 193).
19. Ibid., p. 194.

coherent and organized fashion, and the preferences of the local residents, recreationists, property owners, and environmentalists had been made exceedingly clear. It is somewhat surprising, therefore, that General William F. Cassidy, then chairman of the Board of Engineers for Rivers and Harbors who had traveled over 3,000 miles to have a close look at the sites affected by the proposal and to learn how the local citizens felt about the issues, found the hearing so utterly disappointing.

> We got a lot of opinion, a lot of emotion, but very little in the way of fact. In my mind a good many of the people who talked had not even read the report [three-volume technical report prepared by the Corps], not analyzed [it]; they only picked pieces out of it and out of the news to justify their opinion. . . . There was a great deal of error and misinformation . . . presented here. The Board is not in the position to try and make a judgment from that kind of supposed information.[20]

What General Cassidy apparently had been looking for but had not found was hard information upon which the board could make its decision. The obvious conclusion is that what may be hard information to some is not to others. General Cassidy was clearly of the school that believes that facts based on feelings are not hard enough.

The Project Stymied

Upon returning to Washington, D.C., General Cassidy, along with the other board members (all generals in charge of divisions), decided that the proposal recommended by the Seattle District should go forward. In their letter to the chief of engineers they simply brushed aside the seeming contradiction between developing the Snoqualmie Valley and preserving it as a greenbelt. "The Board notes that there is a real need in the Snoqualmie River valley for flood control and for preservation of the greenbelt of agricultural land below the Snoqualmie River. The proposed dam and reservoir project on the Middle Fork of the Snoqualmie River serves this end."[21] In other words, for reasons that remain unclear the board concluded that the opponents' demand for a greenbelt really did not apply to the Upper Valley. While the Upper Valley would be open for development, the Lower Valley—if appropriate land-use regulation was adopted—could be maintained as a greenbelt.

20. Ibid., pp. 200–201.
21. Letter, chairman of the Board of Engineers for Rivers and Harbors to the chief of engineers, April 28, 1970, p. 8.

When asked by the chief of engineers to review the project proposal, Governor Daniel J. Evans of Washington in turn asked the director of the state Department of Ecology to prepare a position for the state. An environmental review team was assembled and ultimately recommended that the project not be authorized. The governor accepted the team's advice and informed the chief on November 23, 1970: "It is the recommendation of the review team and my recommendation that the Middle Fork project not be authorized at this time." Instead, he suggested that "an in-depth study of all available alternatives and combinations of alternatives should be undertaken by the Corps of Engineers in concert with the appropriate agencies of the State of Washington."[22] The message was clear: the Corps would have to reach an accommodation with the opposition forces or there would be no project.

This was a dramatic setback for the Corps. The chief would never go over the head of the governor and recommend the project to Congress. Thus with the power of the governor behind them, the environmentalists achieved a major victory. In view of the district's many activities, however, it might be able to tolerate the loss of one project. But the environmentalists were on the warpath and, having experienced one important victory, could they be satisfied? Wouldn't they press on to bring the entire construction program of the Seattle District to a halt?

The Advent of Fishbowl Planning

Governor Evans's decision not to endorse the proposal marked a turning point in the flood protection program for the Snoqualmie. It also marked a turning point for the Seattle District. Just before the governor's decision on the Middle Fork, Colonel Howard L. Sargent became district engineer of the Seattle District. Realizing the dire implications of the decision, Sargent decided to accept the governor's invitation to undertake a restudy. This would demonstrate both the district's continuing concern with the problems of the people in the river basin and its open-mindedness in considering all possible alternative solutions.

More important, Sargent viewed the restudy as an opportunity to implement a truly comprehensive public participation and open planning system that he had developed while in a management assignment at the

22. U.S. Department of the Army, Corps of Engineers, Seattle District and State of Washington, Department of Ecology, *Middle Fork Snoqualmie River Joint Study: Report to Governor Evans* (June 1973), p. 2.

Pentagon. It was called fishbowl planning, a sufficiently radical concept to have had little chance of adoption in more tranquil times. With little to lose and much to gain, however, the district staff, under the leadership of Sargent, underwent an almost complete about-face in the conduct of its planning.

Sargent first met with the governor to determine specifically what additional alternatives he wished to have studied. An agreement was reached on the subject of the restudy and on having it conducted by a study team composed of members of both the Corps and the state Department of Ecology. This was unprecedented. Not only were two agencies, one federal and one state, going to undertake a study jointly, but the two involved had previously been archenemies. (The Department of Ecology's review team, after all, had recommended that Evans veto the original Corps proposal.) The agreement of January 1971 between the two agencies called for the participation of the public through Sargent's fishbowl planning technique in reviewing four basic alternatives, including the original Middle Fork proposal. The plan for the restudy was then agreed upon by the OCE. Funding was appropriated by Congress in the budget for fiscal year 1973, and the restudy began in September 1972.[23]

The basic objective of fishbowl planning, as envisioned by Sargent, is "to insure that planning for public-works projects is highly visible to all interested organizations and individuals."[24] Concerned citizens were to be involved in the planning process from the beginning. Throughout the planning process citizens serve as a check on agency planners and contribute ideas, insights, and alternatives of their own. The program was designed to satisfy both the desire of citizens for participation in agency decisions and the necessity, strongly felt by Sargent, to check the subtle biases that agency planners inevitably introduce into proposals. The district could then render decisions on the proposals based on all the facts.

The four formal or procedural components of fishbowl planning are workshops, public meetings, citizen committees, and a brochure on the study. The public meetings provide a forum for citizens, organizations, and agencies to discuss alternative solutions under consideration in a

23. The cost-sharing agreement of the restudy called for the Corps to contribute $40,000 and for the state to contribute $14,000.
24. Colonel Howard L. Sargent, Jr., "Fishbowl Planning Immerses Pacific Northwest Citizens in Corps Projects," Civil Engineering, vol. 42 (September 1972), pp. 54–57.

study. Workshops are smaller gatherings where more informal and particularized discussions take place, and ideally, citizens volunteer to conduct them. The citizen committees are in a sense organizational appendages to the Corps. They are composed of community and organization leaders who can maintain contact with the broader public, mobilize it for meetings, and so on.

The study brochure is an essential, and perhaps the most innovative, component of fishbowl planning. It serves as the central study document, which is available throughout the study, and is continually being modified and updated. It provides a written record of *all* the alternative solutions ever suggested by citizens, agencies, or whomever. As new alternatives are suggested, they are added in subsequent editions of the brochures, of which there are six or seven throughout the life of the study. Even if an alternative is rejected at some point, it is not deleted. Rather, it is retained as proof that it has been examined. The brochures serve as a forum for rational debate about the alternatives. An alternative is described in summary fashion on one page; on the next page a pro and con list is provided. Any person or organization can enter a position. Their names are included with their statements, letting everyone know where they stand. Each edition of the brochure contains a list of the names of all persons who have made comments on the study. Sargent felt that this helps "identify groups that should be participating—but aren't."[25]

Another section of the brochure "identifies the one or two alternatives selected for technical checkout, such as geology, hydrology, or a prediction of effects on fish and wildlife. The District Engineer discusses each alternative in turn, giving reasons for selecting or rejecting the alternative for the detailed checkout."[26] As the result of the checkouts are available, they are incorporated into the brochure and ultimately become the basis for the district engineer's recommendation to higher authorities.

In all, there is a considerable difference between traditional Corps planning and fishbowl planning. Procedurally, the latter includes 15 separate activities designed to draw the public into the planning process; only three of these activities—two public meetings and formal-letter notification of its intentions to other public agencies—were included in traditional Corps planning.

25. Ibid., p. 56.
26. Ibid.

The Joint Study

In one important respect the restudy of the Middle Fork project differed from Sargent's idealized outline for fishbowl planning. The joint study effort did not begin from scratch with a public meeting to determine the concerns and preferences of all interests, with no alternatives presented by the planners. Instead, the Seattle District and the Department of Ecology decided between themselves which alternatives to include in the study and selected four: two versions of the district's original multipurpose dam and reservoir proposal along with a recommendation for a land-use management system; a system of setback levees, floodway acquisition, and a land-use management system; and a totally nonstructural approach utilizing floodway easements and flood insurance.[27] The general public first knew of these alternatives in the initial edition of the study team's brochure.

The study team's decision to review only four alternatives was made for the sake of expediency, but conservationists saw it as an indication of the Corps' unwillingness to entertain all potential alternatives. Obviously a great deal of distrust still existed. The alternatives became the central issue at the initial public workshop held at North Bend on October 3, 1972, following the publication of the first edition of the study brochure. Thirty-six persons attended, representing all contending factions. The representative of the Puget Sound League of Women Voters requested that consideration be given to other alternatives that might be proposed by participating agencies or groups.

Public Consideration of the Restudy

The first large-scale public meeting to discuss the restudy was held in North Bend on the evening of November 9, 1972. Tempers had cooled in the two and a half years since the BERH's public hearing, but the issues remained controversial nonetheless. One hundred and twenty persons attended the two-hour meeting (only a fraction of the thousand who at-

27. Setback levees are those constructed some distance from the edge of the watercourse to contain floodwater within a broad natural channel. A floodway easement is acquired by a public body for the purpose of allowing floodwaters to pass without interruption beyond that caused by existing structures. Title to property, however, remains with the private owner.

tended the six-hour hearing in March 1970). The joint study team members shared the task of bringing the public up to date on their agreements and indicating what they intended to do next. The discussion of the alternatives was basically a rehash of the views expressed at the 1970 hearing, except that this time it centered on why the study team had limited itself to only four alternatives.

Edward Delanty of the Washington Kayak Club noted that "several other potentially viable alternatives" were not being considered. He pointed out that the town of Snoqualmie and part of North Bend constituted the major flood-prone residential areas on the upper floodplain. Therefore, "Why wasn't an alternative being considered which leveed these areas and nothing more? Has the cost of relocating the developments in the upper flood plain, coupled with limited levee work, been considered?" He went on to suggest that participants be permitted to present alternatives and that impact statements be prepared for the alternatives, as called for by the state's new Shoreline Management Act of 1971.[28]

The study team may have restricted itself to four alternatives, but as members claimed at the hearing, they had no intention of excluding the consideration of others. Thus Sydney Steinborn, chief of the Engineering Division for the Seattle District, expressed the team's desire to include in its report to the governor as many alternatives as were proposed. He answered Delanty by saying: "We want those who are proposing alternatives to come to us and take the initiative and we will have mini-workshops on alternatives. We hope to have this in January, so those of you who have alternatives continue to make them known."[29] The problem was whether the time and money available to the study team was sufficient for it to consider other alternatives. As Corps people often lament, public participation is very costly.

What came of the first public meeting, then, was the promise to incorporate additional alternatives into the study report. The burden of examining additional alternatives, however, would fall, not on the study team, but on those proposing them. Recreation advocates and conservationists would thus be given their first opportunity to make a constructive

28. Seattle District, transcript of public meeting on the Middle Fork project, held at North Bend, November 9, 1972, pp. 49–50.
29. Ibid., p. 51.

contribution to the decisionmaking process. Rather than being cast in the negative role of opposing the structural solutions, they now had the opportunity to come up with serious nonstructural ones.

The Mini-Workshops

The second workshop of the study was held in late January 1973 and was attended by some 90 persons. At the request of citizens who were concerned with the study but who lived outside the floodplain, this workshop was not held at North Bend but at Bellevue Community College on the eastern fringe of Seattle.

The issue of considering other alternatives had now been resolved. Dates were announced for a series of mini-workshops of the type promised by Steinborn at the public meeting in November. The workshops would be sponsored by various organizations and persons in the community; the study team would attend, but only in a consulting capacity. As it turned out, most of the mini-workshops were arranged by the groups opposed to the original dam proposal, although the sessions were attended by proponents as well.[30]

The first mini-workshop was conducted by Steven Doyle of the Duvall Valley Commission and was attended by approximately 30 persons. Marvin Vialle, the study coordinator representing the Department of Ecology, and Frank Urabeck, the study coordinator from the Seattle District, reviewed the four original alternatives. The sessions prompted questions about the effects of flooding on floodplains and about the environmental effects of the various alternatives. The second mini-workshop focused more narrowly on the need for, and likelihood of, land-use management systems that could complement the various alternatives being considered. In addition, the state and local laws that pertained to land-use regulations in the Snoqualmie River basin were reviewed.

The third mini-workshop shifted back to North Bend and was sponsored by David Osterholt of the Sierra Club. It was devoted to new alternatives proposed by the Sierra Club and the Alpine Lakes Protection Society (ALPS) that appeared in the next (fourth) edition of the study brochure. The Sierra Club had three suggestions: (1) a comprehensive system of floodplain management permitting current uses of the floodplain to continue but prohibiting new buildings and landfills (this became

30. The discussion of the six mini-workshops is drawn from Seattle District and Department of Ecology, *Joint Study*, sec. 5.

alternative 5); (2) a plan for evacuating the floodplain requiring the permanent evacuation of all habitable structures within the floodway area that were subject to deep and fast-flowing water (alternative 6); and (3) a plan that called for the rigorous application of state and local laws, such as the state's Shoreline Management Act of 1971, that apply to floodplains (alternative 7). ALPS suggested two other alternatives: a comprehensive plan to reduce the level, frequency, and siltation of floods by improving logging practices throughout the Snoqualmie River basin (alternative 8); and the placing of riprap along all sections of the Snoqualmie River banks that are subject to severe soil erosion, together with some local dikes and levees (alternative 9).

The valley farmers attending the mini-workshop felt that none of the five alternatives offered that evening were viable means of reducing flood damage. They persisted in their belief that this could only be accomplished with a dam.

The fourth mini-workshop was devoted to a presentation by Wolf Bauer, long-time conservationist of the region. He argued that turning the Snoqualmie River valley into a European-type resort area would permit it to retain its open-space character while remaining economically viable through tourism and recreation.

The fifth mini-workshop considered an alternative proposed by the Washington Kayak Club. This plan called for designating segments of the Middle Fork above North Bend as "wild, scenic, and recreational rivers" under either a national or state river system; establishing an open-space zone over the 23,000 acres of the Snoqualmie River floodplain; building levees to protect the town of Carnation against the 100-year flood; and allowing setback levees above the falls (alternative 10).

Following these five mini-workshops, the last of the three previously scheduled general workshops was held in North Bend on March 13. It served as a summary session during which all the new alternatives were reviewed. During the sixth and final mini-workshop held the following week, the Department of Ecology reviewed the legislative aspects of each of the alternatives.

The Final Public Meeting

If General Cassidy had sat through the second and final public meeting of the restudy, held at North Bend Elementary School on the evening of May 1, 1973, surely he would have been appalled. Three years had elapsed since the BERH hearing, and barely one "new fact" or the kind of "hard information" on which the Corps could make its decisions had been uncovered. There were more alternatives and more rapport and mutual respect between state agencies and the Corps, between the conservationists and the Corps, and between the proponents and opponents of the dam and reservoir project. But positions on the original Seattle District proposal remained unchanged. Thus while the continual constructive interaction of the fishbowl planning process resulted in the participants' greater appreciation for one another's views, it did not result in any new substantive information or a consensus.

Proponents had not been persuaded that the dam inevitably meant development and the end of the greenbelt nature of the valley. Bill Reams, King County councilman, made this clear.

I have been on the Council for four years and have sat in on many of the meetings, a couple of them with the Department of Ecology, several meetings with our own flood control people, and several that we have had at the King County Council. The Council almost unanimously has voted to reaffirm the sponsorship of this project. We only had one Councilman dissenting. . . .

We are committed to keeping the Snoqualmie Valley in its natural state and keeping the people on the land that have been on the land for the last 80 to 90 years, and we feel that in this discussion the best way to keep the people on the land and allow them to continue farming is to allow this dam to be built. We think that by eliminating some of the severe flooding we will allow people who are having a tough time now, making it, to continue farming.[31]

Some attendees once again reminded the audience that floods were a severe hardship for those who had to endure them, and that therefore the dam should be built. Scott Wallace, after assailing the motives of Brock Evans (who had since moved out of the Seattle area), went on to say:

I don't question the integrity of the opponents of the dam or of their methods or their feelings, they are natural, but the thing that disturbs me a little bit is that they will not honor the years of toil, the thousands and thousands of dollars spent by bona fide organizations, the counties, the state, the federal government and all of these other agencies that have worked on this project for 25 years from its first conception to try to come to a reasonable solution to a problem.[32]

    31. Seattle District, transcript of public meeting on the joint study held at North Bend, May 1, 1973, pp. 15–16.
    32. Ibid., p. 37.

After all, he argued, it was not as though they didn't have the same goal in mind.

The people that have cleared this valley and made it the greenbelt that all of you admire and . . . want to preserve . . . have a common goal: we want to preserve the greenbelt. The county has moved forthrightly to zone it for agriculture, established a floodplain over zone, and this is the use that it will be put to, and as we said in our position paper, our arguments for the dam are very simple, but the arguments against the dam are based on three false assumptions, and I reiterate again those assumptions are, one, the dam will foster . . . industrialization similar to that in the Green River basin, . . . two, the dam reservoir will destroy part of the river and part of the wilderness area, and . . . three, . . . by constantly advancing dubious alternatives the dam will be buried and the valley saved by doing nothing.[33]

So, again, one of the strongest proponents stressed his view that the recreationists were nothing but obstructionists, and misguided ones at that.

Naturally the environmentalists expressed their continuing belief in the social and environmental hazards of building a dam. The Washington Environmental Council endorsed alternative 10, as did the Washington Kayak Club and the Lake Washington Branch of the American Association of University Women. ALPS endorsed its own proposal, alternative 9.

A number of local opponents of the dam and reservoir took the opportunity to voice their views at this meeting, something that had rarely occurred during earlier meetings. The most damning of these came from Jesse Petrich, a real estate salesman from North Bend, and concerned the motives of at least some of those advocating the dam. "The gentleman alongside of me down there, I sold a piece of property of his the other day, and he says, 'Are you against the dam? Gee, if we had that dam my property would be worth twice as much, three times as much, because they could have built on all 650 feet of the river.' "[34] Windfall profits— the motive the environmentalists believed to be behind much of the support of the dam but could never document—was finally raised by one of the local residents themselves.

Petrich related a similar episode.

A funny thing happened today. A lady friend of my daughter's was waiting at the house for her when I got home from the office, and I had never met her before, and right away we got in an argument about this. She started to tell me about a dear friend of hers who had 12 or 13 lots down here on the river

33. Ibid., pp. 37–38.
34. Ibid., p. 27.

and . . . couldn't build on them because of the floodplain controls. And I said,
"You know what it appears to me? She bet on the wrong horse. . . . She
bought a bunch of them to hold and go up in value and make a little money,
and she gambled and lost, and let her take it." And boy, she flounced out of
the house madder than a wet hen, but that's the way I feel. . . . I think we can
get along without a dam.[35]

There were also a number of pleas, however, for a more sympathetic
understanding of the flood victim's position. Richard Zemp, for one, was
convinced that the proposed dam was vital to the area and was willing to
give up his holdings as a sign of his good faith. He owned about a mile
of riverfront property in the Upper Valley and offered to make it available
for sale (at market value) or to trade it for land held by the government
so that the property could be set aside in its natural state. He reasoned
that everyone would lose if a compromise could not be reached. Without
some agreed upon plan, he said: "We are going to have a haphazard pattern of growth and development, and erosion and flood damage is going
to continue. Let's stop the bickering and let's come to some kind of conclusion that we can lay on Governor Dan's desk and say O.K., now you
have some viable alternatives."[36]

Zemp could not have been more correct in his estimation of what it
would take to get an affirmative response from the governor. But a viable
alternative, or even several from which to choose, was not to emerge from
the restudy effort.

The Restudy Ends

This last public meeting was followed by the publication of the final
version of the study brochure in June 1973. The brochure had by then
grown from the original 11 pages to 70, most of which were devoted to a
description of the 11 alternatives.[37]

The study team also terminated its activities and submitted its report
to Governor Evans in June. The report included a copy of the final
brochure, assorted correspondence, new data papers that had been completed during the restudy, and a summary of the evolution of the restudy.

35. Ibid., p. 28.
36. Ibid., p. 56.
37. Seattle District and Department of Ecology, *Joint Study*. The eleventh alternative was not discussed earlier, because it was suggested quite late in the restudy by a
resident of North Bend. It called for channel modification to reduce flooding in the
Upper Valley.

But it did not contain a recommendation by the team favoring one, or even a select few, of the 11 alternatives. Neither the team members nor the broader public had reached anything close to a consensus. The study team did feel, however, that a compromise might have been worked out if there had been just a little more time. After six months of fishbowl planning the contending factions had finally overcome their initial distrust of one another and the agencies involved and had seriously begun to search for some sort of reconciliation. This essentially was their message to the governor. The report states: "While respective positions of proponents and opponents relative to the original Middle Fork proposal did not appear to have changed during the course of the workshops and public meetings, some indication toward compromise was indicated in the public participation period."[38]

Since Governor Evans had suggested the restudy, he was obligated to comment on it. He was not at liberty, however, to give his approval to the Corps to proceed with any of the alternatives. The Corps had formally presented only one proposal to him, the one the chief had asked the governor to comment on back in 1970. After reviewing the restudy the governor advised the Corps that he had again concluded that the environmental risks associated with the Corps' proposal for a dam and reservoir were unacceptably high—therefore, no project.

Local pressure and the Corps' continuing interest in attending to the problem of flooding in the Snohomish River basin kept the issue alive. In 1973 the Community Crisis Intervention Center of St. Louis offered to mediate between the opponents and proponents. Governor Evans accepted the offer, and the mediation effort, begun in the summer of 1974, resulted in a plan agreed upon by the Sierra Club, the Washington Environmental Council, the valley farmers, the League of Women Voters, and the basin communities.

The items in the plan that fell under the purview of the Corps were the construction of a multipurpose storage dam on the North Fork of the Snoqualmie River (a dam much smaller in scale and storage capacity than that originally proposed by the Seattle District for the Middle Fork), the modification of the Seattle reservoir on the South Fork of the Tolt River to include flood storage, and setback levees for the towns of North Bend and Snoqualmie. Other features of the plan that were the responsibility of

38. Ibid., p. 4.

state and local governments called for the purchase of development rights in the floodplain to ensure its rural status, the creation of several public parks in the floodplain, and the protection of the plain where the Snohomish River spills into Puget Sound.

Governor Evans appointed an interim citizens' committee to oversee the implementation of the agreement, and the district office undertook a preliminary feasibility study of the portions of the plan that it would be responsible for. The district found the projects economically justifiable, but just as its study was being completed, a new governor was elected who asked to review the mediated plan. In July 1977 Governor Dixy Lee Ray endorsed the plan and encouraged the Corps to proceed with its feasibility study. However, she also virtually reopened the entire issue by asking that the future of the Cedar River basin (adjoining the Snohomish basin to the south and west) and the long-range water supply needs of Seattle be incorporated into the planning effort. This expanded study, initiated by the Corps and the State of Washington, is scheduled for completion in late 1981. Clearly the controversy is far from over.

Fishbowl Planning Appraised

What can be learned from the fishbowl experience? To begin with, the fishbowl process during the restudy departed in some ways from Sargent's plan, usually in innovative responses to unanticipated problems. For example, a second agency was made a part of the study team, a condition that was required by Governor Evans and one not typical of other Corps studies or of any other government agency's project studies. In addition, the mini-workshops were ad hoc, the result of the desire of citizens to offer alternatives the study team had neither the time nor resources to consider.

Second, Sargent did not consider fishbowl planning simply a strategic response to the controversy over flood management along the Snoqualmie River; he saw it as a format for all agency planning efforts. Therefore, since late 1970 it has been formally required for all Seattle District studies and has become fairly well institutionalized throughout the district.

Despite the inability of fishbowl planning to bring about a consensus on a single alternative in the Middle Fork study, the program is considered worthwhile by the district and by most outside observers. This may be partly because fishbowl planning did not begin with the same basic goal as that of the Office of the Chief of Engineers. It was hoped that in the new era of public participation the chief's guidelines would achieve a clear consensus among all those concerned by facilitating the resolution of conflict.[39] In contrast, fishbowl planning was designed to improve communication among all concerned parties, with the hope that this would lead to greater flexibility on the part of the proponents of each alternative and an atmosphere in which proponents could be encouraged to accommodate the concerns of others, thereby expanding the extent of mutual interest.[40] This may seem a subtle distinction, but as noted earlier, under the OCE guidelines planners were told—and had come to expect—that an elaborate public participation program would produce a consensus on an alternative that all parties accepted as the best solution. Fishbowl planning holds out no such promise; the important point is that it is not judged a failure if a consensus does not emerge.

In sum, the foremost payoff of fishbowl planning in the Middle Fork study was the respect the Corps' Seattle District won from even its strongest critics for opening the decisionmaking process to such an extent. This had never been attempted before.

39. U.S. Department of the Army, Corps of Engineers, Office of the Chief of Engineers, "Water Resources Policies and Authorities: Public Participation in Water Resources Planning," EC 1165-2-100 (May 28, 1971).

40. U.S. Department of the Army, Corps of Engineers, Office of the Chief of Engineers, "Investigation Planning and Development of Water Resources: Public Involvement in Planning," SDR 1120-2-1 (November 10, 1971).

CHAPTER SEVEN

An Evaluation of Open Planning

THE EXTENSIVE public participation programs initiated by the Corps in the early 1970s are illustrated by four of the five studies presented in chapters 4, 5, and 6: the L-15 levee, Cleveland-Akron wastewater management, the Middle Fork of the Snoqualmie River, and the Wildcat and San Pablo creeks. Taken together they shed a good deal of light on how in practice the much debated issues of the scope of representation appropriate for an effective open planning program, the utility of various organizational methods, the delegation of authority to participants, and project separability can be resolved. They also provide a rich source of information on how the public responds to open planning and how in turn a public agency such as the Corps responds. A comparison of these responses suggests that although citizens and the agency can both learn from the planning experience, their ultimate evaluations of the process may differ markedly.

Characteristics of Open Planning

In each of the four instances where an open program was used, the scope of representation was based primarily on geographic considerations. Meetings and workshops were held in most of the areas directly affected by a project, and while the district officers widely publicized the studies, they left it up to those interested to come forward on their own. This seemed to work quite well.

But the specific method of participation varied widely from one study to the next. Only during the Snoqualmie River study, for example, was the public specifically encouraged to design alternatives (which were then incorporated into the joint report of the Corps and the Washington State Department of Ecology), although suggestions by participants did become part of the L-15 compromise plan. In addition, the study brochure developed by the Seattle District provided an ingenious means of communicating the pros and cons of each suggestion and of documenting the evolution of the entire planning process. The brochure is especially helpful in Corps-type planning where activities are drawn out over months and often years and where people enter at different stages and thus are unaware of the range of alternatives already considered and the proponents and opponents of each.

In the Wildcat and San Pablo creeks study, consultation was primarily with the Model Cities personnel and other public officials, a satisfactory arrangement for that situation. Participation was enhanced in the Cleveland-Akron wastewater management study through the use of the "Purewater Press," which served as a brochure to announce meetings and to discuss the alternatives and as a novel means of educating the general public through readable articles on the potentials of comprehensive land treatment and other methods of wastewater management. While the effort was obviously self-serving, it was the only way most participants could learn about the capabilities and costs of these technologies. In all likelihood the journalistic approach used in the articles assured that they would be read by far more people than read the Corps' customary technical reports. This approach is now in widespread use by the Corps.

In none of the four studies was the Corps' authority to make the final decision on a project formally relinquished to the participants in open planning. In practice, authority was shared with other government agencies and with the citizens who participated. The participants in some cases had a de facto veto power over proposals they considered unacceptable, and this is considerable power. They also contributed to the extensive modifications that Corps districts made in their original plans. It is our impression that the participants did not expect more from their efforts. This is suggested in a survey we conducted of the participants in the five major studies we examined. The majority of the respondents felt that first and foremost the Corps of Engineers should be responsible for developing approaches for dealing with problems related to water resources. The next largest vote went to "water resource experts"; "local citizens" and the "general public" were much further down the list.[1]

The issue of separability of the projects in the studies of the Wildcat and San Pablo creeks, Cleveland-Akron, and to a lesser extent the Snoqualmie River, was not nearly as salient as in the studies for the Mississippi River–Gulf Outlet (MR-GO) lock and channel and the Unit L-15 levee.

1. Respondents were asked which of the officials or groups listed below should be

The first three projects are not integral parts of a broader Corps project. The absence of this constraint surely allowed the districts to operate far more freely but did not help in reaching a consensus. Thus despite their innovative participatory planning programs the Seattle District and the Buffalo District were unable to achieve a consensus on a project.

The Public's Evaluation

How did the public respond to the open-planning programs? To obtain the views of participants we spoke with key persons in each of the projects and also conducted an extensive questionnaire survey (see appendix A) of a random sample of participants. The survey included more than 900 persons selected from among the approximately 3,000 who participated in the public meetings, seminars, workshops, discussions, and planning during the five studies discussed in previous chapters. Questionnaire items were mainly closed-ended, and respondents were asked to score each item on a four-point scale (for example, from "strongly agree" to "strongly disagree"). Information was elicited about general orientation toward the Corps, the proper role of citizens in water resource planning, the level of direct participation desired, the extent of participation actually achieved, and motives for participation. The questionnaires were sent out in December 1973 and January 1974; the overall response rate was 53 percent.

Most respondents were quite pleased with their experience in open planning, particularly those who felt they had been excluded from earlier

---

responsible for developing the alternatives for dealing with the water-related problems of a community. Their response was as follows:

	Percent
Corps of Engineers	37.7
Water resource experts	30.8
Local elected officials	10.5
Local citizens	6.2
Regional government	5.1
Conservationists and environmentalists	4.8
General public	4.1
State officials	1.2
Local business	0.5
Congress	0.0
President	0.0

See appendix A for further information about the survey of participants.

Corps decisions and who therefore saw the Corps' changing posture toward the public as very significant. Characteristic was the attitude of Brock Evans, director of the Washington, D.C., office of the Sierra Club, who had served as the club's regional vice-president in the Northwest during the initial stages of the battle over the Snoqualmie River project. Evans rated fishbowl planning as a major victory for the public and for project opponents. He thought that the institutionalization of a decisionmaking process that was truly open and through which all sides could receive a fair public hearing was of great importance. As long as the Corps retained open planning, project opponents had a viable method of challenging the agency. Although they might not succeed in every case, their efforts could not help but have an effect on the Corps.[2]

The participants, however, were not completely satisfied with all the procedures used in the five studies. The survey revealed that they thought there was much room for improvement.

Modes of Participation

There are a number of formal and informal ways for the public to participate in every Corps project decision. The traditional way has been through the large public meetings required for many years by the agency. These continue to be mandatory in every project study. Today, of course, workshops, small meetings, and more interactive exchanges are being introduced. Citizens have also had indirect access to decisionmaking either through their elected political officials or through organized interest groups engaged in active lobbying.

As shown in table 7-1, the survey indicates that large public meetings remain the dominant mode of participation and access even in these more participatory studies; commenting on environmental impact statements and writing government officials trail close behind. Conferences, workshops, and seminars, which are considered to be the most productive form of public participation, have not been available or have not been taken advantage of by a large portion of the activist public. These modes appear at the bottom half of the ranking levels of participation achieved. The modes least used are (1) working through lobbying groups, either for or against the Corps, or (2) meeting with the Corps to establish the scope of water resource needs for the local community.

2. Interview with Evans, January 23, 1974.

Table 7-1. *Modes of Public Participation in Corps Planning,*
Ranked by Survey Respondents

Modes of participation	Rank	
	By preference[a]	By frequency of use
Large public meetings where Corps personnel discuss alternative project proposals with the public.	1	3
Large public meetings where Corps personnel describe the proposed project.	2	1
Meetings with Corps personnel to determine which of the many alternative project proposals under consideration should be studied in depth.	3	8
Meetings with Corps personnel to establish the scope of water resource needs for the local community.	4	12
Small workshops or seminars where Corps personnel discuss details of a proposed project with the public.	5	7
Large public meetings where citizens present their views on a proposed project to the Corps.	6	2
Conferences with Corps personnel attended by representatives of various local interests.	7	6
Commenting on the environmental impact statement of a proposed project.	8	4
Writing letters to government officials about the project proposal.	9	5
Informally meeting with Corps personnel to discuss a proposed project.	10	9
Small conferences with Corps personnel, attended by the members of an organization to which you belong.	11	11
Local elections on proposed projects.	12	b
A citizen oversight board that reviews activities of the Corps.	13	b
Supporting an interest group that usually favors Corps projects.	14	13
Supporting an interest group that usually opposes Corps projects.	15	10

a. Rated on a four-point scale. Order determined according to the mean rating of the mode.
b. Not available to citizens participating in the five project studies examined but used elsewhere as a means of citizen supervision of agencies.

How satisfactory are the available modes of participation? When respondents were asked to rate the desirability of participation via 15 modes (the 13 available to them in the studies plus local elections on the proposed projects and a citizen oversight board), their answers revealed that the level of participation *attained* differed from the level *desired*. As table 7-1 shows, large meetings in which the public can express views and exchange information with the agency were rated highly. The public concurred with the Corps on the need for this forum. On the other hand, the respondents felt they should be given more opportunity to meet with the Corps to "determine which of the many alternative project proposals under consideration should be studied in depth" (ranked third) than was provided in their actual experience in planning (where the item ranked eighth). Similarly, respondents ranked fourth the desire to "meet with the Corps to establish the scope of water resource needs for the local community," but felt they had little opportunity to do so in practice (the item ranked second to the bottom of participation achieved). When asked if they believed that a public referendum on a project or a citizen oversight board to monitor the Corps would be productive, respondents replied in the negative.

Subgroup Comparisons

While it is instructive to see which modes of participation are being used most frequently and which are preferred, a summary index of the participants' overall evaluation of the participatory planning process is needed—an index that can be used to make comparisons among the five studies irrespective of the particular circumstances of each. For this purpose general questions were asked about the tone and substance of the planning sessions attended and about the extent to which participants felt the Corps had included them in a meaningful way. For instance, respondents were asked whether they agreed or disagreed with such statements as "The public meetings were useful because they gave me an opportunity to learn about the alternatives available for solving our local problems," and "The information about the proposed project provided by the Corps can easily be understood by the layman."

All the questionnaire items pertaining to the tone and substance of the participatory experience were then drawn together into an attitudinal scale labeled "evaluation of open planning." The mean response to all questions in the scale provides a convenient and reliable summary index of a respondent's general evaluation of the public participation program.

Table 7-2. *Attitudinal Scales, by Subgroups*

Subgroup	Mean scale score[a]		Number of responses
	Evaluation of open planning	Evaluation of proposed project	
Study			
Wildcat and San Pablo creeks flood control	3.22	3.06	34
Cleveland-Akron wastewater management	3.12	1.96	110
Middle Fork of Snoqualmie River flood control	3.06	2.26	98
Mississippi River–Gulf Outlet lock and connecting channel	2.73	1.98	82
Unit L-15 levee	2.71	2.28	111
Self-Identified Role			
Environmental or conservation	2.79	1.70	78
Concerned citizen	2.90	2.17	254
Business	3.19	2.51	56
Substantive Interest			
Environmental effects[b]	2.87	1.82	254
Direct personal benefit[c]	3.02	3.21	44

a. Based on a four-point scale.
b. Persons who scored 4 (on a four-point scale) on the item in part 6 of the survey questionnaire "I am concerned over the environmental effects of the proposed plan" but less than 4 on the item "My home (or other properties) was recently flooded and I may benefit from the proposed project."
c. Persons who scored 4 on the second item in note b above but less than 4 on the first item.

(For a more detailed discussion of the construction of attitudinal scales, see appendix B.)

With a summary measure of the participants' evaluation of the public participation experience in hand, it is possible to make several types of comparisons. Table 7-2 provides a three-dimensional comparison of the evaluation of participation, by study, by self-identified role, and by substantive interest.

The study-by-study comparison shows that, in general, participants gave higher ratings to the planning process in the studies of flood control on the Wildcat and San Pablo creeks, Cleveland-Akron wastewater management, and flood control on the Middle Fork of the Snoqualmie River than to the process in the L-15 and MR-GO studies. Apparently they felt that the Corps was more candid, that its proposals were more comprehensive and comprehensible, and that its neutrality was more evident in the first three cases.

The second part of table 7-2 reveals that these evaluations are based to some extent on the respondent's self-identified role; respondents were asked if they represented any group or if they were simply concerned citizens. Not surprisingly, those who saw themselves as representing the traditional ally of the Corps, the business community, rated the public participation programs on the average higher than did conservationists and environmentalists. Most of the persons (65 percent) attending the public planning sessions said they did so as concerned citizens rather than as representatives of business (14 percent) or as members of the environmental community (20 percent). Traditional interest groups obviously were represented, but the Corps' programs were available to a large number of ordinary citizens too. Or else respondents chose the most neutral category with which to identify themselves.

In the last part of table 7-2 a distinction is made between those who saw the possibility of direct personal gain and those concerned about the environment. By a slight margin, those who anticipated a direct benefit from the project rated the planning process higher, although the rating given by both groups was appreciable (2.87 and 3.02 respectively). Given the high marks for the planning process, how did the public evaluate the resulting project proposals? As indicated in earlier chapters and in the table, reactions were mixed.

The project evaluation scale was constructed from questionnaire items in much the same manner as the evaluation of the open planning measure, with one exception. In December 1973 and January 1974, when the questionnaire was administered, not all of the five Corps districts had announced their formal recommendation for a project. In the case of the Cleveland-Akron study, despite the district's preference for a comprehensive land disposal system, a series of options was presented from which political leaders could choose. Still, it seems clear that most of the participants had a good idea of what the Corps wanted and would probably recommend. Nevertheless, when asked to react to the Corps' recommended project proposal, some respondents were forced to rely on an educated guess as to what that proposal was going to be.

In evaluating the project, respondents were asked to use a four-point scale ranging from "important reason" (4) to "unimportant reason" (1) to indicate how pertinent several statements were to their involvement in the study. Two of the statements were diametrically opposed: "I am in favor of the project the Corps proposed" and "I oppose the proposed plan." The same respondent sometimes rated both as highly important, and we had to assume that the items either were misread or were answered mistakenly or that the respondent was confused. Whichever the case, 11 respondents gave both the negative and positive statement high ratings of 4 or 3, and were not included in any of the analyses involving the project evaluation. If, however, anyone gave a *low* rating to both items, we simply took this as an indication of indifference to the project, not confusion, and these answers were therefore retained.

A single aspect of project evaluation stands out: *Across the board the rating of proposed projects was lower than for the planning process.* Only those persons who saw a direct personal benefit in a Corps project gave higher marks to the project than to the process. It appears that while the bulk of the participants appreciated the Corps' effort to include the public in planning, they were not nearly so satisfied with substance. Not surprisingly, the disparity is most marked in the Cleveland-Akron study; respondents gave the planning process the second highest rating (3.12) of all the five studies but rated the Corps' preferred (though not formally recommended) project, the large-scale land disposal system, the lowest (1.96). Similarly the planning process in the Snoqualmie River study received a high rating, but the Corps' preferred modified dam and levee proposal received a low one.

The Corps' Evaluation

After the initial experimentation with new forms of public participation and open planning as exemplified in the several studies we examined, the Corps seemed to lose interest in aggressively pursuing the program. A planner from the Kansas City District, for example, said, "The L-15 planning effort was a great program, but we won't be trying it again." He reasoned that it was too costly, requiring too many man-hours for too little payoff, since it did not result in a buildable Corps project. There are exceptions to this view, of course, such as in the San Francisco and Seattle districts, where the creed of open planning is more ingrained and where environmentalists are strong. But the response of these districts to truly open and interactive planning is fairly unrepresentative of that of the other districts and of the headquarters in Washington, D.C.

The Corps' coolness to open and interactive planning is more evident in its deeds than in its words. It has not changed its regulations nor has it publicly changed its views. Yet neither has it pushed beyond the initial series of experimental open-planning efforts (for example, the Cleveland-Akron wastewater management study and the Snoqualmie River study) to ensure that such programs will be adopted agency-wide, nor has it institutionalized fishbowl planning or any other comprehensive method of open planning beyond the Seattle District. The downgrading of the program is also reflected in the changing role played by the Institute for Water Resources (IWR). Its Technical Assistance Program (TAP), so critical in taking the open-planning techniques to the field at the project-study level, has been terminated. In the TAP's place, the IWR now provides a series of in-house short courses in public participation. While these courses serve to sensitize agency personnel to the social and ecological ramifications of Corps activities and the importance of open planning, they do not seem to be much of a substitute for the innovative input of the TAP. Thus while broad public participation remains a part of all Corps project studies, it is not conducted with the same zeal and accorded the same importance as in the 1972–74 period.

This paring back of the program clearly is not due to the participants' cold reception of the initial wave of programs. As we have shown, their enthusiasm for the better efforts was impressive. Yet we believe that their failure to reach a consensus on the best project alternative and to rate highly the alternatives selected by the Corps explains the decline in the agency's enthusiasm for and wide use of the more innovative types of open-planning programs.

Admittedly, there are other conceivable reasons for the retreat: bureaucratic backlash within the agency, the tightening of budgets throughout the federal government, and the shifting political focus in the United States since 1973 away from conservation and environmental issues to solving the nation's energy problems.

On the basis of our research, however, the crucial factor seems to be simply that after several years of experimentation the Corps felt that the cost of the public participation programs was too great if they failed to achieve a consensus on such project proposals as the dam on the Middle Fork, the massive land treatment plan for Cleveland-Akron, or the combined plan for the L-15 levee area. By the summer of 1974 even the strongest proponents of the consensus-building approach were beginning to have doubts. Major General John W. Morris, director of Civil Works, after reiterating his well-known position that open planning was designed to achieve consensus, admitted that "maybe that simply isn't possible."[3] Without a local consensus, of course, the prospect of winning congressional approval of a project—the lifeblood of a public works agency—is virtually nil. Moreover, the failure to win a consensus contradicts all that the agency had been led to expect of public participation from the social psychologists and human relations experts who designed the program as well as from the program's in-house advocates. This, of course, begs the question of why the open-planning efforts failed to build the desired consensus.

Recall that the Corps adopted the strategy of participatory decisionmaking to accomplish three major objectives (see chapter 2): to help legitimize the Corps' role in water resource planning (the public relations objective); to provide the means by which the Corps could learn firsthand the full range of community needs and preferences (the information objective); and most important, to achieve conflict resolution. Thus the Corps was convinced that a positive setting in which all those affected could be brought into the decision process would generate a favorable public attitude toward the agency and would overcome resistance to its goals. Naturally that meant consensus on a water resource project that the Corps could develop.

The Corps Model of Open Planning

The flaw in the Corps' reasoning about open planning, which goes to the heart of its disappointment with the program, can be seen when the basic premise of its decisionmaking model is submitted to systematic examination. First it is necessary to set forth in an initial causal model the Corps' view of the state of affairs in the late 1960s and early 1970s. This is provided in part I of figure 7-1. In this and subsequent figures

A = evaluation of proposed project,
B = evaluation of experience in public participation program,
C = orientation toward Corps,
D = citizen power,
E = extent of environmental concern.

The three components of part I of figure 7-1, of course, represent a simplification, but they depict the factors pertinent to the introduction of participatory decisionmaking: a vocal group of citizens with environ-

3. Interview with Morris, July 25, 1974.

Figure 7-1. *The Corps' Conception of Open Planning*[a]

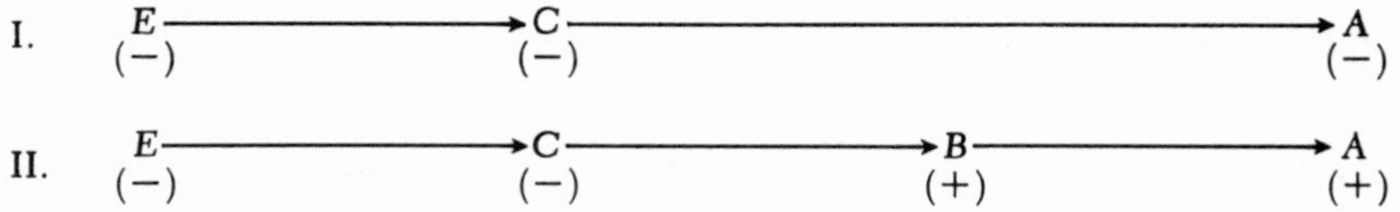

I. E ————————→ C ——————————————————→ A
    $(-)$　　　　　　　　 $(-)$　　　　　　　　　　　　　　　 $(-)$

II. E ————————→ C ———————————→ B ————————→ A
    $(-)$　　　　　　　　 $(-)$　　　　　　　 $(+)$　　　　　　 $(+)$

a. The sign above each factor (see text for definitions) indicates the Corps' view of how support for a project would be affected positively or negatively by that factor.

mental concerns was distressed with the prevailing lack of ecological sensitivity and the growth mentality among their fellow citizens and in government agencies.[4] This placed them in conflict with the traditional mode of thinking and activities of the Corps and led to negative evaluations of Corps' projects.

The model depicted in part II of figure 7-1 shows the anticipated effect of adding participative decisionmaking to the process. It would not necessarily change concerns or orientations toward the Corps, at least not in the short run. It would change evaluations of specific Corps projects, however, and over time should bring about greater satisfaction with the agency per se and public cooperation in accomplishing the goals agreed upon in the participative decision process.

An Expanded Model of Open Planning

In a number of ways the context within which the Corps was attempting to implement the participation thesis was different from those described by the program's proponents in social psychology and industry. It was not an experiment whose substantive outcome would be of little or no consequence to the participants; those who made the effort to attend the Corps' planning sessions could be expected to come with very definite objectives. Nor could it be assumed that the participants concurred on who should be the ultimate judge. They were not members of

4. Although environmentalism is used as the measure of concern in the model, environmentalists are not the only segment of the community interested in Corps projects. If those with commercial or flood protection or other concerns were to be inserted in the model, their orientations toward the Corps and their evaluation of planning and of projects could be expected to differ from those with environmental concerns. A number of interests in a community can usually be counted on to support Corps activities. Their inclusion in participation planning, it could reasonably be assumed in light of the participation thesis, would simply enhance their positive image of the Corps and enthusiasm for its projects.

Figure 7-2. *An Expanded Model of Open Planning*[a]

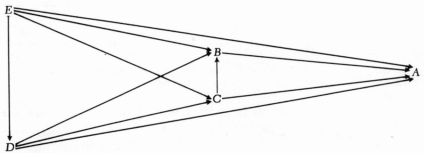

a. Symbols are defined in the text.

the organization and did not feel bound by its assumed authority in rendering ultimate decisions on water resource projects or in determining general agency policy. This is in contrast to experimental settings wherein the participants are usually indifferent to the usurpation of authority by the experimenter, or to the industrial setting, where workers, although given a voice, seldom challenge the inherent right of management to make final decisions.[5]

These differences probably mean that the linkage between the participative experience, B, and project evaluation, A, was not as direct as the Corps might have wished. Involvement in the planning of a project may increase credibility and trust in the agency. Participants may develop an effective rapport with the engineers and may respect the Corps' earnest efforts to reach a consensus. But the greater the extent to which participants enter the planning process with fundamental disagreements over goals and objectives, the less likely a consensus on the proposed project will be. When views are polarized from the outset, the best efforts at compromise and consensus-building fail. Indeed, in extremely divisive situations, if the Corps fails to side with one of the contending groups and attempts to find some middle ground or compromise position, no one may accept its plan.

Figure 7-2, an expanded model of open planning, shows a multiplicity

5. For excellent discussions of the limits of the participative decisionmaking thesis, see Frederick C. Mosher, "Participation and Reorganization," in Frederick C. Mosher, ed., *Governmental Reorganizations: Cases and Commentary* (Bobbs-Merrill for the Inter-University Case Program, 1967); and Sidney Verba, *Small Groups and Political Behavior: A Study of Leadership* (Princeton University Press, 1961).

of direct and indirect linkages leading to A. In essence it is the Corps model, with two important modifications. First, citizen power, D—the propensity of participants to want more decisionmaking powers delegated to citizens—has been included as an independent causal factor affecting the succeeding factors in the planning process. In an era when citizens demand a direct say in the decisions of public agencies, this factor could be expected to stand out as an independent one, particularly influencing the evaluation of the Corps' planning program and the underlying predispositions toward the agency.

Second, when the participants' interests are likely to result in incompatible objectives, participation per se will not bring about generalized support for a plan. Thus the linkage to A is assumed to run along both BA and CA. Consequently, one cannot assume, as did the Corps, that a positive experience in planning will in itself result in a positive evaluation of a proposed project.

Both the Corps model and the expanded model lack feedback loops that, if included, would add a dynamic component. They might indicate, for example, that changes in the kinds of projects the Corps undertakes should eventually bring about changes in the public's attitude toward the Corps, or that changes in Corps planning should eventually dampen demands for citizen power, and so on. They are not included because it is assumed that for a given episode of project planning the process is static, with orientations and evaluations remaining fairly constant. And since the Corps' studies examined in chapters 4, 5, and 6 are single episodes, information on long-term feedback is not available.

A Comparison of Models

A comparison of the two models is made possible through the use of data collected in our survey of the participants in the five project studies. The measures of "evaluation of proposed project," A, and "evaluation of experience in public participation program," B, were introduced earlier in the chapter. Briefly, the remaining components of the models are measured as described below (see appendix B for details).

From the battery of survey items that focused on the reasons for participating in the planning process, three types of participants were identified: those primarily concerned with the environmental effects of proposed projects, those with personal property or commercial and economic interests, and those who appear to have been motivated out of curiosity about the new forms of public decisionmaking being introduced by the Corps (that is, the civic-minded). Taking the mean of a respondent's ratings across all the items that distinguish a given type offered one good measure of his level of concern. These means, for example, provide a measure for comparing the extent to which the respondents' involvement was based on concern with environmental issues or on their own economic well-being. There is little overlap among the three concerns: the correlation between the environmental and the economic benefit measures a negigible 0.05; that between the environmental and civic-minded, 0.12, is somewhat higher yet still minimal; and that between economic interest and civic-minded is 0.07.[6]

In examining models of the planning process, environmentalism, E, will be used as the measure of concern because of the importance of environmentalists to the Corps' efforts. Moreover, preliminary analysis showed that using either of the other two concerns had virtually no effect on the structure of the Corps model or the expanded model.

The component of the expanded model not considered in the Corps' model—or in prior applications of the participation thesis—is the propensity of citizens to want to share authority in public policy decisions. As will become evident, the greater this propensity, the less likely it is that the public will be satisfied with any decisionmaking process that leaves the major decisions in the hands of a government agency. This component is measured by items that statistically cluster together into a "citizen power" scale, D, such as "Citizens should have a greater voice in the planning of water resource projects" and the inverse of "The decisions over which water resource projects are to be built should be left in the hands of the experts."

C is measured by a series of questionnaire items that cluster in a measure of "orientation toward Corps." The items ask respondents about their underlying impressions of the Corps. They show that if one believes that "the Corps is making an honest effort to reconcile the many community interests," he is also likely to believe that "the opinions of citizens greatly influence the actions taken by the Corps," while disagreeing with the statement that the Corps "goes through the motions of consulting citizens but it is not sincerely interested in obtaining their views."

Before proceeding, we should repeat a point made earlier. Asking re-

6. The level of significance of the three correlations is 0.09, 0.01, and 0.17 respectively. All correlations reported here and in the following analysis are calculated by the Pearson product-moment method.

spondents to judge a proposed project before it is formally announced obviously presents some problems in interpreting the results, especially since the official recommendation may differ from what is expected, and this could alter a respondent's project evaluation. For the test of the two models, however, the issue is immaterial. If the planning effort was perceived to be a positive one, then under the assumption of the participation thesis the respondent would approve of and be committed to what he believed to be the project proposal, whether or not the recommended project had been formally announced. With operational measures of A through E, it is now possible to return to the discussion of the adequacy of the Corps model of the planning process.

The Corps felt that it could involve the public in a successful participatory planning program. This proved to be the case. The scale score mean of B (evaluation of experience in public participation program) is equal to that of E (extent of environmental concern) and higher than all the other scales. On the four-point ladder the mean for $B = 2.93$, whereas $A = 2.20$, $C = 2.74$, $D = 2.78$, and $E = 2.94$. Evidently the public regarded the public meetings, workshops, and other activities as constituting a comprehensive and sincere effort at including citizens in the planning process.

Yet this is only part of what the Corps expected. It also assumed that the greater one's environmental concern, the more antipathy toward the agency, and that this was in turn related to project evaluation. But the Corps was persuaded that interjecting participatory decisionmaking into the process would produce a positive evaluation of agency projects. These assumptions will be examined first through the use of simple correlation coefficients between the model components, followed by a path analysis of the model's major causal linkages.

The correlation coefficients of adjacent components of the Corps model shown in figure 7-3 reveal some anticipated findings and one rather surprising finding.[7] As expected, part I of figure 7-3 shows that the CA relationship is strong (0.50). If citizens hold the Corps in low regard, this will be reflected in project evaluation. Part II also shows that the BA relationship is strong (0.42), as expected, though the CB relationship is even stronger (0.77).

If it is true, as the Corps assumed, that those with environmental con-

---

7. Arrows have been deleted from figures 7-3 and 7-4, which show only measures of association, to avoid confusion with the earlier discussions of the models, where arrows are used to identify an inferred causal path.

Figure 7-3. *Correlation Coefficients of the Corps Model of Open Planning*[a]

I. $E \underset{(-0.09)}{\text{------}} C \underset{0.50}{\text{-----------------}} A$ $(R = 0.523; R^2 = 0.274)$

II. $E \underset{(-0.09)}{\text{------}} C \underset{0.77}{\text{-----------}} B \underset{0.42}{\text{----------}} A$ $(R = 0.531; R^2 = 0.282)$

a. Symbols are defined in the text. Coefficients are significant at the 0.01 level, except those in parentheses.

cerns hold the Corps in low regard, then there should be a high negative correlative between the measures of environmental concern and of orientation toward the agency. Contrary to this expectation, the *EC* relationship is a negligible −0.09. Although the sign is negative and thus in the direction expected, the relationship is so low as to be meaningless. There seems to be no *direct* link between concern with environmental issues and attitudes toward the Corps, a point that will be reconsidered in the path analysis.[8]

Simple correlation coefficients provide a good overview of relationships between model components but do not indicate to what extent participatory decisionmaking has a *direct* effect on project evaluation. The useful statistic here is R^2—the square of the multiple correlation coefficient —which gives the proportion of the variation in the dependent variable, *A*, accounted for by one or more of the independent variables, *B* through *E*. R^2 for the initial Corps model in part I of figure 7-3 is 0.274; that is, *E* and *C* account for approximately 28 percent of the variation in *A*. What does *B* add to this? With *B* included, R^2 rises to 0.282, a minuscule increase of 0.008. In other words, when environmentalism and orientation toward the Corps are accounted for, evaluation of the participatory experience adds little to the explanation of the variation in project evaluation.

An examination of the expanded model provides equally interesting results. Like the Corps model, the expanded model assumes a direct *EC* link but also that the relationship is mediated in part by *D*. Like the Corps model, too, it assumes that the all-important *BA* link exists, but that in

8. A similar result followed when the same analysis was run on a subset of 78 self-identified environmental group representatives (in contrast to those persons with environmental concerns). The correlation between the "environmental concern" measure of the environmental representatives and "orientation toward Corps" was a mere −0.14, with a significance level of 0.11.

Figure 7-4. *Correlation Coefficients of the Expanded Model*[a]

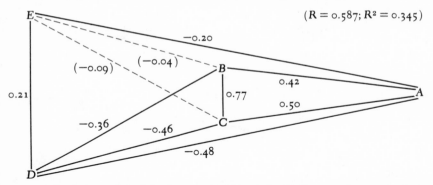

$(R = 0.587; R^2 = 0.345)$

a. Symbols are defined in the text. Coefficients are significant at the 0.01 level, except those in parentheses.

addition there are direct links between *E*, *D*, and *A*. The complex nature of the relationships is borne out in the correlation coefficients in figure 7-4.

It appears that the Corps is correct, after all, in expecting the antipathy of those with environmental concerns. It is just that negative feelings about the agency are filtered through and exacerbated by belief in citizen power. This is indicated by the positive *ED* relationship, followed by the negative *DC* one.

The failure of the very effective public participation efforts to carry over into project evaluation is explained to some extent by the expanded model. Yes, there is an appreciable *BA* relationship, but *CA* is even stronger. It may be, therefore, that despite the participants' experience in the planning programs, their *initial attitude* toward the agency may dictate project evaluation. The extent to which this occurs will be returned to in a moment.

Figure 7-4 also helps to clear up the maze of probable linkages hypothesized by the model. The negligible *EB* and *EC* relationships eliminate them as meaningful links and thus will be considered no further.

With the weakest links eliminated from the model, it is appropriate to ask which of the remaining relationships are nonspurious. Path analysis provides the answer.[9] The technique determines the unique effect of each

9. For two general nonmathematical introductions to path analysis and causal modeling see Hubert M. Blalock, Jr., *Causal Inferences in Nonexperimental Research* (University of North Carolina Press, 1961); and Herbert B. Asher, *Causal Modeling*

Figure 7-5. *Path Coefficients of the Expanded Model*[a]

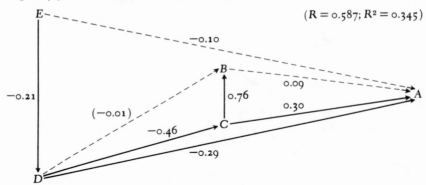

$(R = 0.587; R^2 = 0.345)$

a. Symbols are defined in the text. Coefficients are significant at the 0.01 level except those in parentheses.

independent causal factor on the dependent variable (evaluation of proposed project, A). In essence the relationship between each independent variable and the dependent variable is calculated while holding all others constant. Each arrow in figure 7-5 represents the presumed causal linkage or paths of causal influence remaining in the expanded model. Through the use of standardized regression coefficients, the strength of each path is estimated.

The picture that emerges is somewhat surprising in light of the correlations in figure 7-4. *DB* reduces almost to zero, leaving *C* as the only direct factor influencing *B*. More important, *D* and *C* clearly emerge as the two equally dominant determinants of *A*, whereas *B* and *E*, which correlate moderately well with *A* (0.42 and −0.20 respectively), are

(Sage Publications, 1976). The four basic assumptions of path analysis are that variables are clearly defined as dependent or independent; that the relationships between variables are additive and linear; that other causes of each of the variables in the system are uncorrelated with the other variables in the system; and that the causation being assumed is unidimensional. See Donald J. McCrone and C. F. Cnudde, "Toward a Communications Theory of Democratic Political Development: A Causal Model," in Samuel A. Kirkpatrick, ed., *Quantitative Analysis of Political Data* (Merrill, 1974), p. 208. It is important to note that the calculation of path coefficients does not reveal the causal structure but provides a technique for assessing the assumed causal relations. The specification of the causal flow within the models must be a priori to the application of the path analysis technique.

shown to have no discernible direct impact.[10] The critical variables turn out to be "orientation toward Corps" and "citizen power," not "evaluation of public participation program" or "environmental concerns."

One final question remains. Does the addition of D in the expanded model add to the explained variance in A? Recall that with E, C, and B in the model as the independent variables, $R^2 = 0.282$. Including D increases R^2 to 0.345. While there is no hard and fast rule for judging this difference, it seems to us to be a significant amount. Belief in citizen power does have some independent effect on one's evaluation of a Corps proposed project.

Summary and Conclusion

It should now be clear why the Army Corps of Engineers has reduced the open and interactive planning program that began in the early 1970s. In the tradition of various social psychologists and organizational theorists, it assumed that a well-intentioned, positive, open-planning process would result directly in the participants' greater satisfaction with the agency; that this would in turn foster greater congruence on goals between the individual participants and the agency; and that more effective implementation of the agency's goals would be facilitated. Instead, the participants in the five studies examined clearly distinguished between the planning activities of the Corps, with which they were by and large satisfied, and the Corps' goals, which they rated relatively low. This lack of carry-over from satisfaction with the decisionmaking process to the evaluation of project proposals appears to have baffled and disappointed the Corps.

The failure of the program to produce the anticipated carry-over can be explained by two factors. First is the Corps' uncritical acceptance of the participation thesis. The Corps assumed, at least implicitly, that its environment was analogous to that of the experimental and industrial set-

10. There is no established rule for determining the point below which the influence of a path is considered negligible. Nevertheless, the paths from B (0.09) and E (−0.10) are sufficiently weak for us to assert that they have no discernible impact. See Fred N. Kerlinger and Elazar J. Pedhazur, *Multiple Regression in Behavioral Research* (Holt, Rinehart, and Winston, 1973), p. 318.

tings in which the efficacy of the participation thesis had been demonstrated. It assumed that if all members of the group, defined by the Corps as all people interested in a particular water resource project, were brought together in the decisionmaking process, an identification with the group and the group's goals (which the Corps believed would be congruent with its goals) would result. It assumed that the participants in the decisionmaking process of a public agency would accept the Corps' authority. The Corps further assumed that the kind of esprit de corps generated among the members of the small groups in which the participation thesis had been demonstrated could be replicated in its planning process. There were numerous participants, however, most from outside the agency, and they were therefore far less susceptible to pressures to conform to the group goal and adopt a team spirit.

The differences between the Corps' environment and those in which the participation thesis had been successful are crucial. Most participants came to the Corps' planning program with strong views about the substantive issues under consideration. Many felt the need for a greater sharing of responsibilities between them and the Army engineers in the decisions that affected their lives. Their substantive concerns, belief in sharing responsibilities, and general predisposition toward the Corps all affected their evaluation of the proposed projects. These factors were operative despite the rapport that built up between the participants and the engineers and despite the appreciation of the engineers' efforts to open the decisionmaking process. In short, the participants in the five studies judged the project proposals far more by what they thought of the Corps and by what they wanted the agency to do or not do than by their reactions to the planning process through which the proposals were developed.

Second, and related to the first factor, many of the participants in the five studies (particularly the environmentalists) also began with negative attitudes toward the Corps. They believed the Corps was not especially sympathetic to their concerns and that they had little chance of influencing the agency's behavior. Therefore, despite the open nature of the planning program, their initial low evaluation of the Corps made their low evaluation of the Corps' proposed projects almost a foregone conclusion.

Still, it is not unreasonable to assume that "evaluation of planning" and "orientation toward Corps" are interactive. Thus the positive evaluation of planning that has been expressed by the participants in the studies examined ought to produce feedback and in turn have a positive effect on their attitudes toward the Corps. We believe that if the public could experience more open planning programs, it would eventually have a higher regard for the agency.

"Evaluation of project" and "orientation toward Corps" are also most likely interactive. Thus to the extent that the Corps modifies the nature of its project proposals to accommodate the demands of environmentalists and its other critics, this too would produce feedback and would positively affect attitudes toward the agency, probably even more than a continuation of open planning would.

If there is one lesson to be learned from the studies examined, it is that favor cannot be won for old project ideas or even some innovative ones (such as massive land treatment for sewage sludge disposal) simply by undertaking elaborate open-planning programs. But if the Corps viewed open planning as a long-term educational process for both itself and the public, it could strengthen support for the agency and its proposals. As long as it views open planning as a short-term strategy for coalescing divergent factions around existing missions and projects, however, disappointment is inevitable.

CHAPTER EIGHT

An Appraisal of Organizational Change in the Corps

THAT A PERFORMANCE gap existed in public agencies whose activities directly affected the general environment was self-evident by the late 1960s. They were out of step with those vocal elements of the public who were championing environmental issues. For the Army Corps of Engineers, closing this performance gap meant a broad-based assault on traditional projects, missions, and procedures.

We focused our study on the Corps because it appeared to be reacting to demands for change in a fashion uncharacteristic of large and powerful bureaucracies. Indeed, in the early 1970s the Corps appeared to be responding to the spirit of the demands for more open decisionmaking and for heightened environmental sensitivity much more than its bureaucratic counterparts were. Environmentalism was aimed primarily at changing the substance of the Corps' activities, in making significant changes in the nature of its projects. The open-planning and citizen participation efforts were directed more at procedural changes, at including all interested and affected parties in the decision process. In practice, of course, there was a good deal of overlap among the groups calling for change. The emphasis on participation, while not specifically project oriented, was seen as an indirect but necessary means of attaining a greater degree of environmental awareness: once the environmentalists were allowed to participate in decisions, those decisions would be more likely to reflect their views.

Conceivably, the goals of open planning could be met without achieving more environmentally sensitive projects. Likewise, environmentally sensitive projects might be developed without an extensive public participation effort. In practice, however, these two new goals were developed simultaneously.

Judging Change in the Corps

To gauge the degree of change in the Corps, four criteria of organizational change were established in chapter 1 that we believe are applicable, not only to the Corps, but to most public agencies: (1) changes in organizational objectives; (2) changes in internal structure; (3) changes in output or performance; and (4) changes in the decisionmaking process. The remainder of this chapter is devoted to a summary of and conclusions about each of these four points.

New Objectives

As we show in chapter 2, the Corps responded to new demands by calling for dramatic departures: setting new objectives of environmental awareness and instituting open planning. The greatest push in this direction came from the Office of the Chief of Engineers in both publicizing the departure and charting the new course of action. New agency rules and guidelines were often issued before, and often went beyond, those required by the National Environmental Policy Act (NEPA) of 1969 and the President's Council on Environmental Quality.

The pronouncement of the agency's new mission and the issuance of implementation guides called for a substantial change in the organization. This came very much as a surprise to the Corps' environmental opponents as well as to its traditional allies. We consider it fair, therefore, to judge the first criterion as having been met.

Environmental Considerations and Structural Changes

What of the second criterion—reorganization to meet the new challenge? Several conclusions can be reached regarding the Corps' response to the new environmental mandate in terms of structural changes. To begin with, there were and are significant constraints on the type of changes implied by NEPA and the environmental mandate of the chief of engineers. The very nature of the agency's civil works program, according to some environmental groups and agencies, is opposed to what they perceive as sound environmental policy or sound resource management. In its civil works role the Corps has been and continues to be a construction-oriented agency whose operations have been intended to further the goals of economic development.[1]

Since 1970, however, the agency has had two primary objectives. The first continues to be economic development. Major General John W. Morris, the director of the civil works program, reaffirmed this goal at a ground-breaking ceremony in 1974:

> The future looks bright and the Corps of Engineers is on the threshold of a "new era of dynamic growth in water resources development. . . ."
> I have a sense now of a new direction and a feeling that new initiatives are developing. The recent Water Resources Development Act of 1974 is a strong indication that our Congress is working very hard and fast to move along our power projects—projects which strengthen our economic base, such as navigation, and highly justified damage-prevention flood control actions.[2]

The second goal of the agency now is environmental quality. The two co-exist uneasily. Of the latter objective, the director of civil works said that although some people believe otherwise, the Corps does not take lightly its responsibility for changing the path of nature.

> During our studies, our planning and designing, we listen carefully to the voices of opposition, regardless of how emotional they may be, because it is in the adversary arena where views are exchanged, knowledge is gained and compromises are reached. . . . The right way is to balance actions; consider all sides; and make decisions based upon those considerations which are the greatest benefit to the most people.[3]

Insofar as environmental quality is now a primary objective of the

1. Several studies, however, have challenged the long-standing belief that the Corps' traditional dams and reservoirs add to regional economic productivity. See Charles B. Garrison, "A Case Study of the Local Economic Impact of Reservoir Recreation," *Journal of Leisure Research*, vol. 6 (Winter 1974), pp. 7–19; Bernard D. Shanks, "Missouri River Development Policy and Community Development" (paper presented at the Eleventh American Water Resources Conference, Baton Rouge, Louisiana, November 1975); and Robert H. Haveman and Paula Stephan, "White Elephants, Waterways, and the Transportation Act of 1966," in Robert H. Haveman and Robert D. Hamrin, *The Political Economy of Federal Policy* (Harper and Row, 1973).

2. U.S. Department of the Army, Corps of Engineers, Office of the Chief of Engineers, "Future 'Bright' for Corps of Engineer Water Resource Projects, Maj. Gen. John Morris Tells Tenn-Tom Ground-Breaking Ceremony," news release, May 9, 1974, p. 1.

3. Ibid.

agency, the question then is how and in what ways the Corps changed in order to accommodate the new policy. Has this goal really been given equal status with economic development?

The data in chapter 3 on internal reorganization indicate a considerable effort to create what might be called the infrastructure, or organizational capability, necessary for the incorporation of this new policy within the agency. The Corps has performed well in bringing in new personnel with nonengineering backgrounds.[4] In 1969 there were approximately 75 "environmentalists" in the entire agency; in 1977 there were about 575.[5] Advisory boards composed of planning and environmental professionals and a range of interest group representatives have also been widely used. And unlike the situation before 1970, all the agency's offices now have a distinguishable unit whose primary purpose is to provide environmental input in the agency's planning process. Thus it seems clear that the Corps has made a serious attempt to cope with environmental considerations by altering the organization's formal structure. When the agency's environmental capabilities in the 1960s are compared with those of today, the Corps must be given high marks for reorganization. Yet the capabilities for meeting the agency's traditional missions are still dominant; environmental quality is an auxiliary function of the agency.

Substantive Change: Preliminary Indications

In assessing how well the Corps met the third criterion of organizational change, the important question is what effect personnel and organiational changes had on Corps projects. Are Corps projects any different (or significantly different) from what they would have been without a verbal and organizational commitment to environmental goals? At least two factors make such evaluations difficult, but they should not prevent us from offering as objective an assessment as possible.

First, the nature of the Corps' civil works program makes it difficult to determine with complete certainty whether structural and personnel changes have produced changes in the agency's projects. Most of the

4. Richard A. Liroff also reached this conclusion in *A National Policy for the Environment: NEPA and Its Aftermath* (Indiana University Press, 1976), p. 117. It would be interesting to do a cross-agency study of hiring patterns that were the result of NEPA requirements. To our knowledge, such data are not available, but our impression—based on experience with other resource agencies—is that the Corps has probably done more in this respect than most other federal agencies.
5. Data obtained from the Office of the Chief of Engineers, Washington, D.C.

agency's work load at the time our study was conducted was composed of projects already under way and in various stages of completion. On the average, it takes six years to complete the planning of a project, and construction may take another ten years.[6] Thus the effect of new programs and methods on *ongoing* work is of necessity minimal, and any changes that do result from internal or external pressures will usually be marginal. For example, evaluating the extent of change in an ongoing program, such as the study of the Mississippi River–Gulf Outlet (MR-GO) lock and channel described in chapter 4, is not only methodologically difficult but is likely to show that changes are marginal.

Second, it is very difficult to make a causal connection between personnel and structural changes and specific changes in general agency policies or specific projects.[7] Rather, it must usually be inferred that when a change in the former (for example, the addition of personnel with nonengineering backgrounds) is followed in a reasonable period of time by a change in the latter (for example, the adoption of nonstructural methods of flood control), that one causes the other. While this is not a substitute for a rigorous empirical demonstration of the linkages involved, it is the only strategy currently available in studying change in complex organizations.

With these qualifications in mind, we offer some examples of changes in ongoing projects that were identified by agency personnel as direct results of the commitment to an environmental policy. These examples, unlike the more dramatic ones given in chapters 2, 4, 5, and 6, illustrate the more typical kinds of changes that have occurred as a result of the new policy.

To begin with, few Corps projects in the final planning stages, if any, have been completely halted as a result of NEPA or the chief's new environmental mandate.[8] A considerable number of projects, however, have been delayed or modified, and the agency has kept a record of them. Proj-

6. See Robert David Wolff, "Involving the Public and the Hierarchy in Corps of Engineers' Survey Investigations," Report EEP-45, Program in Engineering–Economic Planning (Stanford University, November 1971), fig. 2-2, p. 30.

7. H. Paul Friesema and Paul J. Culhane speak of Freidrick's "law of anticipated reaction" in agencies that makes a direct linkage in structural and output change difficult. See "Social Impacts, Politics, and the Environmental Impact Statement Process," *Natural Resources Journal*, vol. 16 (April 1976), p. 355.

8. One Corps officer stated categorically that "no project had been stopped as a result of NEPA."

ect modification is the largest category. By May 1, 1973, 175 projects had been modified as a result of NEPA.[9] In the interviews conducted at district and division offices, it was impossible to explore the details of every project modification, but we discussed project changes or halts with Corps personnel in each office.

Personnel in the San Francisco District used the Sonoma Creek project to illustrate the effect of environmental concern on project planning. This project was designed with an "overflow bypass" feature; instead of channelizing the creek, sufficient acreage was left on either side to allow the creek to flow over into greenbelt areas during periods of flooding. The project has been recommended for construction with the bypass feature. Thus, this seems to be a good example of the incorporation of nonstructural features into a project. (The debate about structural versus nonstructural solutions to the problem of flooding is, of course, central to questions of environmental policy within the agency.)

In St. Louis two projects were singled out as having been affected by environmental concern. The first, the Meramec Park Lake project, was a source of frustration because it had been bogged down for so long in litigation even though the agency had made significant modifications to meet the environmentalists' opposition. The second was the Maline Creek project, which, a district employee explained, is "significantly different from what it would have been ten years ago. First we planned a totally structural project. Then we turned around 180 degrees and designed a totally environmentally oriented plan. Finally we've ended up somewhere in between." The Corps' plan for Maline Creek, now characterized as an open sewer running through St. Louis, is to clean it up and make it an attractive recreational feature of the inner city. As of 1978, however, this project was still in the planning stage, having been returned to the St. Louis District for further work after a review by the Board of Engineers for Rivers and Harbors revealed a number of design problems.

Agency people in the Chicago District mentioned the Little Calumet River project as an example of environmental concern. When the project was first authorized for study in the early 1960s, it was for flood control and channel-dredging only. In 1965, however, the study authorization added the benefits of recreation and small boat navigation, inclusions

9. U.S. Department of the Army, Corps of Engineers, Directorate of Civil Works, "Environmental Program," EP 1105-2-500 (June 1973), p. A-1.

that Corps personnel felt significantly changed the nature of the project. In addition, while the Little Calumet River project is still a channelization project, it features a 22-mile-long greenbelt adjacent to the river. A further change was that the agency reduced the number of relocations necessary to carry out the project so that fewer people would be adversely affected. All these modifications were perceived as being related to environmental planning and as representing positive changes in project planning.

A growing problem to the Corps in this age of environmental concern is what to do with the "dredge spoil" that is the result of the agency's dredging activity. Many disposal sites are simply full or are filling up. In this connection, the Detroit District Office mentioned the Point Mouillee disposal facility project, where the agency is experimenting with the possibility of turning what was once considered waste into "environmental profit." In this particular project, the original idea was to build a "metro park" on top of the fill, or spoil. But that idea met with considerable opposition from certain groups in the Detroit vicinity, and so it was dropped. The district then turned to the idea of creating marsh islands, or wetlands, out of the spoil, to the delight of conservationists. The Norfolk District is doing likewise, and also cited its wetlands program in connection with environmental change.

A final illustration of project changes in ongoing Corps studies is a levee project that has been under discussion at the Baltimore District. Levees generally consist of cement walls that are not very attractive and that may block the view of the river for nearby residents. Thus in designing a levee project for Harrisburg, Pennsylvania, the district decided that instead of a three-foot-high cement wall along the river bank fronting the city, it would try designing a "flip wall" with partitions that could be raised and lowered as necessary so that no permanent structure would detract from a historical site along the waterfront or block views of the river. Under this plan, of course, in the event of a flood the agency would have to make sure that all partitions were up and that they would hold. But after considering the pros and cons of a flip wall, it was decided that it would be more practical to reroute the levee around the historical site in question.

These examples of project modifications clearly indicate that changes in ongoing agency programs or projects are at the margin. Meanwhile, battles still rage over many Corps projects, such as the massive Tennessee-Tombigbee waterway and others cited earlier.[10]

Although ongoing projects changed only slightly during the period of our investigation, a substantial effort was made to develop new and more socially and environmentally acceptable programs. The studies discussed in chapters 4, 5, and 6 show how the agency initiated extensive planning efforts for the first time in the fields of wastewater management and non-structural and mixed approaches to floodplain management. It has also shifted much of its attention to the large population centers through its comprehensive urban water use plans. To this list should be added the agency's newly expanded planning responsibilities for shoreline protection. Aggressive action in this program in at least one noteworthy instance has caused a complete reversal of allegiances; developers began lobbying Congress to curtail the Corps' power and environmentalists began fighting to sustain it.[11]

These are promising indications that the agency is translating the environmental mission into new programs. Yet with the long lead time necessary for the planning of Corps projects and the ever present tendency to return to the traditional pattern of operations, it is yet to be seen whether the Corps will want or be able to continue incorporating environmental considerations in its construction activities. The bulk of projects being authorized for construction as of 1976, for example, were traditional navigation and flood protection projects.[12] Moreover, the Corps still has an extensive backlog of previously authorized projects. This situation is of considerable concern to the environmental community's leading "Corps watcher," Brent Blackwelder of the Environmental Policy Center. In an interview he argued that despite the agency's recent efforts, its sunk costs are proving to be an overwhelming barrier to change.

Today we can clobber them on new projects which are poorly conceived. . . . The problem is with all the old boondoggles authorized by Congress back in

10. See Don Moser, "Dig They Must: The Army Engineers—Securing Allies and Acquiring Enemies," *Smithsonian* (December 1976), pp. 40–51; and Karen Elliot House, "Selling of a Dam: Tie between Congress, Engineer Corps Leads to Dubious Projects," *Wall Street Journal,* June 17, 1977.

11. See Don Moser, "Mangrove Island Is Reprieved by Army Engineers," *Smithsonian,* January 1977, pp. 68–77.

12. See Water Resources Development Act of 1976 (90 Stat. 2917).

the Forties and Fifties which are still not built. The Corps clings to them like a bulldog. These projects never die, they just fall into a coma for a while, then get revived. Our fight now is with all these old dogs.[13]

Who wins the fight is up to the Corps. Will it make sufficient compromises to mollify project opponents? Or will it battle to the end on each old project? Only the former strategy, of course, will result in a substantial change in substantive output in the years to come.

Decisionmaking: Experimentation in Open Planning

Political legitimacy in a participatory era requires open planning, as does the charting of new environmental directions in a traditionally construction-oriented agency. Only through open planning can the necessary constant pressure on an agency be sustained. Thus the degree of openness of the decisionmaking process is our fourth criterion of organizational change. As illustrated in the detailed discussions of the Wildcat and San Pablo creeks flood control study, the Cleveland-Akron wastewater management study, and the Middle Fork of the Snoqualmie River flood control study, the Corps has ample capability in this area. The best example, in our estimation, is the Seattle District's "fishbowl" planning.

Fishbowl planning has general applicability. The Seattle District demonstrated in actual practice that such planning can be adapted to the study of all water resource problems. It permits the expression of divergent views, alternative problem definitions, and numerous and nontraditional possible solutions. Citizen groups, as well as the Corps, can participate through fishbowl planning, not only in suggesting ideas, but in conducting workshops and in outlining alternatives. Through the wide dissemination of the brochure that is a part of every fishbowl study, the entire evolution of the planning effort is kept in full public view. Each alternative is presented along with its pros and cons, and the persons or groups supporting and opposing each alternative are identified in the brochure.

Admittedly, fishbowl planning does not achieve the sharing of formal power between citizens and the Corps that some advocates of public participation in bureaucratic decisionmaking would like to see. The fishbowl process permits citizens to advise, recommend, express their views, and seek to persuade the Corps to adopt their preferred position. It is the Corps, however, that in the end must decide among the various alterna-

13. Moser, "Dig They Must," p. 45.

tives and make its recommendations. Protecting this line of authority is necessary if the U.S. system of representative government and the delegation of authority by Congress to federal agencies is to be preserved. Congress has not established the Corps, or for that matter any other federal agency, so that it might in turn hand over its powers to a select number of citizens who happen to express intense preferences on a given project proposal. The Corps, like any bureaucracy, is expected to bring its own expertise to bear on a problem, albeit in light of the best available information about the preferences of contending factions. To delegate authority to citizens would entirely negate the role of bureaucracy as "expert." Fishbowl planning preserves this role for the Corps, while at the same time affording citizens the opportunity to *contribute* to agency decisionmaking. It provides for as open a decisionmaking process as is practicable without actually making private parties decisionmakers within the agency.

But irrespective of the form of open planning adopted in the studies we examined, the effect such planning had on changing the Corps' decisions was appreciable. Although there was no one-to-one correspondence between the degree of openness of the planning process and the resulting project plan, whenever a substantial effort was made (this would include all but the MR-GO study), a greater balance clearly existed between environmental and economic considerations. Further, the Corps developed a greater appreciation of the diversity of interests in the communities in which it operates. The open planning process enabled new and previously ignored interests to directly press their demands and in several instances to contribute previously overlooked alternatives. In short, in the cases examined, open planning served its function in the change process of the Corps. Thus we feel it appropriate to rate the change in decisionmaking that resulted from the chief's pronouncement of a more open decision process as substantial, *where adopted*. Unfortunately, the really comprehensive open planning efforts of the sort reported here have been limited in number. Overall, then, the change in the decision process has been mixed at the field level, depending on both district initiatives and local demands.

In fact, the present coolness of the agency to its experiences with open planning raises the serious question of whether the Corps will make a major effort to continue with it agency-wide. The limited follow-up to the experimentations in open planning of 1972–75 lends credence to the more pessimistic appraisals. Since open planning was by and large an internally generated policy, its continuation is dependent on how it is perceived within the agency, particularly by the leadership. As noted earlier, the Technical Assistance Program launched by the Corps' Institute for Water Resources to assist districts in developing new modes of public participation has been terminated. Where it was used, the Technical Assistance Program proved effective in developing extensive public participation. Little of permanence came out of these experiments, however. There is also the stark fact that of the 36 Corps districts, only one, the Seattle District, has considered extensive public participation sufficiently important to incorporate it formally into the district's planning rules and regulations. Unless such procedures are codified, citizens will have little recourse when recalcitrant district engineers decide to limit public participation to the traditional few large public meetings.

On the other hand, extensive public involvement will probably continue as an integral part of the several dozen urban studies now under way. Urban studies, however, are not necessarily project-directed in the way that a flood control or navigation study is. Therefore, they rarely set off the heated controversies that occur when citizens believe the Corps is seriously considering the actual construction of a project. Thus open decisionmaking in this context may not be as informative or important as it is in others. In other words, open planning in the urban studies program is not very costly to the Corps. It is, of course, a step in the right direction and a way of keeping the concept alive within the agency. There may eventually be spillover from these experiences into more project-oriented studies. Yet the Corps is already doing better than most other federal agencies, even with its modest requirements for public participation in its planning.[14] We strongly suspect, however, that only outside pressure of the sort generated in the late 1960s and early 1970s will prompt

14. Few systematic data are available comparing public participation in planning programs in federal agencies, and thus our conclusion is based largely on our knowledge of numerous federal agencies. Nevertheless, a survey in 1974 did show that federal officials, newspaper editors, and educators familiar with federal public works agencies rated the Corps' public involvement program quite high. Over 50 percent of those sampled felt the Corps' program was better than that of other federal agencies, and 84 percent saw it as good or better. See Colonel Gerald E. Galloway, "The Decision Process of the Civil Works Function of the Army Corps of Engineers," U.S. Army War College Military Research Program Paper (June 1974), p. 51.

the agency to institute an agency-wide open-planning program on the order of fishbowl planning or seek dramatically different forms of public involvement.

Conclusions about the Criteria

Our inability to identify with a high degree of certainty the course the Corps will follow in its decisionmaking process and selection of projects in the coming years obviously leaves a gap in our study. While the nine years that have elapsed since the chief of engineers' call for a rather dramatic change have revealed a great deal about the change effort, it is now apparent that another decade or so will be needed to determine the full impact of current efforts on actual field-level projects. For although it is plausible that the projects being planned today with more consideration for the environment will be those constructed in the future, the Corps conceivably could return to its backlog of more traditional projects if development interests are given free rein.

At the same time, as we have shown, there have been pronouncements of dramatic new missions, a substantial degree of reorganization, and to a lesser extent changes in the agency's decisionmaking process. Further, old projects have been modified and more environmentally sound and socially sensitive ones are on the drawing board. It appears also that the Corps and its critics have reached a modus vivendi with respect to the issues of the environment and public participation. For several years the agency has attempted to reform itself in a manner that would satisfy the environmentalists. There is much room for improvement, but the Corps' efforts to date have been rewarded. Today the Corps has a more positive image than it did, say, 10 years ago when criticism was at its peak. In our opinion, this is largely because of the Corps' efforts to achieve internal change.

The Cycle of Organizational Change

We believe that the Corps' experience reveals a great deal about the potential for change in large public bureaucracies as a whole and the process by which this change occurs. This experience vividly illustrates the state of comfortable equilibrium in which most organizations typically exist and points to the conditions necessary to create a new equilibrium more in keeping with changing public needs and wishes. Yet the Corps has not remained in a perpetual state of change, nor is it likely that any agency could. Thus the process involved may best be thought of as a cyclical one.

The cycle begins when sovereigns, clientele groups, or others important to an agency voice new demands. Inasmuch as no organization is totally homogeneous and every member is not completely programmed, some insiders will become sensitive to the need for change, and some may even see the need for a dramatic overhaul of practices or programs. The motives or personalities of the change-seekers need not be very different from those of persons who resist change; they can be just as loyal and as dedicated to the organization and as concerned with their status and job security. Yet their perceptions of the world around them and of the role of their organization in it are sufficiently different to lead them to seek change as a method of survival. The result is a greater degree of overt tension among the members of the organization.

At this point in the cycle the accumulation of rules and regulations must be modified if the organization is to change to an appreciable extent. Those persons seeking to change the organization must then emancipate it from the web of rules and regulations that has enveloped it. First, however, those seeking change must win the trust of their colleagues: trust that they will respect the traditional values and missions of the agency and will not embarrass their superiors and colleagues or reflect poorly upon the organization. The extension of this trust throughout the agency is a key ingredient of change. Without it, attempts to change will invariably be subverted from within, irrespective of the formal authority of the change-seekers.

Next, those seeking to substantially modify the organization must identify their goals with a process-related concept. They need a catchword. In recent years the concept of open planning has often taken on this new, change-oriented meaning. Open planning is no longer a matter of routine project and engineering design (as it was traditionally defined in the case of public works agencies such as the Corps of Engineers). Rather, it has become a comprehensive long-range endeavor aimed at determining the future roles of the organization. This stage of the cycle is a time of reflection and sometimes of bold departures; the resources and attention given to planning are important for both their symbolic effect and their substantive result. The message to those inside and outside the organization is clear: the organization is seriously rethinking its traditional missions and is searching for goals more compatible with the needs of its changing external environment.

If new missions are to be adopted, or even if old ones are to be carried out in a more efficient or more equitable fashion, traditional patterns of behavior must be modified. Reorganization is used to accomplish this by disrupting the established chain of command, the status ordering, and the communications patterns. Reorganization can also disrupt the unofficial constraints on behavior that constitute the informal systems of power and communication that ordinarily cannot be reached by other means. In addition, the recruitment of people with unorthodox viewpoints, new ideas, and different professional training and experiences causes the organization to become more heterogeneous. This, of course, facilitates the introduction of new procedures and programs.

This is also the time when the organization solicits new clientele groups—in the private sector as consumers and in the public sector as potential beneficiaries of proposed new services. Such solicitation would occur with or without formal or legal mandates to consult with the public. Whereas private organizations need be concerned only with those they intend to serve directly, public agencies must also reckon with those actually or potentially opposed to their activities. For public agencies, then, part of the change effort rests on public participation and citizen input as major strategies. The focus on new or broader input in part is to placate previously hostile groups whose attacks may have prompted internal reassessment in the first place. But just as often, the agency is seeking broad-based support for its new missions. Finally, a new clientele may be solicited to satisfy the need for agency credibility and legitimacy in the eyes of both its sovereign and the general public. A price the agency may have to pay to win this support and to execute its new missions effectively is a basic reformulation of its decisionmaking processes. This may mean some decentralization of authority or the development of a more open decisionmaking process to accommodate the new clientele.

Once the new missions are identified and new groups are granted access to agency decisions, a new equilibrium, albeit often uneasy, is established. This does not necessarily mean that all controversies have been resolved between the agency, its competing constituencies, and attentive publics; but only that a new level of accommodation has been achieved—that is, a good deal of change has occurred. Moreover, the long-term survival of most agencies periodically requires such new accommodations.

The Corps is noteworthy for managing to go through a change cycle while reconciling or at least juggling seemingly irreconcilable demands for water resource development, environmental protection, and open planning. After making a decision to change, the agency moved expeditiously and rather successfully to accommodate itself to a changing social and political environment. Thus this study serves as a classic illustration of the process of mutual accommodation that occurs between an agency and its attentive publics in a changing world. In observing this particular example of change, one cannot help but note also that the Army Corps of Engineers has once again proved to be a most politically astute organization.

The Questionnaire

THE ITEMS in the questionnaire discussed in chapter 7 follow directly from our research interests. Part I of the questionnaire asks who the respondent represented in the planning process. Part II includes a wide range of questions about general attitudes toward the Corps of Engineers, the planning experience, and the anticipated Corps project. Part III focuses more closely on the kind of planning activities the respondent was involved in, while Part IV seeks to determine the kinds of planning of activities thought desirable. Part V raises the issue of who should have ultimate planning responsibilities for a community project. Part VI inquires into the reasons for a respondent's participation in the planning process, and Part VII includes more detailed questions about one's personal experiences in the planning of a specific project and knowledge of the contending forces involved. Finally, Part VIII presents a set of demographic and personal questions.

Questionnaires were mailed to a randomly selected group of persons involved in each of the five project studies discussed in chapters 4, 5, and 6: to 200 in the wastewater management study for the Cleveland-Akron and Three Rivers Watershed areas; 200 in the study of Unit L-15 of the Missouri River Levee System; 195 in the Mississippi River–Gulf Outlet (MR-GO) new lock and connecting channel study; 138 in the study of flood control and related water resource problems on the Wildcat and San Pablo creeks; and 184 in the study of flood control problems along the Middle Fork of the Snoqualmie River. Questionnaires not returned within four weeks were followed by a single postcard reminder.

The response rate was computed by dividing all returned questionnaires (470) by the total mailed out (917) less those returned undelivered by the Postal Service (29). The response rate varied by study: 36 percent for the Wildcat and San Pablo creeks study, 48 percent for the MR-GO study,

58 percent for the L-15 levee study and the Cleveland-Akron wastewater management study, and 59 percent for the Snoqualmie River study. Because some respondents failed to complete the questionnaire either correctly or fully, 35 of them have been excluded from the analysis. An examination of these questionnaires indicates that some of the older and less educated respondents—those with less than a high school education—had difficulty in completing the questionnaire. It must be assumed, therefore, that this segment of the participant population in Corps planning is underrepresented in our response set. The education factor may also account for the unusually low response rate for the San Pablo Creek study, since many participants come from the Model Cities area of San Pablo and North Richmond. This would also explain why 14 of the 35 excluded questionnaires were from participants in that study. The history of such questionnaires has shown that "the biases in mail samples are toward those respondents with more education and those who are most interested in the topic."[1] Given the length of the questionnaire, however, we consider ourselves fortunate to have achieved as high an overall response rate as we did.

The complete questionnaire follows.

1. Seymour Sudman, *Applied Sampling* (Academic Press, 1976), p. 30.

PUBLIC PARTICIPATION OPINION SURVEY

You have received this questionnaire because your name is one among the many that have been drawn from the attendance lists of public meetings held by the Army Corps of Engineers. Although the Corps has provided the attendance lists from its public meetings, it is not responsible for either the contents or the use of the questionnaire.

The questions asked are about your experience in the planning of a Corps project. This is not a test. There are no right or wrong answers. The names of respondents will remain anonymous. All that is wanted is your frank and honest opinions about the Corps' citizen participation program. Your cooperation is most appreciated.

Daniel A. Mazmanian, Director
Citizen Participation Project
The Brookings Institution
1775 Massachusetts Ave., N.W.
Washington, D.C. 20036

PART I

Many people have attended the public meetings, workshops, seminars, and activities that are part of the project planning process of the Corps of Engineers. Some have come as representatives of interest groups, some as representatives of government, and others as concerned citizens. In what capacity did you attend?

Check one

(a) I attended as a representative of a government agency.   ☐

(b) I attended as a representative of a business organization.   ☐

(c) I attended as a representative of a labor organization.   ☐

(d) I attended as a representative of a conservation or
     environmental organization.   ☐

(e) I attended solely as an interested citizen.   ☐

(f) Other (specify) _____
     _____   ☐

PART II

Opinions vary on the recent attempts by the Corps to involve citizens more directly in the planning of public projects. Listed below are a number of typical statements one hears. At the right is a picture of a ladder which says "Agree" at the top and "Disagree" at the bottom. The steps in between are numbered from "4" to "1." For example, "4" means that you agree completely with the statement and "1" means that you disagree completely. Please insert in the space provided next to each statement the number along the ladder that indicates your reaction to the statement.

Agree

— 4 —

— 3 —

— 2 —

— 1 —

Disagree

Rating

1. The information about the proposed project provided by the Corps can easily be understood by the layman. _____
2. The Corps was not really interested in my point of view. _____
3. I learned much about the Corps' activities in water resources management through participating in the planning of a project. _____
4. All the important points of view are evaluated in the Corps' project planning process. _____
5. The public meetings were not very helpful in informing me about the costs and benefits of the alternatives being considered. _____
6. It was difficult attending the public meetings because of the inconvenient time (or the inconvenient location) of the meeting. _____
7. The Corps goes through the motions of consulting citizens, but it is not sincerely interested in obtaining their views. _____
8. The Corps' study manager appreciated my point of view. _____
9. The information about the project provided by the Corps was too technical. _____
10. The public meetings were useful because they gave me an opportunity to learn about the alternatives available for solving our local problems. _____
11. The opinions of citizens greatly influence the actions taken by the Corps. _____
12. There is little that I can do to affect the Corps. _____
13. The Corps relies heavily on the wishes of citizens directly affected by a proposed project. _____
14. Citizens should be given greater authority to choose which plan will be implemented. _____

15. The Corps attempts to please local business interests above all
    others.   _____
16. The decision over which water resource projects are to be built
    should be left in the hands of the experts.   _____
17. The Corps did not provide sufficient information to allow me
    to decide which alternative plan to support.   _____
18. The Corps is making an honest effort to reconcile the many
    community interests.   _____
19. I intend to participate in future project planning programs. _____
20. Every citizen should be able to take the Corps to court and
    bring to a halt an unwanted project.   _____
21. The Corps is very concerned over problems of conservation
    and pollution.   _____
22. I see no reason for taking part in any future Corps-sponsored
    citizen involvement programs.   _____
23. Throughout the project planning it was never obvious which
    of the alternative plans the Corps supported.   _____
24. Citizens should have a greater voice in the planning of public
    water resource projects.   _____
25. The most important role for citizens to play is preventing
    unwanted projects.   _____
26. On the whole the Corps is doing a good job.   _____
27. Corps personnel usually tried to avoid any open discussion at
    public meetings of the most controversial issues surrounding
    the proposed project.   _____

PART III

Listed below are the leading ways in which the public can   *Very active*
participate in the planning process of a Corps of Engineers   *in*
project. Not all these ways are available for every project.
At the right is a picture of a ladder which says "Very active in"   ___ 4 ___
at the top and "Not active in" at the bottom. The steps in
between are numbered from "4" to "1" and represent   ___ 3 ___
different degrees of participation. For example, "4" means
that you think you were quite active in an activity, "3"   ___ 2 ___
means that you were moderately active, and "1" means
that you did not participate at all. Insert in the space   ___ 1 ___
provided after each statement the number along the ladder
that best reflects the extent of your participation in the   *Not active*
activity.   *in*

                                                                     Rating

1. Large public meetings where Corps personnel described the
   proposed project.   _____
2. Large public meetings where the public presented its views on
   a proposed project to the Corps.   _____
3. Large public meetings where Corps personnel discussed
   alternative project proposals with the public.   _____
4. Small workshops or seminars where Corps personnel discussed
   details of a proposed project with the public.   _____
5. Conferences with Corps personnel, attended by representatives
   of various local interests.   _____
6. Small conferences with Corps personnel, attended by the
   members of an organization to which you belong.   _____
7. Meetings with Corps personnel to establish the scope of water
   resource needs for the local community.   _____
8. Meetings with Corps personnel to determine which of the
   many alternative project proposals under consideration should
   be studied in depth.   _____
9. Commenting on the environmental impact statement of a
   proposed project.   _____
10. Writing letters to government officials about the project
    proposal.   _____
11. Supporting an interest group that usually favors Corps
    projects.   _____
12. Supporting an interest group that usually opposes Corps
    projects.   _____
13. Informally meeting with Corps personnel to discuss a proposed
    project.   _____
14. Other (specify) _____
                                                                  _____

PART IV

The list of methods of public participation presented in
Part III is repeated below, along with some additional ways
for the public to become involved. At the right is a
picture of a ladder which says "Good way" *at the top and* "Poor
way" *at the bottom. Consider how well each method provides*
the public with an opportunity to learn about and influence
the outcome of a project. For instance, if you feel the
method is a very good way of learning about and influencing
a project, you would mark "4" *in the space provided to the*
right of the statement.

Good way

— 4 —

— 3 —

— 2 —

— 1 —

Poor way

Rating

1. Large public meetings where Corps personnel described the proposed project. _____
2. Large public meetings where the public presented its views on a proposed project to the Corps. _____
3. Large public meetings where Corps personnel discussed alternative project proposals with the public. _____
4. Small workshops or seminars where Corps personnel discussed details of a proposed project with the public. _____
5. Conferences with Corps personnel, attended by representatives of various local interests. _____
6. Small conference with Corps personnel, attended by the members of an organization to which you belong. _____
7. Meetings with Corps personnel to establish the scope of water resource needs for the local community. _____
8. Meetings with Corps personnel to determine which of the many alternative project proposals under consideration should be studied in depth. _____
9. Commenting on the environmental impact statement of a proposed project. _____
10. Writing letters to government officials about the project proposal. _____
11. Supporting an interest group that usually favors Corps projects. _____
12. Supporting an interest group that usually opposes Corps projects. _____
13. Informally meeting with Corps personnel to discuss a proposed project. _____
14. Local elections on proposed projects. _____
15. A citizen oversight board that reviews activities of the Corps. _____
16. Other (specify) _____ _____

PART V

There are three major stages to every public water resource project. The first stage is deciding what problems exist and which public agency is responsible for dealing with them. The second stage involves deciding which of the many alternative approaches that could be employed to deal with the problem will be adopted. Finally, after a project is completed its effectiveness must be evaluated. Listed below are the various persons who conceivably could be responsible for making the decisions at each stage in the progress of a project:

1. *Local elected officials*
2. *The Corps of Engineers*
3. *Water resource experts*
4. *The general public*
5. *State officials*
6. *Congress*
7. *Regional government*
8. *Local citizens*
9. *The President*
10. *Local businessmen*
11. *Conservationists and environmentalists*

Drawing from the list above, mark in the space provided at the right of each statement the code (1–11 above) designating who should be responsible for:

1. Deciding what are the water-related problems of a community. _____
2. Developing the alternative approaches for dealing with these problems. _____
3. Overseeing and evaluating the projects that are undertaken to deal with the problems. _____

PART VI

Important
reason

Listed below are a number of the reasons given by citizens for   __ 4 __
participating in the planning of a Corps project. To the right is a
ladder numbered from "4" to "1," which says "Important reason"   __ 3 __
at the top and "Unimportant reason" at the bottom. Insert in the
space provided after each statement the number along the ladder   __ 2 __
that indicates how important a reason this was in motivating you
to participate in the planning of a Corps project.   __ 1 __

Unimportant
reason

Rating

1. The project under consideration affected my home (or other
   properties).   _____
2. I am interested in the commercial opportunities in the study
   area.   _____
3. I am interested in preserving areas for fishing and hunting that
   the Corps was considering for its project.   _____
4. I am interested in questions of wastewater management.   _____
5. I am concerned over the environmental effects of the proposed
   plans.   _____
6. I am in favor of the project the Corps proposed.   _____
7. My home (or other properties) was recently flooded and I may
   benefit from the proposed project.   _____
8. I follow Corps activities as part of my job.   _____
9. The Corps was under attack and needed to be defended.   _____
10. Citizen involvement programs are new to this community and
    I was curious as to how they work.   _____
11. I oppose the proposed plans.   _____
12. Other (specify) _____
    _____   _____

PART VII

The next set of questions is about the details of your personal experience in the planning process.

1. Regarding your most recent experience in project planning, what is the number of public meetings, including seminars and workshops, that you attended?   _____

2. In total, how many hours were you able to devote to the project familiarizing yourself with the details of the alternative plans, attending meetings, commenting on the project in writing, or in any other manner?

Hours devoted to project	*Check one*
0–9	_____
10–19	_____
20–29	_____
30–39	_____
40–49	_____
50–59	_____
60–69	_____
70–79	_____
80 or more	

3. How were you notified that the planning of this project was under way?

	Check as many as apply
Corps circulars, letters, or flyers	_____
Newspapers or magazine coverage	_____
Television or radio coverage	_____
By an organized interest group	_____
By a neighborhood or local government association	_____
By word of mouth	_____
Other (specify) _____	_____

4. At what point in the project planning process did you become involved? (Check one.)

   Early _____ Midway _____ Late _____ Don't know _____

5. Did you attend the first, second, or third public meeting held to consider the proposed project? (Check as many as apply. If you do not know the number of the meeting you attended, mark "don't know.")

I attended the first public meeting	_____
I attended the second public meeting	_____
I attended the third public meeting	_____
Don't know	_____

6. Did you know that under the National Environmental Policy Act of 1969 the Corps is required to develop an environmental impact statement fully disclosing the positive and negative effects of a proposed project? (Check one.)

   Yes _____   No _____

   (a) Have you ever seen the enviromental impact statement on the proposed project? (Check one.)

   Yes _____   No _____

   (b) Have you submitted written comments to be included as part of the official environmental impact statement record? (Check one.)

   Yes _____   No _____

7. Do you know what has become of the project you helped plan? (Check one.)

   Yes _____   No _____

   If you answered yes to question 7, continue. If you answered no, please go on to question 8.

   (a) Has the district Corps office forwarded its recommendations to the division office? (Check one.)

   Yes _____   No _____   Don't know _____

   (b) Has the division office forwarded its recommendation on the project to the Board of Engineers for Rivers and Harbors? (Check one.)

   Yes _____   No _____   Don't know _____

   (c) Has Congress approved the project? (Check one.)

   Yes _____   No _____   Don't know _____

   (d) Has construction begun on the project? (Check one.)

   Yes _____   No _____   Don't know _____

   (e) How have you stayed informed of developments on the project?

                                                              Check as many
                                                              as apply

   Corps circulars, letters, or flyers   _____
   Newspaper or magazine coverage   _____
   Television or radio coverage   _____
   By an organized interest group   _____
   By neighborhood or local government association   _____
   By word of mouth   _____
   Other (specify) _____   _____

8. Do you know if the Corps ever modified or changed its plans for the project you participated in as a result of suggestions made by citizens? (Check one.)

   Yes _____   No _____   Don't know _____

*If you answered yes to question 8, continue. If you answered
no, please go on to question 9.*

(a) Check the numbered step along the   *Major changes made*
ladder to the right that best indicates the
extent of changes brought about as a   4 ——————
result of suggestions made by citizens.   3 ——————
                                                              2 ——————
                                                              1 ——————
                                                     Minor changes made

(b) Are you satisfied with the project plan   *Completely satisfied*
that was ultimately decided upon by the
Corps? Check the numbered step along   4 ——————
the ladder to the right that best   3 ——————
indicates the extent of your satisfaction.   2 ——————
                                                              1 ——————
                                                         Not satisfied

(c) If you are not completely satisfied with the plan finally
decided upon by the Corps, can you state in a few words
what it is that you prefer to be done.

————————————————————————————————
————————————————————————————————
————————————————————————————————

9. Which groups in your community usually support Corps
activities? Do you know the names of their leading spokesmen?
Please list as many groups as come to mind.

Group	*Spokesman*
———————	———————
———————	———————
———————	———————
———————	———————

Which groups in your community usually oppose Corps
activities? Do you know the names of their leading spokesman?
Please list as many groups as come to mind.

Group	*Spokesman*
———————	———————
———————	———————
———————	———————
———————	———————

10. For how many years have you been actively interested in Corps
project planning? (Check one.)

            Less than one year   ————
            One to three years   ————
            Three to five years   ————
            More than five years   ————

PART VIII

The last set of questions is about you.
1. How old are you to your nearest birthday? _____
2. How many years of education have you completed? _____
3. Sex: Male _____ Female _____
4. Residence: Own _____ Rent or lease _____
5. Number of years at present address: _____
6. Number of years in the state or region: _____
7. Are you currently retired or not employed? Yes _____ No _____
8. What is your occupation, or if you are either retired or not working, what was your occupation?

	Check one
Professional, executive	_____
White collar, sales	_____
Skilled labor	_____
Semiskilled labor	_____
Housewife	_____
Student	_____
Other (specify) _____	_____

9. Are you a member of any organizations? If so, please list them under the categories provided below.
   Types of organizations

Business	_____
Labor	_____
Fraternal or social	_____
Conservation or environmental	_____
Hunting or fishing	_____
Other (specify)	_____

10. What was your family income last year? (Check one.)

$0–$6,999	_____
$ 7,000–$9,999	_____
$10,000–$12,999	_____
$13,000–$15,999	_____
$16,000–$19,999	_____
$20,000–$29,999	_____
$30,000 and above	_____

APPENDIX B

Measures of the Model Components

THE QUESTIONNAIRE in appendix A asked participants of the five studies an array of questions about their substantive concerns, attitudes toward the Corps, and so on. Through the use of cluster analysis (a statistical technique similar to factor analysis) and qualitative judgments, the questions were grouped together into several general scales that in turn are used as the measures of the components of the two models of decision-making shown in chapter 7.[1] The items included in each scale are presented below.

Extent of Environmental Concern

Those who participated had had little previous opportunity to be involved in the planning process of water resource agencies. They were not coerced, although many participated because of the prompting of friends and associates. None were paid by the Corps for their time and efforts. When asked why they bothered to participate 71.8 percent of the respondents said it was because of concern over the environmental effects of the proposed plans. As shown in table B-1, concern about how a project might affect one's home or other properties was a reason given by 55.7 percent of the participants. Concern about wastewater management ranked third (47.9 percent).

The most theoretically interesting of these concerns are those that distinguish between the known (or at least stereotyped) competing factions engaged in the Corps' public participation program: the environmentalists and those who expected to receive a direct commercial or personal

1. Clusters (scales) were determined by grouping items according to their highest pair-wise correlation coefficient. The specific technique employed was designed and programmed by Michael R. Leavitt; see program abstract "MULTYP/Multiple Typal Analysis: A Clustering Program," *Behavioral Science*, vol. 16 (July 1971), pp. 417–18.

Table B-1. *Survey Respondents' Reasons for Participating in Corps Planning*

Reason for participation	Percent of respondents giving item a top rating of 4[a]
1. I am concerned about the environmental effects of the proposed plans.	71.8
2. The project under consideration affected my home or other properties.	55.7
3. I am interested in questions of wastewater management.	47.9
4. I am interested in preserving areas for fishing and hunting that the Corps was considering for its project.	31.2
5. My home (or other properties) was recently flooded and I may benefit from the proposed project.	23.1
6. I am interested in the commercial opportunities in the study area.	17.9
7. Citizen involvement programs are new to this community and I was curious about how they work.	16.3
8. I follow Corps activities as part of my job.	13.9

a. The items were rated on a four-point scale. Only items receiving a rating of 4 are used in the rank ordering above, based on absolute frequencies. If items with ratings of four and three are combined and then ranked, the order changes slightly; the third and second items are reversed, the fifth and fourth are reversed, and the seventh moves to the fifth position.

benefit from a project. The extent to which these two groups agree or disagree on their evaluations of the Corps and its direction of water resource projects should have an enormous bearing on the success of the public participation efforts in achieving a consensus about projects. The extent to which those who participated did so out of a sense of public-mindedness is also of some interest, as well as the extent to which these persons are like the other two types.

The three concerns of participants identified below with our means of measuring them tap quite distinct kinds of interest:

Concern	Measure
Environment	The average of the responses on a four-point scale to items 1, 3, and 4 in table B-1.
Civic-mindedness	Responses to item 7 in table B-1.
Economic benefit	The average of the respondent's rating given to items 5 and 6 in table B-1.

Taking a mean of a respondent's ratings across all the items that relate to environmentalism, for example, provides a good measure of the respondent's level of concern in that area. These means, hereafter referred to as "scale scores," make it possible to compare the extent to which the respondents' involvement is based on concern with environmental issues, on their own economic well-being, or on their civic-mindedness. The correlation between environment and economic benefit measures a negligible 0.05, that between environment and civic-mindedness is a somewhat higher yet still minimal 0.12, and that between economic interest and civic-mindedness is 0.07.[2]

In examining the two models of the planning process in chapter 7, environmentalism (E) is used as the measure of concern because it is central to the Corps' new planning efforts. Using either economic benefit or civic-mindedness as the measure of concern has virtually no effect on the structure of the two models.

Citizen Power

The component of the expanded model not considered in the Corps model and in prior applications of the participation thesis is the propensity of citizens to want to share authority in public policy decisions (D). The greater this tendency, the less likely it is that the public will be satisfied with any decisionmaking process that leaves the major decisions in the hands of the Corps. The extent to which this tendency is present is reflected in the answers to such items as 1 and the inverse of 3 in the citizen action scale below:[3]

1. Citizens should have a greater voice in the planning of public water resource projects.

2. Citizens should be given greater authority to choose which plan will be implemented.

3. Deciding which water resource projects are to be built should be left in the hands of the experts.

---

2. The level of significance of the three correlations reported is 0.09, 0.01, and 0.17 respectively. (The lower the degree of significance, the more statistically reliable the correlation coefficient.) All correlation coefficients reported are calculated by the Pearson product-moment method.

3. Items were rated on a four-point scale. For item 3, the actual scores were inverted when the scale scores were calculated.

4. The most important role for citizens to play is preventing unwanted projects.

5. Every citizen should be able to take the Corps to court and bring to a halt an unwanted project.

Orientation toward Corps

A person's general orientation toward the Corps is revealed in responses to the following items that scale (cluster) together regarding attitudes about the Corps' openness and tone and about its receptivity to citizens (C):[4]

1. The Corps was not really interested in my point of view.

2. The Corps is making an honest effort to reconcile the many community interests.

3. The Corps attempts to please local business interests above all others.

4. On the whole the Corps is doing a good job.

5. The Corps is very concerned about problems of conservation and pollution.

6. The Corps goes through the motions of consulting citizens, but it is not sincerely interested in obtaining their views.

7. All the important points of view are evaluated in the Corps' project-planning process.

8. There is little that I can do to affect the Corps.

9. The Corps relies heavily on the wishes of citizens directly affected by a proposed project.

10. The opinions of citizens greatly influence the actions taken by the Corps.

For example, if one believes that item 2 is true, he will also be likely to agree with item 10, while disagreeing with item 6.

4. Items were rated on a four-point scale. For items 1, 3, 6, and 8, the actual scores were inverted when the scale scores were calculated. As in psychology, "orientation" here is synonymous with "attitude," which is defined as "learned predispositions to respond to an object or class of objects in a favorable or unfavorable way." (Martin Fishbein, "A Consideration of Beliefs, and Their Role in Attitude Measurement," in Martin Fishbein, ed., *Readings in Attitude Theory and Measurement* [John Wiley, 1967], p. 257.)

Evaluation of Experience in Public Participation Program

Throughout the planning, participants formed opinions about many aspects of the process, such as which modes of participation were to be preferred, the Corps' seriousness in consulting with the public, and how effectively the Corps communicates information and ideas to the public. This is reflected in part in the preferences for some modes of participation over others. In order to test the two models of participatory decision-making, however, a summary view, or "operational indicator," of the participants' overall evaluation of the planning experience was needed. Thus the group of items below that inquire into the substance of the Corps' participatory planning program as actually experienced by the respondents gave us the means to evaluate the respondents' experience in the public participation program (B):[5]

1. The information about the project provided by the Corps was too technical.

2. Corps personnel usually tried to avoid any open discussion at public meetings of the most controversial issues surrounding the proposed project.

3. The public meetings were useful because they gave me an opportunity to learn about the alternatives available for solving our local problems.

4. The Corps did not provide sufficient information to allow me to decide which alternative plan to support.

5. The public meetings were not very helpful in informing me about the costs and benefits of the alternatives being considered.

6. The information about the proposed project provided by the Corps can easily be understood by the layman.

7. The Corps' study manager appreciated my point of view.

8. I learned much about the Corps' activities in water resources management through participating in the planning of a project.

5. Items were rated on a four-point scale. For items 1, 2, 4, and 5, the actual scores were inverted when the scale scores were calculated. The scale is primarily based on a clustering of items. Items 2 and 3, however, were added to the machine-generated cluster, given their substantive content. A check on this modification was accomplished by correlating each item of the measure with the measure itself. The correlations between the measure and the two added items are above 0.55 and are equivalent in size to those of the original items in the cluster.

These items attempt to gauge what actually transpired at the planning sessions and to what extent the respondents felt the agency had included them in a meaningful way.

Evaluation of Proposed Project

The most difficult component of the models to measure is the evaluation of the Corps' recommended project (A) because some districts had not announced their recommendation by the time the questionnaire was administered. Or, as in the Cleveland-Akron study, the district presented political leaders with a series of options. Although it is evident that during the planning process virtually all the participants had some idea of what the Corps' preferred plan was, many had to rely on an educated guess to identify it when asked to react to the Corps' recommended project proposal.[6]

Asking respondents to judge a proposed project before it is formally announced obviously presents some problems in interpreting the responses, especially since the official recommendation may differ from what is anticipated, and this could alter a respondent's evaluation. For the test of the two models, however, the issue is immaterial. If the planning effort was perceived to be a positive one and the respondents thought they knew which alternative was going to be recommended, under the assumption of the participation thesis a commitment to and approval of the project would be predicted.

The two items constituting the evaluation-of-project measure are:[7]

1. I oppose the proposed plans.
2. I am in favor of the project the Corps proposed.

Since all respondents were asked to answer both items, which are diametrically opposed, it is conceivable that a person could give a high rating to both. If so, one would have to assume that either the items were misread or that the respondent was confused on the issue. Whichever the

6. Only 5 percent of the respondents failed to express an opinion about the proposed project. Approximately the same proportion failed to answer most of the other items on the questionnaire.

7. Items are rated on a four-point score. For item 1, the actual scores were inverted when the scale scores were calculated.

case, in the 11 instances when a respondent gave a high rating of 4 or 3 to both items, the observation was deleted from the analysis. The reverse does not logically follow. That is, a low rating on both items could simply be an indication of indifference to the project, not confusion, and these cases were therefore retained.

Index

Alford, Robert A., 33n
Allee, David J., 114–15n
Allerton Park, 21
Allerton, Robert, 21
Alpine Lakes Protection Society (ALPS), 138, 150, 151, 153
ALPS. *See* Alpine Lakes Protection Society
Alton Lake Committee, 77
Arnstein, Sherry R., 35n
Ashbrook, John M., 130
Ash, C. Grant, 52n
Asher, Herbert B., 175–76n
Auburg, Joseph D., 65n
Audubon Society. *See* National Audubon Society

Bauer, Wolf, 151
Benefit-cost analyses, 13–16; Oakley reservoir project, 22–23; Snoqualmie River project, 137–38, 140–41; Unit L-15 Levee project, 76, 77, 78–79; Wildcat and San Pablo creeks project, 111
BERH. *See* Board of Engineers for Rivers and Harbors
Bernstein, Marilyn, 2n
Beyers, William B., 140
Bishop, A. Bruce, 32n
Blackwelder, Brent, 187–88
Blake, Robert R., 5n
Blalock, Hubert M., Jr., 175n
Board of Commissioners of the Port of New Orleans, 81, 83–87, 91–93
Board of Engineers for Rivers and Harbors (BERH), 17, 112, 185; and Snoqualmie River project, 137, 138–44
Bond, Christopher S., 66
Borton, Thomas E., 32n

Bowers, David G., 5n
Braybrooke, David, 4n
Breaden, John, 107n
Brochures: fishbowl planning tool, 146, 147, 158–59; Snoqualmie River project, 148, 154, 158–59; Three Rivers Watershed project, 121–22, 123–24, 159; Unit L-15 Levee project, 75, 78; Wildcat and San Pablo creeks project, 108
Broussalian, V. L., 13n
Brown, Gardner, Jr., 141
Buffalo District. *See* Three Rivers Watershed project
Bureau of Reclamation, 64
Bureau of Sports Fisheries and Wildlife, 51

Carter, Jimmy, 97
Cassidy, William F., 144
Centroport, U.S.A., 81–82
Chambers of commerce: and Mississippi River–Gulf Outlet channel, 84; and Three Rivers Watershed project, 125, 129–30
Chicago District. *See* Oakley reservoir project
Chief of engineers. *See* Office of the Chief of Engineers
Citizen advisory committees, 38–39, 74–75, 146, 183
Clarke, Frederick J., 25–26, 27–28, 62n
Clement, Roland C., 26n
Cleveland-Akron and Three Rivers Watershed project. *See* Three Rivers Watershed project
Cnudde, C. F., 176n
Coalition for the Environment, 71, 78
Committee on Allerton Park, 21–23

CAN ORGANIZATIONS CHANGE?